Don't Think Twice

Don't Think Twice

ADVENTURE AND HEALING AT
100 MILES PER HOUR

BARBARA SCHUICHET

G. P. PUTNAM'S SONS
NEW YORK

G. P. PUTNAM'S SONS
Publishers Since 1838
An imprint of Penguin Random House LLC
375 Hudson Street
New York, New York 10014

ISBN: 9781101981801

Printed in the United States of America
1   3   5   7   9   10   8   6   4   2

Book design by Amanda Dewey

Penguin is committed to publishing works of quality and integrity. In
that spirit, we are proud to offer this book to our readers; however,
the story, the experiences, and the words are the author's alone.

To Bob Dylan and my mother

AUTHOR'S NOTE

As you will read in chapter 19, "Catch and Release," I purposely erased all notes and photographs I took during my trip. But on December 17, 2008, before I began writing this memoir, I flew back to Buffalo, New York, and redid the same journey to Los Angeles by car. At that time I retook photographs of several places I'd visited and consulted a few people who appear in the book, but for the most part, I relied upon my memory to re-create conversations and events that took place while I was on the road. For flashbacks, I called upon both my memory as well as those of my sisters, oftentimes writing a composite of all our recollections. In some instances, I've changed the names and modified identifying characteristics of individuals who appear in the story, to preserve anonymity and privacy.

Because my journey covered 3,988 miles, I was unable to include many of the places where I stopped. To all the people who impacted my journey, those who appear in the book, as well as those I had to omit, I offer my heartfelt thanks.

Don't Think Twice

One

Motorcycle Therapy

———◆———

Bart Mange swaggered into the classroom reeking of cigarette smoke and scratching his bed head. He was a mutt of a man, middle-aged, kind of like Nick Nolte's mug shot come to life, except his hair was red and I don't think he was drunk.

"Good morning, *lady* . . . and gentlemen." He threw me a grin. "I'll be your motorcycle instructor, and if I do my job right, you're all gonna live." He looked around the room, attitude up the wazoo, sneering at everyone. "Anybody wanna leave?"

I sat there, the only woman in a room full of guys. They all looked like they'd just gotten out of jail, and I looked like their grandmother. We had nothing in common except a desire to learn how to ride and an instant fear of the Dirty Harry doppelgänger who was supposed to teach us. At least he wasn't two or three decades younger than me. In fact, the tread marks on Bart Mange's face were proof he'd logged lots of mileage on and off the road. Weathered like indoor furniture left outside, his skin was as leathery as the outfit he wore, and whatever age he was, he looked ten years older than that.

I liked him immediately. He looked like he wanted to punish some-one, and I didn't have to think twice to know I was in the right place. I was used to pain.

Just a year ago, riding a bike meant sweating my ass off in a spinning class, but my life had gone awry since then, and I needed to go beyond my comfort zone to regain my equilibrium. I'm not sure why balancing atop a machine that could kill me seemed like a good way to stop wanting to die, but it was worth a try since everything else had failed to kindle my inter-est in living.

Bart tapped his name on the chalkboard. "My friends call me Bart Mange, but none of you will ever be my friend, so you can call me Mr. Mange or Sir."

He ran his fingers through his hair and blinked like he was trying to stay awake. It was probably just nicotine withdrawal, since moments before class I'd seen him standing outside sucking so hard on a cigarette I thought he might inhale it.

"Okay, the first thing I want you to do is look at how I'm dressed." He beat his chest. "Leather jacket." He slapped his thigh. "Leather chaps." He stamped his foot and clapped his hands. "Leather boots and leather gloves. I smell like a cow, don't I?"

"More like a Camel." One of the guys in the back snickered. "Or a Marlboro."

Bart pointed his stubbly chin at the guy's chest, thick and muscled in his wife-beater undershirt. "My friend thinks this is all a big joke, but I'm serious as the stomach flu. Anyone not wearing an extra layer of skin tomorrow doesn't get on a bike."

I raised my hand to inform Mr. Mange that tomorrow's schedule said we wouldn't actually be *on* the motorcycles until after lunch.

"And your point is . . . ?"

"Well, it's supposed to be ninety-five tomorrow and this classroom isn't air-conditioned."

"Uh-huh." He sat on the edge of his desk and crossed his arms.

"I was just saying—"

"Look, lady. I'm a *nice* guy. I want you covered in cowhide to remind you that your *own* hide is vulnerable each and every time you're on a motorcycle." He slapped his butt and looked around the room. "Got it?"

"Got it!" we all yelled, except for the guy next to me, who just popped his gum.

Bart was on him like a crow on carrion. "You—the clown with the gum—you don't get it, do you?"

"My name is John, Mr. Mange, and I definitely get it."

"*Jawn* will *really* get it when he doesn't wear a jacket and scrapes off an elbow!"

Everybody laughed nervously.

"You think that's funny? I knew a guy who wore tennis shoes one day and scraped off a toe. Funny, huh?"

Everyone gasped, and one person quietly left the room.

"One down . . . Anyone else?" Bart shook his head and chuckled. "Man, I saw some idiot wearing flip-flops and shorts doing eighty up the coast the other day. I wanted to drive him into the ocean myself!"

He stared wistfully out the window as if the idea of killing someone was pleasing, then he clapped his hands and grinned. "Okay, let's get real. You might start out one morning dressed in full gear, and you're warm and cozy because it's a little nippy out. But as you're riding along—*la-di-da*—all of a sudden the cool air disappears and the sun starts frying you like a chicken breast. What do you do?"

"Whip off a layer!" one of the gangbangers slouching two rows over called out.

"Okay. Aerosol Can over there would just peel himself like a banana, but what if you don't have saddlebags? Do you toss your leathers by the side of the road?" He waited, then screamed, "*You do nothing!* You grow a set of balls and you just keep on riding!"

I felt a disturbing twinge between my legs as I imagined how uncomfortable testicles must be. But what was even more disquieting was the unsettling itch Bart had ignited in me. For the first time in months, I was excited about something. I sat on the edge of my seat and listened to Bart like he was the Dalai Lama.

"Now, keep in mind, children, even if you *do* have a place to stow your gear, sometimes the road is just too rough to ride without protection. You get my meaning? If you go down, it won't be clothes you'll scrape off."

A bald guy with *HAIR* tattooed on his scalp called out, "What if—?"

"There are no what-ifs in motorcycling. If the road is smooth as a snake's belly, you wear leather. If you're afraid of helmet hair, you still wear a full-on brain bucket with a face mask. Those boys in Nazi beanies are just vegetables waiting to happen."

Bart let the image sink in and then smiled. "Listen, the truth is there are two kinds of bikers—those who've had a wreck and those who are going to. You have a better chance of not turning into a piece of broccoli wearing protective gear, okay?"

I gulped hard. If Bart wasn't wearing a helmet and did a face-plant on the 405, he'd probably just leave a tobacco stain; if I did the same, I'd wind up brain-dead. I shook off the image, then felt a strange wave of relief. Maybe that wouldn't be so bad . . . not feeling anything.

I must have drifted off because suddenly I felt a hand on my shoulder. "You okay, buttercup?" Bart laid a workbook on my desk. "You're looking a little green."

"I'm fine. I always look sick to my stomach when I'm excited."

"Well, don't get *too* excited." He gave me a gentle pat, then grinned at the class. "Okay, children, tomorrow we ride. Today we dissect the motorcycle like a guinea pig."

For the next couple of hours Bart browbeat information into us. We learned the parts of a motorcycle from headlight to tailpipe. We learned which part of the road we were supposed to occupy in order to be more visible, and that most drivers wouldn't see us anyway. And despite describing every possible way we could wind up crushed beyond recognition, Bart also left us with the main reason why motorcycling was worth the risk.

"*Freedom*," he said with a huge grin. "Freedom with a big, fat, fucking *F*."

As it turned out, there was a Harley dealership near my house, so after class, I raided the place with the help of a gnarly-looking saleswoman who could have been Bart's twin sister. She also smelled like a pack of cigarettes and looked like she'd just crawled out of bed. Her name tag read Proud Mary but she said I could call her PM.

"I call my old man AM 'cause we're like night and day." She winked, coughed, and chuckled at the same time. "His real name is Punk."

I followed her around as she talked me into buying a lot more gear than I needed. She would have talked me into a bike, if my therapist Muriel hadn't called while I was eyeing a set of Harley-Davidson dinnerware.

"You wouldn't believe how cool all this shit is!" I wrapped a scarf imprinted with tiny skulls around my neck. "I swear, I look like Amelia Earhart!"

"Take a deep breath and cut your credit card in half," Muriel said calmly. "Are you still coming in to see me tonight?"

I told her I was, then I told PM to take the Harley shot glasses off my bill. The clothing was enough, and I wore everything out of the store, feeling more comfortable than I had in months. The jacket, the chaps, the boots, the gloves, and especially the helmet—they all seemed to contain me. They'd keep me focused on staying intact, on keeping it together, on not falling apart. And best of all, they'd keep me covered.

Two

The Catalyst

———◆———

We've all had them—those unbelievably bad years in which one thing after another happens, and we begin to think that something greater than ourselves is trying to tell us something. In my case, it seemed like I was taunting disaster, because before my life went to hell, I was completely unaware I was heading for a storm.

"If it's true that God gives people exactly what they can handle," I used to say, "then I guess I can't handle anything."

That's how good I thought my life was before it wasn't. I had a great job writing publicity for a major studio, and even though juggling egos was tough, I loved what I did. And I had a wonderful family that accepted my hellcat of a girlfriend. We'd been together for six years, and even though she was a bossy little thing, she was unbelievably cute and I adored her. I was blissfully unaware of the winds beginning to stir.

And they were.

Anyone could've predicted what was coming by the songs on my iPod. It makes sense now that I got chills hearing "A Hard Rain's A-Gonna Fall," or went hoarse yelling, *"Hey, you! Get off of my cloud!"* But when asked why I chose songs portending doom or preaching defiance, I maintained I was just reliving my often angst-ridden, sometimes rebellious, high school days. On weekends I slept till noon and buried my face in fiction. I was happy with my adequate life and clung to it like a toddler to a pants leg. I needed a kick in the pants, a *potch* in the tush, before I'd open my eyes to anything happening or *not* happening around me.

Then *kick-potch*, one of the head tyrants at the studio called me into her office and told me I was being sacrificed in a merger. This was code for "a younger person is going to take your place." I went into my office, closed my door, and cried. People kept poking their heads in to see if I was okay, but all I wanted was to get to my girlfriend's house so she could comfort me. I called her on the way over but got her voice mail, so I left a message saying I needed to see her right away. She called me three hours later.

"Holy shit, that's terrible," she said, "and I feel just *awful* I can't be there for you tonight, but I've already made dinner plans with Gayle."

It was the third time that month that she and her hairdresser had gone out.

"Can't you cancel?" I asked. "I really need to see you tonight."

"Listen, I'll try to come over after dinner, okay?"

At midnight I called my friend Lynn.

"She is *not* having dinner!" Lynn screamed. "Leave her before she leaves you."

Throughout the next week, I suffered through my unemployment alone. Then one day my girlfriend called to say she was coming over to give me my Christmas present.

"Christmas isn't for another week," I said. "I haven't gotten you anything yet."

"Don't worry about it. What time should I come over?"

"What do you mean, don't worry about it?"

She sighed. "Do you really want to do this over the phone?"

"Do what?" I was starting to feel the same way I had just before my boss told me I'd been laid off. I gripped the phone. "You can't be serious. You can't be thinking about what I think you're thinking about."

She laughed. "You are such a nutcase. I think that's why I love you, but . . ." She took a deep breath. "Please, can't I just come over?"

I was only forty-nine, not menopausal yet, but I felt such a rush of heat blast through me I was sure I was having a hot flash. "Yeah, come over." I tried to keep my voice from shaking. "Around seven. I'll pick up some Thai."

She said she wasn't sure she could make it by seven, and though I told her not to worry about it, *I* worried about it . . . especially when she didn't ring the doorbell until after ten.

"What's with the doorbell?" I asked, standing before her sweating in my new suede jacket, the one I'd just bought to wear to her house on Christmas Day. "Why didn't you use your key?"

She walked in, sat on my couch, and handed me an Abercrombie & Fitch sweatshirt unwrapped in a paper bag. "Merry Christmas, Happy Chanukah." She smiled weakly. Then she took my key off her keychain. "I'm sorry, honey."

I sat next to her on the couch, a little drunk with nothing but a half-bottle of wine in me. "I'm guessing you've eaten," I said, trying not to sound bitter, trying not to slur. "There's ice-cold Thai on the kitchen counter, help yourself."

"I'm not hungry, but I could use a glass of wine." She grabbed my empty glass off the coffee table, went into my kitchen, and split what was left in the bottle between us. "Why don't I fix you a plate? You really should eat something."

I sat there holding my brand-new sweatshirt to my chest and thinking of the beautifully wrapped present that was now under her pillow on my bed. I hadn't had time to shop for a proper gift, pick up dinner, and shave my legs before seven, so I'd slipped my diamond stud earrings into a silk pouch and tied it with a lace ribbon.

"No, thanks," I said. "I think I'll just drink."

"Come on, Barb." She put a glass of wine and a plate of Thai on the coffee table in front of me. Then she took her place on the couch and squeezed my hand. "I think we both know this has been over for a while."

"The only thing I *know* is that you've got unbelievably bad timing." I took a gulp of wine. "For fuck's sake, I just lost my job."

She didn't say a word. She just took the glass of wine out of my hand, grabbed her own glass, and headed for the bedroom.

"You've got to be kidding," I said. *"That's* what you want to do now?"

She stopped halfway down the hall, turned, and gave me that look she always did when she was trying to get away with something. "Come on," she said. "Once more for old time's sake?"

Oh, yeah . . . she got the earrings.

I got through Christmas by going to a friend's party, drinking shots of tequila, and thinking seriously about going back to men. I got through New Year's Eve by telling everyone I had a date, then bringing home lobster risotto from my favorite Italian restaurant and eating it in front of my TV with a bottle of expensive chardonnay. The risotto tasted like Elmer's glue, the wine like water, and the white roses I sent to myself on Valentine's Day made me laugh and cry at the same time. The card, which I'd dictated to the salesperson over the phone, was sweet, pathetic, and stolen from Bob Dylan.

"You don't have to worry anymore. I'll be your baby tonight."

Over the next few weeks I changed the songs on my iPod to whiny country music like "I Don't Know Whether to Kill Myself or Go Bowling" and "Sleeping Single in a Double Bed." I started wearing a cowboy hat to cover my unkempt hair, and when I wasn't howling like Patsy Cline, I was declaring to anyone who would listen that my life was going to change for the better.

"No corporation will vacuum my brain again," I informed the mailman.

"People are finding soul mates in their laptops," I told the kid who bagged my groceries. "True love is just a mouse click away."

Inwardly I was a mess, but glass-half-full-of-Scotch woman that I was, I was handling things okay. I started getting up every morning at seven and made it my job to look for a job. I joined two online employment services and three dating sites, and I developed a true appreciation for casual sex. Then one day I was surfing from CareerBuilder.com to Match.com when my doorbell rang.

I scrambled into the bathroom to brush my teeth and then opened the door to a city building inspector who informed me that the guesthouse I'd converted my garage into was illegal.

"Are you aware that your neighborhood isn't zoned for rentals and that there's a fine for creating unsafe housing?"

I told him I was not aware.

He peered past me as if my illegal guesthouse were in my living room. "I'm sorry, but you have thirty days to kick out your tenant and turn that unit back into a garage."

"Look, I just lost my job and I need that income to get by. Besides, there's a nice guy living back there who would lose his home." I tightened the sash on my robe. "What if I decide to fight this?"

He looked up from his clipboard. "Your fines will build up . . . and you'll lose."

"You wouldn't consider taking—"

He held up his hand. "Don't finish that thought."

"I was going to ask you to take pity on me, not offer you a bribe."

He gave me a wry smile, then handed me a citation. "Look, I'm a busy man. Your paperwork could *easily* get lost on my desk. Do you understand what I'm saying?"

"So you might not follow up on this?"

"Don't push it, lady." He handed me his card. "Just call me when you find a job."

I looked into his kind eyes. "You, sir, are a saint."

He looked into my tired eyes. "I'm just doing my job and trying to sleep at night."

As soon as the inspector drove off, I ran down the block to my neighbor's house.

"I'm Chicken Little!" I cried the minute he opened the door. "I'm afraid to cross the street!"

Frank, a ninety-one-year-old producer who hadn't made a movie since he was thirty, invited me in. "What happened now? Your roof cave in?"

I told him about the building inspector who might "lose" my paperwork.

"And you didn't have to sleep with him?" He pushed open his screen door. "Come in and have a snort to celebrate."

"It's only ten-thirty. I don't drink until noon."

He shrugged. "So you can watch me."

I followed him into the kitchen, where he poured himself two fingers of whiskey. "Look, you still have all your teeth. Everything will be fine."

"Right," I said, wincing as I sat down. "Maybe I will have a drink."

"Why are you making faces like an old lady?" He flexed his muscles. "Join a gym. You'll get girls and maybe you'll give me one." He gulped down his snort and poured a shot for me. "And start drinking more, for God's sake."

I tossed back my whiskey and coughed so hard my back went out.

The next day I saw a chiropractor. "Wow," he said, shaking his head at my fifth lumbar. "You must have a tremendous threshold for pain."

I thought so too, until I got that five a.m. call. Until my life spun off its axis. Until the sky fell. I had a dream that my mom died . . . and then she did.

It had been five months and three weeks since I lost my job, five months and two weeks since my girlfriend trashed my heart. I should have known better on that June morning than to answer that call. Everyone knows a phone ringing in the dark isn't good news.

When my phone jolted me awake, I knew it was trouble. Only finding out you've won the lottery is worth getting ripped from sleep. My life was noisy with bills, my wardrobe crying for an update. All I wanted was quiet, and here that damn phone was ringing, making it impossible for me to go back to my dream that was so real.

"Wake up, little bug."

Through the sheets I could see the silhouette of my mother standing over me.

"Time to get cracking," she said. "You've got a big day ahead of you."

Somehow in the night I'd shed forty years and ninety pounds. Now I was a skinny fourth grader not ready for summer to be over.

"Please, Mom," I begged. "Give me more time."

Though my eyes were closed, I could see that my house, my bed, my walls were all different. My mattress had shrunk to a twin; my smooth adobe bricks were covered with ugly wallpaper. My surroundings, though familiar, were unsettling. Only my bookshelves, teeming with ceramic and plastic Clydesdales, palominos, and bays, calmed me down. Yes, there was my piebald, with white socks and blaze, my wild-eyed mustang, and docile mare. Even in my dreams, everything equine calmed me down . . . and I did need calming.

"Go away, Mom," I said. "Let me sleep a little more."

She pulled back my covers and grinned. "I'm gonna get mean."

"Nooooo!" I squealed, wriggling from her grasp.

But instead of tickling my ribs, she kissed the creases of my middle-aged brow.

"Now, wake up," she said firmly, and as she drew away, she began whispering answers to questions I'd been asking for years.

But I couldn't hear her—the damn phone was ringing.

"What?" I grumbled into the receiver.

"Barb?"

My sister was on the other end of the line asking me who I was. I didn't have to ask *which* sister because I knew it would be Sandra. She was closest in age to me. Harriet, the eldest, would call Naomi, who would call Sandra, who would call me.

My heart fluttered; my eyes groped the room for my horse collection, now boxed in the basement. I didn't want to ask the question, but I did anyway. "What's wrong?"

"It's Mom."

Of course it was Mom. Hadn't she just kissed me goodbye? I struggled to keep from throwing the phone across the room.

"Naomi called me about ten minutes ago." Sandra burst into tears. "Mom died."

Damn her, I thought, and then I whispered, "Oh my God."

"I know . . . it's unbelievable. I just spoke to her a couple of days ago."

The fragile teacup that was my life was already wobbling. Now it was rocking out of its groove. "I talked to her too. She said she was feeling okay. I was going to book a flight for a visit, but—"

"Look, I'm sorry. I've got to call my kids. Are you okay?"

I was up and pacing now. "Wait . . . just tell me what happened."

"I don't know," Sandra whispered.

"Did she fall? Did she have a stroke?"

"Barbara, I *don't* know."

"Damn it."

"Yeah, damn it."

We tossed the silence back and forth until Sandra said she had to let her kids know so they could make plane reservations. "I'm sorry, I really do have to go." She burst into tears again. "You're okay, aren't you?"

My stomach clenched. "Yeah, go on. I'm okay."

"You're sure you're not just saying that?"

"Of course I'm just saying that!" I took a breath. "I'm fine. Go call your kids."

We hung up and there I stood, naked in my dark bedroom with no one to call.

"The hell I'm okay," I grumbled, wandering into the bathroom, where I stared in the mirror at my ridiculous hair and silly face. "Cry, goddamn it. Your mom just died."

I cupped water into my mouth and wandered back into my bedroom, leaving the old lady with a dead mother behind. My dogs were sitting on my bed staring at me. "Why can't I cry?" I asked their blank faces. "Why am I so angry with her?"

Beau, my half-blind dachshund, burrowed under the covers and came up with a filthy tennis ball. Dudley, my neurotic beagle, glanced toward the kitchen, where his food bowl was. They didn't care if I was a monster, I was *their* monster, and I was up earlier than usual.

The truth was, I was furious with my mother. Four days ago, she had been diagnosed with pancreatic cancer, but the doctors had given her six months to a year. I mean, the woman couldn't be on time for a car pool, a school play, or a piano recital, but given the chance to die early, she was all over that.

I flopped back onto my bed, loathing myself. How sick was I to want her to live through a full death sentence just so I could clear up a few things? What kind of daughter needed a therapeutic breakthrough so badly she wanted her mother to endure bedpans and morphine drips, diapers and bedsores—for what, *clarity*?

My stomach circled. *I* was that kind of daughter. I wanted to drill a hole through my mother and excavate some kind of epiphany. I was certain she was rich with answers, certain she knew why I hadn't made more of my life, and now she had died, taking with her whatever it was I so desperately needed to know.

"Wake up, little bug. Time to get cracking."

I curled into a ball as a memory kicked me in the stomach. I covered my ears to keep her voice out, but what if I never heard her again?

"I'm gonna get mean."

I hugged my ribs, but what if her touch slipped away forever?

Confused, I crawled between the sheets, and like a willful child, I fell back asleep.

Again the phone.

Just moments ago, I had been a six-year-old running down the hall of our Texas ranch house in El Paso, my mother sprinting after me with a dripping spoon in her hand.

"Just one bite!" she insisted. "You'll like it!"

I trudged back to my mother offering me her latest concoction. The job of taste-tester, passed down from Harriet to Naomi to Sandra to me, was to lick spatulas and spoons, then decide if something wound up on the dinner table or in the trash. But before I could sample whatever weird thing my mother had dreamed up, the damn phone rang.

"Hello," I grumbled into the receiver, surprised by my grown-up voice.

"Barb?"

I looked at the caller ID, wondering who wanted me to identify myself this time. Startled, I saw my mother's number and, in a panic, raced around my head to find the logic in this. Of course: Harriet, who still lived in El Paso, was at my mother's house, taking care of everything. You could light Harriet's hair on fire and she'd stay calm and get things done. Me, I'd run around like a human matchstick igniting the curtains.

"Are you okay?" Harriet asked.

"I'm okay. I was just asleep."

"You're unbelievable, Barbara. How could you go back to sleep? Sandra called you, didn't she?"

Four years, eight years, and twelve years older than me, my sisters still believed I was the spoiled baby of the family. But it was more like I was overcooked than overindulged, left on the counter untouched and unsavored.

I struggled back to Harriet from the undertow of self-pity. "Yeah, Sandra called. Do you remember Mom's cream cheese brownies? I was just dreaming about them."

Harriet laughed. "I loved her cherry maraschino cake. The woman could bake, but she sure couldn't cook. Thank God for Chef Boyardee."

An image flashed through my brain, of my mother mincing garlic and onions to go with my dad's dinner every night.

Your father thinks he's still in Russia. She chuckled, wiping away a tear. *So why am I the one who's suffering?*

My throat clutched. "Sandra didn't know what happened. Do you?"

"Not really. Mom was pretty much gone by the time I got there. The paramedics tried to revive her, but I told them to let her go. When they took her away, I started calling everyone."

"Took her away? Where?"

"I don't know, Barbara. Where do you think? Kmart?" She paused, and I could tell she was holding back tears. "Look, I'm sorry. They took her to the hospital. The people from the funeral home will pick her up from there."

I felt a sudden urge to start bawling because my big sister had yelled at me. "Was she alone?" I asked. "God, I hate to think she died alone."

"No, Chula was with her. Poor thing's pretty shaken up. I think she thinks we blame her. Would you talk to her? Your Spanish is better than mine."

As I sat there listening to Harriet assure my mother's housekeeper that it was Barbara in Los Angeles and not the Border Patrol, I thought of Juana, two housekeepers prior. I used to ride her vacuum cleaner like it was a locomotive, pop out of closets like a demonic clown, perch on top of the refrigerator like a vulture—anything to get her to play with me. It was Juana to whom I ran when I fell down the arroyo, Juana who found my stash of marijuana and shamed me into dumping it down the toilet, Juana who played Go Fish and I Spy. My mother was playing mah-jongg or shuffling cards somewhere.

"Barbara?"

Chula's voice dragged me away from the past like a brat from a roller coaster.

"¡Ah, mi amor!" she wailed. *"¡Es un día triste para todos!"*

I let her gather herself and wail a little more before I asked her what had happened.

"Su madre me llamó en la noche," she said. *"Y me preguntó, ¿Qué pasa?'"*

"¿Y nada más?"

Then according to Chula, my mom looked at her with *ojos grandes, como de una niña chiquita,* like a little girl with big eyes, and then she slid to the floor *como una muñeca de trapo,* like a rag doll.

I spoke to Chula for a few more minutes, but she kept dissolving into tears, so I asked her to give the phone back to my sister.

"My God, what did you say to her?" Harriet asked. "She's hysterical."

"I told her the truth. That Mom considered her a good friend."

"It's true. They were close. Did she tell you anything?"

"Not really. Just that Mom kept asking what was happening."

"God, she was probably scared half to death."

"More like completely to death." I chuckled, instantly stunned that the words in my head had come out of my mouth.

Harriet sighed. "I don't know what's wrong with you, Barbara. I really don't."

A prickly silence set in. I didn't know what was wrong with me either.

"Well, at least she didn't suffer," Harriet finally said.

"No, Chula said she looked excited. Like a little girl going on a big trip."

"Mom was *excited* to die?"

"Actually, Chula said *extática*. Apparently Mom was ecstatic to get out of here."

"Wow," Harriet gasped.

"Yeah, wow."

I sat there in Los Angeles, in my shadowy bedroom, picturing Harriet in my mother's bedroom, now streaked with sun. "Do you wanna know what I think?"

"What? Mom's in heaven playing canasta with Grandma?"

"No," I said. "I think she saw Dad, and that's why she looked so excited. I think he swooped down and whisked her away."

"*Whoosh!*" Harriet said, laughing. "Off into the cosmos!"

"*Zoom!*" I said, giggling with my big sister. "He swept her right off to heaven!"

"Just like he whirled me around the dance floor at my wedding." Harriet sniffled.

"Just like he twirled me around at my bat mitzvah," I said, falling silent, my eyes dry as sandpaper.

After Harriet had a good cry and we hung up, Naomi called and we had almost the same conversation. She wound up in tears, talking about how Mom was so loving, so giving, so there for us, and I hung up wondering whose mother she was talking about.

My mother was Queen Elizabeth right down to the shoes and purse. She was regal even when wearing a stained apron—the epitome of grace, whether balancing a checkbook or cleaning up dog vomit. But loving, giving, *there* for us? I remember her giving me a fully packed suitcase when I wanted to run away from home, wishing me luck, and telling me to send a postcard even though I had only just learned to write my name. I remember how she told me to get in the backseat and buckle up before she took me to Sunday School, but drove off before I got in the car, and how she'd left me behind at the grocery store, not realizing what she'd done until I didn't show up for dinner.

It wasn't that my sisters were loved any more than I was; it's just that their mom wasn't as exhausted as mine. Their mom had the energy to assemble elaborate Halloween costumes, while mine draped a white sheet over my head and cut out eyeholes. Their mom wore black dresses to fish funerals, while mine flushed floaters down the toilet. Their mom did the "mom thing," while mine had moved on. In fact, I'm convinced that if Sandra had been a boy, I never would have seen the light of day.

Witness my absence on film. I found no photos of me tucked in a drawer or stashed in a shoe box. No images of me graced a wall or sat framed on a coffee table. I appeared on no nightstands, wasn't pasted in albums, or slipped into any wallets. And I kind of missed the whole celluloid window between home movies and camcorders. I remember my excitement and ultimate letdown each time our family gathered around the film projector, turned off the lights in the living room, and watched old black-and-white reels of family outings. There were Harriet, Naomi, and Sandra sledding in Cloudcroft or tumbling down the dunes of chalk-white gypsum at White Sands National Monument. And there was my mother trying to control a checkered tablecloth as it whipped around in the wind at a family picnic, or my father sneaking a piece of fried chicken out of a slatted wooden basket.

"Where am I?" I would ask, sitting on the carpet with my six-year-old legs tucked under me Indian-style.

"You'll show up in a minute," my father would say, threading another reel into the projector. "Just try to be patient."

"Oh, no, Ben," my mother would say. "She wasn't born yet." Or, "Don't you remember? We left Barbara with the sitter."

To be fair, I'm sure wrangling three daughters on family excursions was hard enough without dealing with a fourth one who couldn't walk yet. And certainly, now as an adult I understand that a crying baby might ruin a nice piece of footage. Certainly one should expect a natural dwindling in the number of photos taken of the mesmerizing first daughter to the been-there-done-that fourth, but I swear there was little record I'd ever left the womb.

This was made glaringly clear to me one day when I was home from graduate school on a break. I was reading on the living room couch under a shrine of three large wedding portraits when one of the women who delivered Meals on Wheels with my mother walked in and changed everything.

"Oh my God!" Helga Bloomberg gasped, turning to my mother. "You have three lovely daughters!" She held her hand to her mouth as if the trio of portraits hanging above me had the power to make her teeth fall out.

I looked up from my book. "She has *four*."

Poor Mrs. Bloomberg looked like a startled guppy.

"Well, of course!" My mother glared at me. "This is Barbara, daughter number four. She's home for spring break."

I tipped an imaginary hat. "Don't mind me. I'm here for only another week."

Mrs. Bloomberg turned pink. "Um, what are you studying?"

"Family counseling."

"Oh, she's just kidding." My mother threw an arm around her friend and began leading her away. "Barbara is studying journalism."

"Not anymore." I grinned. "I've found a new calling."

Mrs. Bloomberg began digging through her purse. "Here they are!" She held up a set of keys. "Oh, dear, I've forgotten an appointment. Let's have coffee another time."

For a moment, my mother stood at the door, waving at her friend's exhaust fumes. Then she slowly turned, gave me a confused look, and drifted from the room. She made it halfway down the hall before I heard her heels make an about-face and click toward me. I expected to get a lecture, an apology, anything but the truth.

"You know, wedding gowns are really impractical." She sat next to me on the couch. "You wear them once, and for what you pay, you could buy ten pantsuits. So how about we go shopping tomorrow and buy the most expensive outfit we can find?" She paused. "Then let's have a gorgeous portrait of you taken. Okay?"

We sat there, she waiting for an answer; I determined not to give her one.

"Don't go away." She patted my knee. "I'll be right back."

Though I wanted to catch the next plane, I stayed on the couch, pretending to read. Then minutes later my mother returned and sat next to me.

She took my hand and dropped a pair of diamond studs in my palm. "I was saving these for your wedding day. I guess now is as good a time as any to give them to you."

I looked at the tiny earrings in my hand and understood exactly what she was saying. Although I hadn't come out yet, I had abandoned wearing dresses, and this was her way of saying she had accepted that I might never find a man. "Thanks, Mom," I muttered. "They're beautiful."

"You know, marriage isn't all it's cracked up to be. You're going to have adventures your sisters will never have."

I pictured myself jostling in a jeep across the Serengeti, following a Sherpa up Mount Everest, flinging myself off the Golden Gate Bridge tethered to a bungee cord.

"I ask only one thing." She glanced toward the symbols of my spinsterhood in my palm. "Will you please wear those instead of your feathers for the portrait?"

And so there we were two weeks later, the four Schoichet daughters, hanging over the living room couch, three in wedding gowns with matching silk shoes, one in a pantsuit with rattlesnake cowboy boots. All of us had diamond studs in our ears; one of us had a blue feather in her hair. Yes, there we hung until we sold my mother's house—the first three daughters happily married, with several grown children; the fourth fated to have trouble settling down, with a dachshund, a beagle, and a pond full of koi.

And my mom, well, she was right to have given me those studs when she did. There was surely no wedding in my future. In fact, not long after what became known as "The Helgaberg Incident," I wound up heading back to graduate school, where I had my first serious affair. It was with my nineteenth-century Russian literature professor. She was my first love, a handsome woman twice my age, and a dead ringer for my dad.

And the earrings, well, they'd always been a symbol of failure from the afternoon my mother gave them to me . . . to the night I dropped them in a silk pouch and gave them away.

It was nearly seven a.m., and a sliver of light from a gap in my drapes was keeping me from sleep, forcing me to face that phone call from two hours before. I got up and thought about calling some friends, but it was too early and I was still too unsettled. I knew I wanted something warm and soothing to fill me up. And though I wanted comfort, not stimulation, I headed to the kitchen to brew a pot of espresso.

By the grace of God, I saw a bottle of Glenlivet and figured it would either knock me out or help me settle into my new reality. With my dad gone nine years and my mom gone just a few hours, I was an orphan. Without warning, I felt as though I'd been kicked to the curb like an empty can, dumped by the side of the universe while my mom raced off to be with my dad in another realm. I felt too small for this, too young to handle it. I wanted to run from the house, bolt into the street right in front of a car. I wanted to get someone's attention. Surely *someone* would run after me.

My hand trembled as I poured myself a drink—didn't anyone see I needed a hug?

Luckily, the Scotch was the perfect thing to calm me down. It soothed the ache that began in my chest and spread like a grassfire throughout my body. Each sip slapped me in the face and blanketed me with a delicious comfort. It was like being caressed by the same hand that had just hit me. It was like my mother stroking my cheek at night as she apologized for accidentally digging her nails into my arm as she dragged me from a toy store.

As I drank my Scotch on my broken bench on my collapsing porch, I let it swaddle me in a blanket of liquid warmth as I watched the sun rise higher in the sky.

"I'm handling this okay," I whispered, and for just a moment, I felt like running to tell my mother what a big girl I was, how great I was at dealing with this whole death thing. Then, smiling at my little-girl self, I finally burst into tears.

Three

It's Not the End of the World

———

When the fortification of the Scotch wore off on the morning of my mother's death, I finally started calling friends, but their lives proved to be as porcelain as mine. If they weren't already in the club no one wants to join—the one in which losing a parent is the initiation—they tried to be there for me, but really they acted as if they were afraid they were going to catch what I had just got. I understood completely. I felt the same way when I saw people wobbling around in the ruins of a life-changing event. I was repelled by their fragility, and even if I wanted to hug them, they looked like they might break.

Now, though I was the one who longed for an embrace, I seemed to project just the opposite. It was like I'd sprouted porcupine quills, and friends began to put barriers between my anguish and their normalcy. Self-help books, coupons for spa treatments, and even a jar of bubble bath appeared in my mailbox. I tried everything. I even wore a medallion of the archangel Raphael, patron saint of mental illness, that I found on my porch.

But it was when I was coming out of a hypnotist's office—where nothing happened except I fell asleep—that I noticed a flyer for a grief support center, pinned onto a corkboard. I copied down the number, and called immediately.

"I'm sorry, but we can't just put you in a group," the receptionist said. "You have to meet with one of our clinicians first and complete an intake evaluation."

"I'm not sure you understand. I need help *now*. A lot has happened and . . ."

I couldn't finish my sentence. Even *I* couldn't hear my story again. My grief had sucked every thought that wasn't sorrowful out of my brain. Friends didn't know what to say to me anymore. My sisters dove into their families. And my ex, who had actually stepped up on the day my mom died by coming over and letting me cry in her arms, was now completely immersed in her new girlfriend and probably getting free haircuts.

"I realize you're in pain," the receptionist said, dialing her voice to a kinder setting. "Loss is powerful."

I began to cry. "I'm actually afraid of it. I don't think I can handle any more."

"Let me see if I can find a counselor to do an intake today." Her voice became a healing salve. "There's a new group for people who are grieving a parent starting in a week. Maybe she can get you in."

I babbled out several different forms of thank you, and squeezed the bridge of my nose so I wouldn't start bawling again.

"You are aware I can't make any promises." She clicked away on her keyboard. "You do understand, don't you?"

I wanted to scream that I didn't understand *anything* . . . that my mommy had just died and I didn't have a job that would occupy my mind for a few hours. I wanted to tell her that *I* felt dead, vacant like an abandoned house with no girlfriend, stressed-out sisters, and worried friends who used to drive me crazy and now were dwindling away.

I took a deep breath. "Sure . . . I understand. But can we at least do the evaluation today? I rarely leave my couch and it would be nice to have someplace to go."

There was a long silence. Had she heard what was in my head? Did she think I was in danger of hurting myself? *Was* I in danger of hurting myself?

"Well, it must be your lucky day. One of our counselors has had a cancelation this afternoon."

I felt such a wave of relief I almost fell over. "Just tell me what time to be there."

Since I was now an expert on grief I sailed through the intake and landed in a group of five women, including myself, and three guys. We met every other week for a *very* long ninety minutes, and I said nothing after introducing myself at our first meeting until two sessions later. I thought I might explode with a gusher of slimy hot pain, or let loose a spray of shrapnel if someone exposed the sour anger buried in my stomach. We sat in a circle in a dimly lit room with lots of pillows, and to be honest, all of their names, faces, backgrounds, and ages have escaped me . . . except one.

Sixty-something Emily had recently retired from teaching to spend more time with her husband, who was dying of cancer, and I think I connected to her most because we were older than everyone else, and now "adult orphans" with the recent death of our second parent. Like me, she had lost her mother, and I think she was even more pissed than I was. To this day, I thank her for having the courage to speak up and guide me through my own bewildering rage.

"My relationship with my mother was, well, complicated," she said, hugging a pillow. "I loved her, sure, but I can't tell you the kind of venom I have boiling inside me." She chuckled, then looked around the room uncomfortably. "Sometimes I go in my garage and scream at her."

"I don't yell at my mom . . . at least not yet," I said quietly. "But pretty much every time I look in the mirror I talk to her. It feels like she abandoned me."

The facilitator for our group was a young woman in her mid-thirties, a little too perky for my taste, and I hated the way she seemed to always be whispering. "A certain kind of anger isn't uncommon after a death," she said. "Often it's directed at God."

"God, schmod." Emily rolled her eyes. "Did God make my mother refuse to get live-in help? Did God make her break her hip and refuse proper medical treatment? There's no cure for my husband's kind of cancer. There *is* a cure for her kind of stubbornness. Just *stop* being stubborn!"

She started to sniffle and someone passed her a box of Kleenex.

"I am *not* going to cry!" she snapped. "And I will never forgive my goddamned mother for not being here to help me get through my husband's goddamned death."

"Your mother is with you in spirit," the woman next to me said, and I thought Emily might hit her.

"Spirit, my ass!" Emily said. "If she's anywhere, she's in fucking heaven having a cocktail with my dad."

I burst out laughing and it felt great. If Emily didn't have to rush off to her dying husband, I'd have asked her out for a drink. "I'll bet our parents are sitting together in some kind of living room on a cloud getting wasted. I'll bet they—" I stopped as a blistering pang of anger bubbled from my mouth. "I don't think my mother gave a second thought to leaving me."

"That's good, Barbara," the counselor said. "Let out your feelings."

She had touched my knee and I jumped like she had hit me.

"No," I said. "I'm done."

"I'm not saying your anger isn't justified," she said. "I'm just trying to clarify it."

I looked around the room at all these kind, suffering people. None of us wanted to be there. All of us just wanted out of the hell we were in. "She left me," I said quietly. "She left me before I got to know her . . . before she got to know me."

Everyone in the group started talking at once and I didn't hear a word they were saying. I'd fallen into a place within myself where I waited until the group finally ended. While everyone stood around, I walked out, wanting to call my mom to see if she was really dead, but instead I just stared at her name in my phone as I did at least once a day. When the elevator came, I dove inside before anyone else from my group had left the room.

As the doors slowly closed, I found myself encased in metal and standing silently next to a rail-thin girl. Stooped over like an elderly woman, she couldn't have been more than a teenager, her stringy blond hair clearly unwashed. She was dressed like a hippie—headband, tie-dyed blouse, long skirt, and sandals—and when I got into the elevator, she took a step back into the far corner as if I might lunge at her with one of the hugs everyone around the place was always passing out.

"Hi," I said, instantly uncomfortable. It was as though we were both prisoners in a holding cell, and if I'd been my old self I'd have said something silly like, *What are you in for?* Instead I just stood there, not feeling like anyone I knew.

"Hi," she muttered, quickly looking at her shoes.

But seconds before our two-word exchange, we'd had a moment of eye contact, and I'd seen a ripple of guilt pass through her. Straightaway, my discomfort vanished. I too had been a shy teenager, mortified by my awkwardness around adults I didn't know.

"I haven't seen you here before," I said, and though I doubted the center would hire someone so young and unkempt, I asked if she worked there anyway.

She shook her head and cracked a timid smile. "No, I'm in a different group than yours. I'm a multiple."

I thought she meant personalities, and I must have looked confused. We were in a Santa Monica grief support center, not the psychiatric ward at Bellevue.

Her face reddened and I thought she might burst into tears. Instead she smiled and offered me a broken laugh. "You probably think I'm Sybil or something." Her smile fell and her eyes darted to the floor. "No, I don't have some kind of disorder. I'm in a group with people mourning more than one death. My whole family was killed in a car wreck."

"Oh, my God." I put my hand over my mouth to cover my shock. "I'm so sorry."

She actually chuckled, as if she enjoyed my unease, but then I realized what I had perceived before as guilt or shyness was really her way of trying to save me from listening to her terrible disclosure.

"I can't really talk about it, but I'm learning to," she said, leveling a strong gaze right at me just as the elevator doors opened. "This place has been a godsend."

"Yes," I said. "It has."

I tried to walk calmly into the lobby, to not look back because there were no words for this girl. But I did stop and turn around to see her once more, to take in a bit of her pain, because I suddenly realized I had a small amount of room in myself to absorb at least some of her grief.

Once outside the building, when I was sure she couldn't see me, I broke into a run. It was the kind of sprinting I did when I was in grade school—fast and effortless. My sadness, which I'd been lugging around like extra weight, had fallen off like a snakeskin, and I was free of it . . . until the sun peeked through my blinds the next morning.

I pulled the covers around me and watched the light slowly take over part of my dark bedroom, and then I got up.

"It's not the end of the world," I said to myself in the bathroom mirror. "Only the end of the world is the end of the world."

. . .

Seven weeks after burying my mom I turned fifty, and on the morning of my birthday, I woke up with a terrible thought. Someone was going to want to celebrate. And right on cue, my sister Naomi called, with Sandra and Harriet conferenced in.

"We're taking you to Las Vegas in three days," she said. "And you're not allowed to say no because we've already got the tickets."

"No," I said. "No, no, and no."

"Come on," said Sandra. "We've booked Caesars Palace, and gotten front-row tickets to Elton John."

"Have fun," I said. "I'm not celebrating anything."

"Yes, you will," said Harriet. "You're going to celebrate your birthday with us in Las Vegas if we have to fly to Los Angeles, kidnap you, and drag you onto the plane."

This was not a hollow threat. My sisters had kidnapped me before. Well, not *kidnapped* me, but they did corner me in my apartment when I was twenty-two, fresh out of college, and disillusioned. It seemed that journalism jobs weren't falling out of the sky like my career counselor had promised, so I was waitressing in two restaurants, pretending I was a suffering writer, and smoking a lot of pot. I had moved to San Francisco because Naomi and her husband were there, and I figured they were good for a home-cooked meal whenever I needed one. But I guess I spent too many nights sitting on my fire escape, staring at Alcatraz, sipping Kahlúa, and complaining to Naomi. Apparently she had become increasingly worried about my tipsy phone calls and all the dark poetry I shared with her, because one day she called to say that Harriet and Sandra were coming into town the next day, and we were all going to have lunch.

"They're just flying in for no reason?" I asked. "What's the occasion?"

"We thought we'd have a little sister time," Naomi said brightly. "You've been so down lately, I called everyone to come cheer you up."

I bought her answer completely. Naomi was the glass-half-full sister, always finding something pleasing to focus on. It was no wonder that she used my depression as an opportunity for us all to get together. And I could see how Harriet and Sandra would be up for a visit too. Harriet was the sister who would empty most of her glass into yours, making sure you had enough to drink before she'd take a sip. Sandra was the sister who had to examine the contents of everyone's glass to make sure no harm came to anyone. What if the drink was too hot and someone got burned? What if it was too cold and someone got a brain freeze? As for me, well, I was the sister who grabbed the glass and drank without thinking. I'd never see a crack in the side, a jagged lip, or shards floating beneath the surface. I was always too quick to quench my thirst.

"So it was just a spur-of-the-moment thing between you guys?" I bit my lip, struggling not to slip into baby sister mode. "And nobody thought about mentioning it to me? I mean, I'll be happy to see everyone, but I could have had plans."

If Naomi had been Harriet, she'd have said she was sorry, that she should have taken my schedule into consideration. If she had been Sandra, she'd have scoffed at even the *idea* that I had plans. But because she was Naomi she said, "It's a surprise! We're meeting at your apartment at noon."

It was definitely a surprise. The next day they all showed up at the same time, walked into the postage stamp I lived in, and delivered an ultimatum.

"We're not going to lunch until you agree to see a psychiatrist," Harriet announced. "Naomi told us how down you've been, and we're worried about you."

"This is ridiculous," I said. "I'm not *that* down. And besides, I see a therapist."

"It has to be a psychiatrist," Sandra said. "Someone who can prescribe drugs." She walked around my tiny apartment, and then plopped into my armchair. "Wow, I'd be depressed here too. You can't even stretch without hitting a wall."

I looked at Naomi. "Our conversations were private."

"It's just Dr. Meddleman. You've heard me talk about him before." She looked at her shoes, the latest from Prada. "He's helped me get over a lot of my guilt."

Drop-dead gorgeous, Naomi married a man who became quite successful and looked like he stepped right out of *GQ*. They were both generous people, beautiful inside and out, but my sister's heart of platinum was restless, always concerned that others might not see her for who she is because she has so much.

"I don't need a psychiatrist," I said. "I *need* a hamburger. I didn't have breakfast because I thought we were having an early lunch."

"You're not eating?" they all said at once.

I burst out laughing. "This is ridiculous. I'm surprised Mom and Dad aren't here."

"They bought our plane tickets," Sandra said. "We didn't want to ambush you."

"Oh, really," I said, looking at Harriet standing in front of the door with her arms folded. "What is this? A tea party?"

"Please, just agree to see someone," Harriet said. "It was Naomi's idea that you go to Meddleman because she knows him, but you can see anyone."

I couldn't help smiling at my big sister. With her arms folded and blinking nervously, she looked like a genie trying to grant a wish. That was Harriet being tough, when conflict of any kind usually made her break into a coughing fit.

"Well, I'm starving too," said Sandra, now standing by the door next to Harriet and Naomi. "Come on, lots of people have a hard time right after college. Just say you'll go, and quit when you want. We'll never know the difference."

And so I went to Dr. Meddleman, but I was too young and sarcastic to take him seriously. When he handed me a rubber bat and recommended I beat a pillow, sure, I hit it a few times, but I usually burst out laughing. Once I actually did feel better when I clobbered a sofa cushion I pretended was Mr. Cohen. He was my high school English teacher, who suggested I play the lead in *Cyrano de Bergerac* because I wouldn't have to wear a prosthetic nose. He did apologize later for making a joke at my expense, but I never forgave him, and got a nose job the next summer for my birthday.

"I could have been another Barbra Streisand!" I yelled at the cushion, and whacked it across the room. "Now I'll never know what I might have looked like."

Really, though, the best thing about seeing Dr. Meddleman was the Prozac he prescribed. It kicked in about the third week and bounced me right out of my depression. It was as though a hand suddenly reached inside my brain, picked out all the feelings of inadequacy, and threw them in the air like confetti.

Don't dwell on the bad stuff, the Prozac said. *Just dwell.*

It was good advice twenty-eight years ago, and it was good advice now. There was nothing I could do about the last six months, and certainly nothing I could do about turning fifty. And so without being kidnapped, I willingly went to Las Vegas, where many of us in the front row of Elton John's concert got up onstage and stood around his red piano. We sang classics like "Rocket Man," "Daniel," and "Goodbye Yellow Brick

Road." We sang all of his old hits, and then suddenly I heard myself singing, "Madman Across the Water" and the lyrics really got to me.

"Will they come again next week?" I screeched. *"Can my mind really take it?"*

Every question pointed right at my life. People had been stopping by or calling for the past few months, but their visits were tapering off. I could see it in their faces, hear it in their voices . . . They were exhausted in their efforts to cheer me up. Peering into my bleak life, they probably couldn't wait to drive off or hang up. There were no right words, no way for anyone to get me through this, and people stopped trying. That's kind of what I wanted—to be left alone. I couldn't take one more platitude or hear one more suggestion. I couldn't watch another person watching me be sad, and I was worn out trying to be cheerful for someone else.

It was sweet of my sisters to whisk me away from my computer, to get me out of my house and away from the classifieds and dating sites. But I was now a middle-aged orphan, and there was no escaping that. My sisters, my friends, everyone on my block and in my neighborhood looked at me like I was someone they used to know, someone they wanted back. And it just made me more despondent because I felt the same way whenever I looked in the mirror.

After the show, as I lay in bed in my hotel room, I couldn't sleep, so I got up and looked down at the Las Vegas Strip churning below. The traffic was nonstop, bumper-to-bumper most of the time, and people shouted and banged on their horns . . . But why? Everyone knows you can't move past a car three inches in front of you. You can't even change lanes, and if you do, you're just blocked by different cars.

And then I saw something wonderful, *powerful*, agile, and just plain cool.

It was a guy dressed in black and blazing past everyone . . . or was it a girl? Yes, it *was* a girl, with a long ponytail whipping in the wind behind her. She was splitting lanes, weaving through traffic, and making a *lot* of noise. I watched her from the moment her headlight zoomed in and began darting between the cars. And I kept my eyes fixed on her taillight as it vanished in the distance. I was mesmerized by how her engine still roared in my ears, how I had *heard* her before she arrived and *felt* her long after she had left.

"*Turning back she just laughs,*" I sang under my breath, feeling the hairs on my forearms quiver like tiny dancers. "*The boulevard is not that bad.*"

Four

Something Right

———◆———

Before I went to bed that night I had a handful of roasted almonds, a stack of Pringles, and a tiny bottle of Johnnie Walker Red mixed with Pellegrino, adding a forty-four-dollar minibar charge to my hotel bill. I had something to celebrate. My life back in Los Angeles might look like a freeway pileup, but I could get through it by ignoring it. Why bother looking for a job when my age was going to wipe out my experience anyway? Why not do all the crazy shit I couldn't do while I was busy working? When my savings ran out I could drink an expensive bottle of wine, play some Billie Holiday, and do the humane thing—put myself down like a dog.

It was a freeing thought. I was never going to have another relationship, not when I couldn't get past the first question every date was bound to ask: *So, what do you do?* And my mom wasn't around anymore to stop me from, well, *anything*. Why not have fun . . . even if it was dangerous.

And so, on the last night we were in Las Vegas, when my sisters took me out to celebrate my birthday, I silently rejoiced in the thought of doing something entirely out of my comfort zone. I was going to live, goddamn it, or die trying. But first, I needed to show my sisters I was okay so they'd quit trying to cheer me up. I raised my glass of wine and made a toast.

"You three are my life, and even though this has been the worst birthday I've ever had, it's also been the best." I reached under my chair for a bag that held four small blue boxes from Tiffany. I placed a box in front of each of us and declared, "Happy Birthday to all of us!"

In minutes, we were all crying. Inside each box was a sterling silver poker chip engraved on one side with *Sisters* and with *Something Right* on the other. Our parents always used to say that they must have done "something right" when it came to raising us. Unlike so many siblings, we were unbelievably close, and even though my sisters didn't know it, they were no longer going to have to worry about me.

"It's beautiful, Barbara," Harriet said. "I'm going to put it in my wallet and carry it with me wherever I go."

Naomi and Sandra agreed to do the same, and I told them I'd flip the poker chip before making any important decisions. If it landed on *Something Right*, I'd go ahead and do it. But if it landed on *Sisters*, I'd think of each of them before moving forward.

I lost my wallet—with the silver coin in the side pocket—shortly after I got home from Las Vegas.

Two weeks after turning fifty, with my first motorcycle class already under my belt, I left Bartel's Harley-Davidson with a ton of new gear and called my neighbor Lynn on the way home. She was a divorced, single mom in her fifties with money problems and health care issues— enough setbacks to make her completely get my depression. Unlike my other friends, she did not make me feel guilty if I suddenly broke into tears. I had thought Lynn would understand why I wanted to rattle my cage and blast by all those cowards in cars. She, I was sure, would be excited—maybe a little envious—when I told her I wanted to become a motorcycle chick. My therapist, the only other person I had told, was less than supportive. And my sisters, well, they certainly couldn't know. They were trying to convince me I should stop driving altogether.

"Motorcycle lessons?" Lynn screamed into the phone. "Can't you at least *try* to handle your problems like a normal person? Go lie on Muriel's couch. Pour out your heart to a bartender. Go to a day spa!"

"I have an appointment with Muriel in an hour. And why are you so worked up? I'm learning to ride a motorcycle, not wrestle alligators."

"Hang on a minute," Lynn said. "I've got to put you on hold."

I paced around my house in my brand-new leathers, checked myself out in the mirror a few times, and waited for Lynn to come back on the line. It was August, and I was beginning to sweat, so I cranked up my air conditioner, and then the doorbell rang.

"You can hang up now." Lynn stood on my front porch grinning. "This is a conversation that *has* to be in person . . . By the way, you look really cool in that outfit."

"Thanks, I think so too." I caught another glimpse of myself in her sunglasses as she brushed past me. "I'm starting to feel pretty comfortable in animal skins."

She plopped on my couch and began typing on her cell phone. "Okay, listen to this. There were more than forty-five hundred motorcycle deaths just this year—and *that* was only in the United States. If we factor in Europe, I'll bet there are a million idiots who wound up half-dead in the hospital. Probably most of them will be amputees."

"What'd you do? Google 'ways to scare Barbara'? Why don't you check how many people died of cancer?"

"You're not learning how to get cancer!" She got up to leave. "I'm going home."

"Wait a minute. You just got here. Let's Google 'car wrecks.'"

She stopped at the front door and glared at me. "You might think you're funny, but I'll be the one sitting by your bedside when the doctors pronounce you brain-dead."

I watched Lynn walk across the street to her house, but the vision she left me with—my body broken, bandaged, and connected to tubes—was freaking me out. For a moment, I actually thought about canceling my lessons, and then I realized something. I wasn't that much better off.

The truth was, I had felt comatose ever since my mom died. But now, with just the *idea* of motorcycling, I felt wicked with the thrill of getting away with something. Just hearing Bart *talk* about motorcycles gave me a Russian roulette quiver of excitement. I couldn't wait to risk my life if only it would goad my mother out of hiding. It was as though she'd been kidnapped, and I half-expected someone to call demanding ransom for her release. Maybe flying around on a death machine would stop me from thinking she was still out there, because if she was, she'd surely try to stop me.

Muriel certainly didn't know what to do with me. I was so agitated during the whole session I had trouble sitting down.

"You said I needed to refocus my life." I paced around her office, stopping to glance at the August 1, 2005, issue of *Time* magazine with an eyewitness to Hiroshima on the cover. "Wow, can you believe they dropped the bomb sixty years ago?"

"Yes, it's hard to believe. Try to stick with what you were saying . . . something about refocusing your life?"

"Right. Don't you think balancing on two wheels should just about do the trick?" I flopped on the couch and grinned like a lunatic. "Tomorrow we start riding!"

"Okay, this is the most animated I've seen you in weeks, but I think you're overreacting." She glanced at the clock. "True, your losses have had you cornered, but jumping on a motorcycle and running away from them isn't sensible—*therapy* is."

Muriel was wrong. It was time to make a run for freedom, time to pull a Steve McQueen and bust out of my stalag.

"Grief has you in its grip." Muriel leaned forward with intent. "It's time to pry yourself loose, time to claw your way back to happiness."

My ankle was beginning to itch. I could feel the jaws of grief clamped around it.

"We're all just animals at the core, but—" Muriel stopped abruptly and put her head in her hands. "I can't go on. It's over ninety degrees outside. *Why* are you dressed like a Hells Angel?"

"My motorcycle instructor says we have to start getting used to wearing our gear. We're supposed to feel naked without padding over every inch of our body." I shrugged. "I have to admit I kind of like it."

Muriel smiled as though I was a bird who'd fallen from a nest. "Look, you're reacting like anyone would after being hit with so much loss. Withdraw, regroup, and bolt to something new. But motorcycling is so . . ."

Dangerous, I thought, my mind wafting out of her office. Already I was a happy drifter on the open road. I'd stewed in my losses long enough. I was marinating in antidepressants, and no amount of therapy was going to change things. I needed to take action and dare to become the person I was going to be.

As Muriel droned on about dealing with loss, I heard the drone of the Harley I'd soon be straddling, a Sportster 1200 Custom I would buy with my inheritance, on eBay. I'd be whizzing along anonymously through towns with names like Needles and pumping gas at stations along Route 66. No longer worried about making a living, I'd simply *be* living. I didn't have to fall into the gap my losses had created. I could ride past my grief, do something beyond the pain, and become a whole new person.

I told Muriel I was taking a sabbatical from therapy and I'd call if I needed to. I didn't tell her what I was going to do because at the time I didn't know. All I knew was that even before I actually lived the images in my mind's eye, I just couldn't see how sitting on a leather couch and dwelling on things could be any better than *wearing* leather and focusing on the road not taken.

Five

Seeds of a Rebel

———————

When I was six, my eighteen-year-old sister, Harriet, transformed from a prom queen into a rebel in a single day. She flew out the door with a maniacal grin, and I raced to the window to see what she was up to. I'll never forget the wonder I felt as I watched her hoist herself behind a dark figure astride a huge mechanical roach. Today, I know I was looking at my first crotch rocket, but back then, all I saw was a man in black riding a smoking insect with my sister attached to his back. Good Harriet had become *Bad*.

When she returned with her hair sticking out like Einstein's, she was either madly in love or scared out of her mind. My other sisters, fourteen-year-old Naomi and ten-year-old Sandra, were drooling over the guy, and I would have been too if I didn't already worship my PE teacher. In any case, Naomi, Sandra, and I listened in rapt attention to Harriet and my parents screaming at one another behind closed doors. We were all wishing we were our big sister—and glad we weren't.

Then one day Harriet retreated to her room and didn't come out for a week. Years later, I found out my parents had bought off her bad boy with a plane ticket to New York. To Harriet's surprise, he swaggered out of her life forever, his helmet tucked under his arm like a severed head. Poor Harriet didn't know whom to hate more—Easy Rider or our parents—and I think she settled on hating all three. But a few years later, when she married Marvin, a life insurance salesman who looked like Clark Kent, she thanked my parents for running what's-his-name out of her life. To this day, that's what we call him, because Harriet would never utter his name again.

Though Harriet's handsome roach rider remained in my little-girl consciousness for many years, motorcycles didn't come back into my life until my junior year of high school when my friend Mike let me drive his dirt bike and I rode it right into a ditch. Mike's Yamaha took the worst of it, and all I got was a sprained finger. At first I was sure my parents were going to ground me, but instead they got crafty.

I was in my room working on a paper about Edgar Allan Poe when my mom appeared in the doorway. "Come into the den," she said. "Daddy and I want to have a word with you."

I followed her down the hall, wondering if I was in trouble because of the accident or because I'd been out with a non-Jewish boy.

"Look, Mike and I are just friends," I said, trailing after her. "I'm not going to marry him."

My mother stopped and turned around. "You're not going to marry *anybody* until after college. Anyway, that's not what this is about."

We walked into the den, where my dad sat behind a newspaper and a wall of cigar smoke. "Well, there she is, my daredevil daughter." He put the paper down. "What are you going to do next? Get blown out of a cannon?"

I looked at my left hand with the splint on my index finger. "So you heard about my little accident."

"Little? According to your mother, it involved a trip to the emergency room." He motioned to the sofa across from his easy chair. "Sit down. I've got good news and bad news. What do you want first?"

"If the bad news is I'm not supposed to see Mike anymore, you can't really stop me. He's in most of my classes. So what's the good news?"

"Pretty cocky for a kid who's going to get her own car when she passes her driver's test." My father frowned, then broke into a grin. "Whaddya think of that?"

"Really? Wow, I don't care what the bad news is!" I jumped off the sofa and gave both my parents a hug. "Thank you!"

My mother was all smiles. "Okay, but it comes with one stipulation."

My dad tried to look stern, but he was clearly enjoying my excitement. "Now as you know, none of your sisters got a car until they went to college." He pointed his cigar at me. "But you—you're different. Your mother and I don't trust you."

"You're buying me a car because you *don't* trust me?"

"What your dad means is, we don't trust you *not* to try riding Mike's bike again." My mom threw me a hard look. "Do you know you could've killed yourself?"

"So here's how it's going to be." My dad crushed his cigar into an ashtray. "We're going to fix that boy's bike and you're going to get a car . . . *if* you promise *never* to ride *his* motorcycle—or *any* motorcycle—again."

"And that's your bad news?" I looked back and forth to each of my parents. "You're kidding, right?"

My dad wagged a finger at me. "This is serious, Barbara. Promise you won't *ever* ride a motorcycle again or the car deal is off."

I put my unsplinted hand over my heart and solemnly swore that I wouldn't straddle anything with a motor. And I didn't until years later . . . *many* years later.

I was living in Santa Fe and waitressing at the Hilton while I figured out what to do with a master's in creative writing, when I befriended a big-boned girl named Carla, the first diesel dyke I'd ever met. That moniker would have been an insult to some women, but Carla loved every inch of her stereotype, from the diamond in her nose and her buzz-cut do to the fuzz on her lip and the beer gut falling over her tight black jeans.

"Keeps me warm astride my ride," she used to say, patting her jelly belly. "Insulation against cold weather and nearly every man."

I was fascinated by her, grossed out by her, and in some ways, envious of her, and even though she was more comfortable in her bulky skin than I would ever be in my scrawny one, she still freaked me out. She was one of those women who didn't just identify as a lesbian—she pretty much screamed out dyke wherever she went.

Still, despite doing my best to dislike her on sight, I became fast friends with Carla one night when I "accidentally" wound up at a gay bar on the outskirts of town. Carla, who was clearly there on purpose, asked me to dance, and when I feigned an upset stomach, she knew right away I was lying. Still, she played my game.

"How about some fresh air?" she suggested. "Maybe it'll settle your stomach."

I couldn't exactly say no to that without offending her, so out the back we went and—*boom*—I fell in love.

"Purrrdy, isn't she?" Carla stroked her gorgeous Fat Boy. "Ever ride a Harley?"

"Never even considered it."

"Then throw a leg over and we'll go for a spin. If that doesn't settle your stomach, at least it'll empty it."

I smiled weakly and threw myself behind Carla's bulk; then I squeezed the life out of her for thirteen minutes that felt like sixty seconds.

"Why'd we come back so soon?" I yelled, still shouting even though she'd turned off the engine. "I was just getting used to blind fear!"

"Cool as air-conditioning, isn't it?" She patted her Harley as though it were a Thoroughbred.

"Better than pizza," I replied, suddenly aware that my arms were still clasped around her waist. "Let's go again!"

"Sorry, doll. My girlfriend will kill me." She wrestled out of my grip. "Promised her I'd be home before eleven."

Reluctantly I got off the bike and almost fell over.

Carla grinned. "Kinda makes you feel drunk, doesn't it?"

I nodded, completely intoxicated. I was a changed woman. I wanted to be a biker babe, a Road Angel, a chopper chick.

A week or so later, Carla crashed. The news was all over the gay community, and though I was still wrestling with my sexuality and not a part of that crowd, I heard about it at the bar. Apparently she wasn't wearing a helmet and was going about seventy when she hit a mattress on the highway. Witnesses said she slid with the bike on top of her the length of a football field. When she finally came to a stop, no one could believe she was still alive.

I'd met her only that one night, but in that short encounter I quickly considered her a friend. And so, over the next few months, I visited her at the hospital, and each time I went, the big-boned girl had wasted away a little more until she was nothing but bones. I don't know if she ever came out of her coma. I had met someone, had fallen in love, and already screwed it up by leaving Santa Fe in pursuit of a PhD. I went on with my life. I forgot about Carla, but the image of her on life-support stayed wallpapered in my head. It remains there today, and it's probably that image that protects me even more than my leathers. It reminds me to respect the machine I'm straddling. It also helps me understand why my parents made me promise I'd never ride a motorcycle again. But they're gone now. I'm no one's little girl anymore, and I don't have to honor anyone's wishes but my own.

Six

A Clutch Situation

The *morning after* my last session with Muriel, I went to the second day of my three-day motorcycle course, which was missing a few thugs who'd probably gotten arrested. Everyone else, including me, was decked out in leather, and after sweating through the indoor portion of class, the remaining punks, delinquents, and I were more than ready to straddle the saddle. Like prisoners with parole papers, we waddled into the parking lot after Bart, all of us reeking of cowhide, and me reeking of fear.

From the second I spotted the line of beat-up motorcycles, I began to hyperventilate. Still, I bravely slid onto the little red Nighthawk assigned to me and waited patiently to die.

First, however, I had to listen to Bart go over every inch of the machine that was going to kill me. From the ignition switch and hand-brake to the clutch and footbrake, he dissected the silent beast between my legs. Then he strode across the parking lot, waved a red flag over his head, and yelled, "Okay, children. Start your engines!"

I'd either peed in my chaps or sweat was dripping down my legs. Still, I turned on the ignition and felt a thrilling roar race from my crotch to my heart. I could only imagine what would happen when I wasn't in neutral. Luckily I was, because the guy next to me was in first gear and his bike leapt from beneath him like a dolphin.

Bart jogged over and stood beside the poor guy who'd straddled nothing but air before he fell over backward onto the ground. Almost everyone was laughing, and I thought Bart would too, but instead he offered the guy his hand, yanked him to his feet, and threw a beefy arm around his neck.

"Thanks for showing everyone what *not* to do. Fire in gear, land on your rear!" He slapped the guy on his backside. "Don't begin till you see that *N*, right buddy?"

"Uh-huh," he grunted, trying not to look completely embarrassed.

Bart looked up and down the line at the rest of us. "Now, who wants to help my pal here lift his bike?"

Four brownnosers raised their hands. I was not among them.

"You on the red tricycle. Front and center!"

Nobody moved. Bart was pointing at me.

Slowly I got off my bike and walked over to the fallen motorcycle. I was just about to bend down to help lift it, when Bart yelled, "Mistake number two!"

I jumped away from the bike as though it had bitten me. "What'd I do?"

Bart rolled his eyes to the sky. "You left your bike running. You might as well *give* it away."

"Fine." I made a U-turn to my bike, turned off the ignition, and then headed back to help my poor classmate, standing over his motorcycle as though he'd murdered it.

"Mistake number three!" Bart crowed.

"What?!" I screamed.

Bart pushed the guy away from his fallen bike, lifted it with one hand like it was made of aluminum, and then strolled over to my tiny Nighthawk to finish humiliating me.

"Better invest in some fancy insurance, buttercup." He yanked the keys out of the ignition and dangled them over his head like mistletoe. "Now, I've been hard on you, little lady." He patted my shoulder and gave me a fatherly smile. "So how would you like the honor of being the first off the line?"

Before I could answer, Bart flipped the keys over to me and I managed to catch them. Then I strode back to my bike, unusually proud to have been singled out. But the second my butt hit leather, I lost all confidence. Body part by body part, I was dissolving into a metaphor. From head to toe—or at least to upper thigh—my whole body began to do to itself what I found difficult to do with my foot—*clutch.*

With just the rev of the engine, my fingers became talons on the handgrips, my thighs a vise around the gas tank, but my foot, which had been clutching stick-shift cars since I was seventeen, suddenly couldn't grasp the way a motorcycle clutched, no matter how patiently or impatiently Bart tried to explain it.

He noticed right away that I was in trouble when he signaled from across the parking lot and I just sat there.

"I can't seem to get it out of neutral," I called out. "I think it's stuck."

"Buttercup, baby, you're too tense," Bart cooed. "You've got to *feeeeeel* the clutch. You've got to stroke it like a lover."

Still, I sat there, until he came swaggering over. That's when I figured it out and lurched forward, sending Bart diving to the asphalt like a soldier toward a foxhole.

"You can try to kill me, Grandma, but I *will* teach you to ride!" He got to his feet and shot me a look. "And by the way, your name's Chickenshit now."

I lifted my visor and smiled. "Cluck you!"

Bart grinned like a mule. "I like you, Chickenshit, and I'm gonna get you to ride that mother *clucking* motorcycle or die trying." He walked across the lot. "Now get over here—*pronto!*"

I liked Bart too. He was like the father figure I would have had if I'd been born in a trailer park. Suddenly I wanted to impress him. "Hey, badass!" I yelled. "Watch out!"

I revved my Nighthawk and did a bump and grind across the lot, taking down several orange cones along the way. Everyone clapped . . . and then the bike fell over. I lay beneath the three-hundred-pound machine wondering when the tailpipe that was burning through my boot would reach my flesh.

In a flash, Bart was by my side, lifting the bike and hoisting me to my feet in what seemed like one swift motion.

"See that?" He pointed to my smoking ankle and glared at all the gaping faces now gathered around us. "A good boot is worth every penny you spend on it." He put his finger through the smoldering polyurethane. "Ha! It hasn't even hit her sock!" He gave my shoulder a squeeze and whispered in my ear, "*Breathe*, sweetheart. You're okay."

I think he thought I was going to cry, but I felt great, the same way I felt the first time I wiped out on skis or got bucked off a horse. After doing a face-plant in the snow I could ski any black diamond. After eating dust, I could ride any horse. All those years of risking my life to get my parents' attention had paid off, and now I knew that Nietzsche was right. If motorcycling didn't kill me, it would make me stronger.

Bart let the class out early that day since everyone, except me, was pretty worn out. Our final lesson was scheduled for the next day at seven a.m. At that time we were to do a bunch of maneuvers around cones and over speed bumps, stop within three feet of a yellow line while barreling toward it as fast as we could, and swerve to avoid several strategically placed hazards, one of which was a friend of Bart's pretending to be a tree.

"Sleep well, children!" he yelled. "Tomorrow I will do everything I can to fail you. *Nobody* leaves my class to be a menace on the road."

I went home and washed down a sleeping pill with two glasses of wine. I was in bed thirty minutes after dinner, asleep by eight-thirty, and up by five. By six-thirty, I had wedged myself into my leathers and boots—the one with the hole in the ankle now a badge of honor—and by seven I was well on my way to becoming an awesome biker chick.

"You're okay, EK," Bart said, when the test was over. "First to fall and the bravest of all."

"EK?" I asked. "For Evel Knievel?"

"No, for fish disease! Of course it's for Evel Knievel. There's one in every class."

With certificate in hand, I was at the DMV a week later to take my written exam. I was ready for anything the road had to offer—as long as it wasn't more than thirty-five miles per hour.

Seven

Losing Your Bearings

———◆———

I've always been impulsive, a trait my mother loved about me but also hated. She liked my spontaneity, but always worried it might get me hurt.

"You came out of the womb an independent little soul," she said. "You'd see something you wanted and you'd lunge for it. Just getting a diaper on you before you rolled off the changing table was a miracle."

It was New Year's Eve 2000 and my mother and I were reminiscing after a night of gambling at the Inn of the Mountain Gods near Ruidoso, New Mexico, about two hours north of El Paso. We'd met there for two reasons—my girlfriend (now my ex) had an odd aversion to celebrating New Year's Eve, and my therapist (two before Muriel) suggested that I do something with my mom.

"It's time the two of you got to know each other." Nureeth grinned the way therapists do when they're about to reel off another platitude. "Neither of you is getting any younger, and besides, your mother might be able to clear up a few things."

"Like why my girlfriend keeps me at arm's length?" I asked. "Like why I crave attention as though it's fresh water on a deserted island?"

Nureeth rolled her eyes. "Why don't you just start by asking her what you were like as a little girl and go from there."

And so I called my mom to ask her if she'd ring in the new millennium with me, and to my surprise she accepted. In fact, she thought it was a great idea.

"It'll be my treat, a chance for the two of us to spend some alone time." She paused, and I pictured her leaning back in the ergonomically correct easy chair that had once been my father's and was now hers. "Do you know your sisters once told Daddy and me we needed to pay more attention to you?"

"You're kidding!?" I almost dropped the phone. "When was that?"

"I think you were about thirteen. Harriet was already married, Naomi was away at college in Tucson, and Sandra was leaving for Austin. You were suddenly home alone in that big empty house. It was around the time you found Frisky dead in the backyard."

"Frederick Von Schoichet," I said wistfully, recalling how I'd snuck up on him sunning in the grass only to find him stiff and covered with flies. "I loved that little guy."

"Yeah, well, he picked a terrible time to die. With your sisters just gone, I think you felt kind of abandoned. Your dad and I didn't know what to do, and I'm not sure we handled things right."

"You cried when Frisky died. You arranged for a funeral at a pet cemetery . . . That was sweet."

"I still feel awful. You were pretty despondent . . . And then your dad and I went on a trip to Europe. It was bad timing, but we couldn't change the tickets."

My grown-up self wanted to say that it was all right, that I understood, but the child in me won out. "Yeah, I remember—I got braces and glasses in the same year. It was awful."

"Well, I'm sorry." She sounded apologetic but firm. "So you arrange the weekend, and I'll pay. We'll spend some real mother-daughter time, okay?"

And so, because my mom and I both liked to gamble, and Ruidoso would be less crazy than Las Vegas, we ended up staring at each other in an outdated casino hotel room on the Mescalero Apache Reservation. There was my mom in her navy-blue pantsuit, sitting on her double bed with her legs crossed like a lady, and there I was across from her, my head propped up on a pillow, lounging in a running suit and sneakers. We didn't know what to say to each other, until after I took Nureeth's advice. Then memories poured out of my mother, stories I was astonished she could recall.

"Remember how you went through that phase when you were convinced you were a horse in another life? You used to pile up all kinds of things—toys, chairs, stuffed animals—then you'd gallop down the hall toward them whinnying at the top of your lungs."

"I did *not* whinny. I was a stallion—I snorted."

We both laughed, a little uncomfortable at first, then almost like we were friends.

"Fine, you snorted. Anyway, you'd hurdle over that pile, scaring the life out of me, and after you cleared it, you'd put something else on the stack until you couldn't make it over and finally fell." She shook her head. "I have no idea how you didn't break something."

We were giggling like schoolgirls now, having more fun than I could ever have imagined, until some of Nureeth's psychobabble fell out of my mouth. "I just wanted you to notice me. I don't know, maybe try to stop me."

"*Stop* you?" My mother refused to bring down the mood. "You were a cyclone. You didn't walk into a room. You blew into it."

"Juana used to catch me as I ran by and fold me into her arms. I can still smell the grease on her apron."

My mother frowned. "Please tell me we're not going to go through this again? I'm sorry, I'm just not a hugger."

I rolled my eyes. "I know, Grandpa had tuberculosis and you weren't allowed to get too close to him. You come from a long line of uptight anti-huggers. That was decades ago, Mom."

"Fine, you want an *ug*?" She got up and put out her arms. "Come here, little girl."

I just sat there feeling ridiculous. I couldn't tell if she was making fun of me or actually trying to be affectionate. I grinned. "An *ug*? You can't even say the word."

"Don't push it." She waved me toward her. "I'm doing the best I can."

Realizing that I was just as uncomfortable as she was, I got up and carefully let my mother put her arms around my waist. It lasted a very awkward four or five seconds.

When it was over she plopped on her bed as if the effort of hugging me had worn her out. "Why do you torture me? Was I really *that* bad of a mother?"

"Of course not. You had a lot to deal with—three perfect daughters and one gigantic pain in the ass."

"Oh, your sisters were far from perfect." She chuckled to herself. "You were like a toy doll they manipulated into doing things. Remember when they made you pretend you'd drowned in the bathtub? I wanted to kill them."

I smiled, picturing my five-year-old self lying naked, soaking wet, and totally unresponsive on the bathroom rug. "I would do anything they told me to do."

My mother, who had been laughing, suddenly wiped a tear from her eye. "You scared the hell out of me." She reached across the expanse from her bed to mine and did something she'd never done before—she took my hand. "So will you do just *one* thing for me?"

I was sure she was going to ask me to forgive her for being such a lousy mother, sure she was going to say she'd done her best, and I was going to say, "You were a great mom. What's to forgive?" But instead she asked me to do something that completely surprised me.

"Would you promise to watch out for yourself, Barbara?" She shook her head and laughed. "You're like one of those butterflies that slams into a windshield. You've got to start looking out for the glass."

I knew exactly what she was talking about. My sisters all had husbands—men to protect them—and to her I was still the weird little kid she'd seen smashed into bug juice in grade school. One day I'd come home without my jacket because I'd given it away to some kid I wanted to like me, another day she was racing me to the emergency room because I'd jumped off a concrete staircase to impress someone. And high school was worse. I was oblivious to the nastiness of my classmates until it flew in my face, thinking that when a group of popular kids called me squirrel they thought I was cute, until one day I found a pile of nuts in my locker.

"Don't worry," my mom assured me throughout my adolescence. "Later in life you're allowed to be different. I just wouldn't flaunt it if I were you."

Thankfully she was right. I began thriving after my sophomore year in college, bouncing off upset, deflecting disappointment, and doing lots of drugs so I didn't care anyway. I grew into my sexuality in my twenties and thirties; and in my forties, time started flying by so nothing mattered. Maybe that's why I never saw anything coming during those terrible six months—not the first blow from my employer, not the second from my lover, and certainly not the sucker punch from my mom.

Her death was much more disorienting than my father's. When he died, my sisters and I were too busy keeping our mom afloat to grieve. It wasn't that his death meant less, it was that I experienced it as some kind of natural pruning of our family tree. Both sets of grandparents were gone, followed by a few aunts and uncles, and so it was expected that my dad, the senior member of the clan, would drop off next.

As I grew older, losing loved ones, like losing physical capabilities, became part of the aging process. One minute I was reading menus without glasses, the next I needed bifocals. One Passover, Grandpa Kopilowitz led the Seder; the next year Uncle Bernie took his place. But when my mom died, it wasn't like coming home to find another relative missing; it was like coming home to find my home was gone. The bewilderment ran deep. I didn't feel a loss, I felt lost. I wasn't confused, I was paralyzed, as frozen as the first time I lost my parents in a crowded mall. As a kid I was pretty sure I'd find them, but now I knew they were gone forever.

Well, not exactly.

You see, a weird thing happened when my mom died. My father returned. I saw him *everywhere*—in coffee shops, at stoplights, even on the plane going home for my mom's funeral. Each time, I longed to ask him questions, if only he could answer, and I wouldn't be hauled off in a straitjacket.

Is Mom with you?

Are the two of you young again?

Would you consider popping in on my ex and scaring her to death?

It was unsettling to feel his presence so strongly when over the past nine years the pain of his death had all but faded away. Now it was my dad who loomed large in my mom's house when my sisters and I went to clean it out, and he who made us linger over a scarf or a shoe. My mom was nearly absent throughout the whole process, until we got to my dad's closet and began packing up things she'd been unable to give away. Then, if we so much as touched a cuff link, I could feel her trying to snatch it out of our grasp.

The really spooky thing was when they both showed up at the same time, just as they did when Harriet discovered their wedding outfits in the back of a cedar closet.

"Wow," she gasped. "Come here and look at this."

As Naomi, Sandra, and I emerged from different parts of the house, I swear my mother's heels *click-click-clicked* down the hall behind us. There too was my dad, just as he was in my childhood home, a whiff of cigar smoke, the rustle of a newspaper.

"What are we going to do with them?" Sandra asked.

"You feel them too?" I exclaimed. "I thought I was going crazy!"

Sandra stared at me. "You *are* crazy. I was talking about these clothes. What were you talking about?"

I stepped back and coughed. The mixture of cigar smoke and mothballs was toxic.

"We can't just give them away." Naomi lifted the cellophane and touched some beaded fabric. "Think of the history behind each piece."

We were staring at my dad's army uniform and the simple dress my mom wore at their wedding. Perfectly preserved, they hung next to my mother's ivory linen suit and my dad's white tuxedo. Our parents had worn these outfits a half-century apart. On April 11, 1948, my dad, in his sergeant's khaki coat, married my mom, in her hand-stitched gown, at Fort Bliss in El Paso, Texas. Fifty years later, on the same day, they renewed their vows in B'nai Zion Synagogue with the four of us standing under the huppah beside them. He was wearing the white tuxedo and she was wearing her suit.

Harriet sighed. "These clothes belong in a museum."

"Yeah," I said. "They're relics from the days when marriages actually lasted."

Instantly I felt my parents vanish. It was as if my sharpness had pierced the delicate fabric between our worlds.

"You know something, Barbara," Harriet whispered in my ear. "I knew what you meant a while ago about feeling Mom and Dad here."

A chill ran through me. "You did?"

"Yup, and I felt them disappear just now too." She smiled like only a big sister can. "Let me tell you a little secret. You don't have to be so tough all the time. Cynicism drives people away—living or dead."

Sitting on the airplane the next day, wearing my mother's diamond pendant and my father's signet ring, I felt my sister's words, my mother's death, and my father's sudden return weighing heavy on me. My whole life felt heavier, and by the time we landed, it was all I could do to wade through the thick air and fall into a cab. It was worse at home; the atmosphere was so gelatinous I couldn't get out of bed. Often I'd stare at a photograph of my parents, trying to imagine them reconnecting in the heavens, and it was that belief that if they could find each other in the great beyond, I too could find myself here on Earth. Then maybe I'd be able to reactivate my compass and navigate back to my life.

Eight

Two Daves and a Sensei in Santa Fe

———◆———

A *week after I* got my motorcycle license, a month after I turned fifty, I started to fantasize in earnest about taking a long trip. This was progress because up until then pretty much everything—my physical, mental, and emotional efforts—had all but stopped. Now I was starting to go out more often, take walks around the block, and even make it through the day without crying. My friends were delighted.

But along with my steps toward healing came an onslaught of confusing epiphanies. It was as though the powers that be had finally stopped torturing me, and now were fucking with me, playing a weird game of keep-away by tossing faith and reality back and forth just out of reach. Suddenly I was making odd connections everywhere—like the time I saw my mother's name, Florence, on the back of a football jersey during a San Diego/Denver game. I was sure she was trying to make contact with me . . . until someone gently pointed out that cornerback Drayton Florence had been playing for the Chargers since 2003.

Soon my friends were backing away at parties, afraid I'd find some oth-erworldly sign in the guacamole. Eventually no one would go to the movies with me, fearing I'd make connections with the characters on-screen. Finally, I had one last epiphany: I was going to end up alone if I didn't con-tain my thoughts, and what better way to do that than inside a helmet.

It was time to buy my first bike, to stop fantasizing about a trip and start visualizing one. Even if it was a simple jaunt up the California coast, maybe a hundred miles or so up to Santa Barbara, I was ready to put my biker's license to use . . . if only I could stop breaking into a sweat when I walked into a motorcycle showroom.

To be sure, my fear of bikes was tremendous, but so was my draw to them. So even before I bought a motorcycle, I drew up a will just in case one killed me. I also took my eldest niece, Lisa, out to dinner to see if she'd be my point person on the road. Lisa, who was a lawyer, would be the only family member I would tell about any of my motorcycle dreams, not because I didn't want to worry anyone, but because I didn't want to be stopped.

"Point person?" Lisa whined. "Why me?"

"Because you're tough. You've got the guts to pull the plug."

"Oh, for God's sake," she gasped. "Nothing's going to happen to you."

"But if it does, you'd have the courage to let me go, right?"

"You're being ridiculous." She rolled her eyes. "This is an awful thing you're asking of me."

"Come on, I'd do it for you."

"Fine, I'll kill you, you kill me. See you in heaven."

"I'm serious, Lisa. All I ask is that you do a couple of things first."

"What? Wash my hands?"

"I'm glad you think this is all a big joke, but I've actually prepared a will." I produced a handwritten document I'd drafted. "I'll get this typed up and notarized in the next couple of days so everything is all legal."

"You don't have to get it notarized, you just need two witnesses."

I pointed my knife at her. "See? I picked the right person. Now, you can be one witness, and—"

"Wait a minute. Neither witness can be a beneficiary." She grinned. "I'm assuming that disqualifies me, right?"

I sighed. "Fine, maybe you can ask two of your lawyer friends." I began skimming through the will. "But first there's just a few points I want to go over with you about removing life-support. Here it is: If I'm ever in a coma, put a donut and a cup of coffee under my nose. If I don't respond—*boom!* Pull the plug."

"You're insane. You didn't actually write that."

"I most certainly did. Now that's only if you're making this decision in the morning. If it's after five, uncork some wine and let me hear you pour it. Spend at least thirty bucks, then put the glass—do *not* use a paper cup— under my nose with a piece of cheese, and if I don't respond, yank the plug."

"Let me see that." Lisa reached for the will. "Does it say how much I should spend on the cheese?"

"Actually, I didn't specify, but a simple Jarlsberg will do. If you're bringing crackers, I really prefer Brie."

"You are the most bizarre person I know." She tucked my will into her briefcase. "I'm going to go over this later, okay?"

"Thank you. I really appreciate it." I waved for the check. "And dinner's on me."

Lisa looked worried. It couldn't be easy agreeing to off your aunt.

"Look, I'll be fine. I'm just taking precautions."

We rose to go and she gave me a hug. "Promise you'll call me before you go anywhere so I can try to stop you, okay?"

"I haven't even bought a bike yet, but I promise you this: if you even mention to anyone that I've gotten my license, when I actually *do* go on a trip no one—not even you—will know I've left."

. . .

Since I'd ridden only a 250 Nighthawk, which was one step up from a Vespa, and since I hadn't gone farther than the parking lot of my motorcycle school, I settled on a 1986 Honda Rebel a neighbor was selling just a few blocks from my house. It was only a thousand dollars and low enough to the ground that I could drag my feet while idling it back home.

A solid 331 pounds when fueled to the gills with 3 gallons of gas and 3 quarts of oil, "Bob" was 87.8 inches from front to rear, and sported a faded black frame with a skull on the tank. He was adorable, and if a motorcycle could be called cuddly, Bob was. In fact, if I could have hauled my little Rebel up my porch steps and into my bedroom, I'd have slept with him.

When I finally worked up the courage to ride up and down my street, then venture into my neighborhood, and finally explore streets large enough to have intersections with stoplights, I realized that Bob, not any human, was going to make my troubles go away. It was Bob who restored my confidence, Bob who gave me moments of peace, Bob who fueled my fantasies. Cranking up to speeds of thirty-five, forty-five, and once a heart stopping fifty, I was a movie star, a thief, a mental patient on the run. I was anyone I wanted to be, but after a few months, I was already bored.

Yes, Bob and I began to burn out just after Halloween. Inseparable at first, blowing through piles of leaves, weaving around pumpkin guts, we went everywhere a surface street could be found. But as anyone driving in Los Angeles knows, to get anywhere, you eventually have to get on a freeway. It was the difference between fooling around and going all the way, and Bob and I were ready to take our relationship to the next level— the 405—or we'd be done by Thanksgiving.

Known for the infamous O.J. Simpson car chase in 1994, the 405 was not for virgins. Still, Bob and I managed to fight our way into the traffic flow, heading north from Santa Monica toward Sherman Oaks. But after a few miles, I realized we might not make it. The crowded freeway some call the "Slow-O-Five" felt like the Daytona 500, so we scurried off at the next exit and idled on a side street, defeated and ashamed.

I knew I needed more than Bob had to offer. I needed a Thorough-bred, not a Shetland—a stud, not a gelding. I wanted horsepower between my legs, a stallion that demanded respect. That's why, when the 405 spat me out like phlegm, I went after clout and muscle. Like a toddler out-growing training wheels, I was ready to ditch cute and cuddly for hand-some and hunky. I wanted a bike that would stare down big rigs and sneer at SUVs. I wanted a Harley.

Now, looking for a motorcycle online is not so different from looking for a lover. You type in your age and weight parameters, your color prefer-ences, and the distance you're willing to travel to meet your new bike. Ultimately, as with any search for "the one," you have to endure a lot of disappointments. Pictures tend to lie. Descriptions often are exaggerated, and no one wants to admit any wear and tear. Though Los Angeles was a very large pool from which to search, it proved to be far too shallow for me to find just the right Harley, so I widened my search radius, first out-side of Los Angeles, and then out of California altogether. I wanted a bike that looked smart but was streetwise too, and wouldn't you know it, I found her in New York.

There she sat on eBay—a bigger girl than I thought I'd end up with—no Fat Boy, to be sure, but definitely a hefty ride. With her big teal tank and maroon pinstriping, she wasn't the less powerful Sportster 883 I'd intended to find, but a big honking 1200 Custom. And though I was looking for a bike with no miles on her—I wanted to be the first—this girl had only a little over five thousand under her belt, and her chrome was, well, *sexy*.

I contacted the seller in Buffalo, a guy named Dave, and asked for a Buy-It-Now price. We settled on a modest eighty-five hundred dollars (I'd have paid more), and shook virtual hands. Then, like someone eager to meet a mail-order bride, I started planning to get my buxom beauty to Los Angeles. She wasn't going to come cheap or easy.

As it turns out, it's probably simpler to smuggle contraband into the United States than it is to bring a motorcycle across the California state line. In fact, it's illegal to bring any used motor vehicle with fewer than seventy-five hundred miles on it into the state of California. Yes, I said *fewer,* not more. The Department of Motor Vehicles will not allow you to register a car or motorcycle with one mile *under* that figure on the odometer. Why? Officials at the DMV had a hard time explaining it to me, but after a little research, I found out that it's because of California's stricter-than-average smog-emission restrictions. It seems that a used vehicle with *fewer* than seventy-five hundred miles on it is considered to be "new," which makes it subject to current California emission standards.

So even though I was ready and willing to pay the shipping charge of more than five hundred bucks to haul my bike from Buffalo to Los Angeles, I couldn't, because once it got here, I wouldn't be able to register it. There was only one solution—put mileage on the bike. And there were only four ways to do that, two of which were legal.

Illegally, I could turn *up* the odometer or replace it with one from an older bike. Legally, I could obtain a temporary registration from New York and hire someone to ride the bike across the country. Or I could do it myself.

It was a no-brainer.

Impulsive? Sure. Rash? Maybe. But the reality of my split-second decision was followed by a lot of preparation. In fact, I spent the entire holiday season looking online at lots of cool accessories—heated insoles for my boots, extra cushioning for my saddle, hard plastic inserts to slide behind my jeans to support my back—but I didn't buy any of them. Instead I opted to spend my money on my head, purchasing a helmet that would not only protect but also entertain me.

Though some headgear can run well over fifteen hundred dollars, nothing is going to keep you from becoming a mashed potato if it's you versus a four-wheeler, so I bought a helmet for three fifty made of nearly unstoppable Kevlar and filled with all kinds of fun gadgets. It was jet-black and glossy, replete with slots that slid open to let in air on either side and on the top. It also had a removable breath box that kept your visor from fogging, and a chin curtain that was supposed to keep bugs and dust from flying up your neck into your face. They both made you look badass, but I wasn't sure if I was going to use them because they were uncomfortable and made me claustrophobic.

My favorite feature was the helmet's Bluetooth capability, with built-in speakers and a microphone. With the touch of a button on the left side, I could make or answer calls. It looked simple to operate in the instructions, but I had to practice a lot, so I wore my fancy-schmancy helmet around the house every chance I got, making calls to the two people I intended to communicate with on the road—my niece Lisa, whose number was in my wallet in case I was hospitalized, and Lynn, who had agreed to stay with my dogs and to keep them if I died.

I also bought a new cell phone with talking navigation and a built-in MP3 player, both of which connected to my Bluetooth, and I began wearing my supercool skid lid (Bart's name for a helmet) while driving my car so I could get the hang of using it. Everything was starting to get expensive, but I didn't care. Why save money when I might not be coming back?

I laughed when I made this comment to Burle. He was the salesman at Bartel's Harley-Davidson who sold me all the gear he deemed essential for my trip. Though he chuckled when I said it, I think I kind of freaked him out.

"You damn well better return from this cockamamie trip," he said. "I don't want to read about you in the papers."

I grinned. "You're just jealous."

"You're probably right." He tugged on the handlebar of his mustache and grabbed a shopping cart. "Now I want you to buy everything I throw in here, no questions asked."

Burle looked like a hairy tree stump, and I followed his bulky body all over the store, accepting almost all of his suggestions, and only arguing over things I knew I'd never use.

"You've got to be kidding." I took the tool kit and ground cloth out of the cart. "I just learned how to ride, I'm not about to learn how to fix anything."

"Fine, but you're taking this." He handed me an orange-and-black Harley-Davidson pup tent.

I put the hundred-twenty-dollar item back on the shelf. "Sorry, Burle. *You* might go camping after all day on a bike, but I'm going to be soaking in a bathtub."

"You might not make it to a tub if your bike breaks down and you don't have any tools to fix it." He threw me a wink. "By the way, it's hard to hail a cab on the highway."

"I am not going to break down. Besides, I'm sure some Good Samaritan will—"

He threw his hands over his ears. "Do *not* finish that sentence. I can't handle it. Let's just assume you won't break down. Now, when are you going?"

"I was thinking of spring, maybe the end of March or mid-April."

He raised an eyebrow. "You are aware that New York isn't sunny California?"

"Fine, maybe I'll go in May, is that all right with you?"

"May is better, but I'd still wait till summer. Maybe by then you'll find some guy to tag along."

I laughed. "Maybe I should mount a crash test dummy behind me?"

"Not a bad idea." He threw a can of Mace in the cart along with some pepper spray. "Just in case an asshole stops instead of a Good Samaritan."

I spent the rest of my time with Burle talking about biker luggage. Since my Sportster didn't have saddlebags, he suggested T-bags—one small for essentials like a toothbrush, underwear, socks, and flip-flops; one large for an extra pair of jeans, a couple of T-shirts, and some walk-around shoes.

"Make those knuckleheads who sold you the bike show you how to strap everything down properly." He threw a handful of bungee cords into the cart. "And take along this little tank bag—the magnets hold it down—so you can get to stuff like money, snacks, lip balm, and aspirin without tunneling through all your shit."

As we walked over to the cash register, Burle looked kind of sad, so I assured him I was going to be fine.

"Oh, I know that. I'm just afraid I forgot something." He looked me up and down. "Maybe you should think about some knee braces."

"Why? I plan on sitting down the whole way."

He grinned. "You'll see."

By the time April came around, I was antsy to leave. I was making and accepting calls inside my helmet like a pro, and Bob and I had logged more than a hundred miles. I was ready to go, and decided it was time to take Lisa out to dinner again to tell her I'd bought a Harley and would be making a slightly longer trip than up the coast.

"Have you lost your mind?" She pointed a bread stick at me. "What if this *Dave* is a psycho? What if he hasn't even got a bike?"

"I'm not an idiot. I saw photos of it on eBay. Besides, I haven't sent any money."

"What if he's not after money? What if the bike was some kind of . . . *bait*?"

Now I was getting upset. Harriet's kid was treating me like an infant. "Look, Lisa, I appreciate your concern, but this whole role-reversal thing isn't working."

"Then don't lay so much responsibility on me. At least let me tell my mom."

I did feel bad about putting the entire burden on my niece, but if I let her tell Harriet, it was as good as telling all my sisters. United, they could guilt me out of anything. "Okay, I promise to call everyone once I'm on the road. Now, can you at least be a *little* excited for me?"

Lisa twirled her napkin in the air. "Whoop-de-do."

Poles apart, we gazed in silence across the table. Having just come from court, Lisa looked like the public defender that she was, dressed in a proper business suit and stylish pumps. Having just left my couch dressed in sweats and sneakers, I looked like one of her clients out on parole. It was an understatement to say we were different, and yet we had respect for each other's strengths. She valued my free spirit; I respected her common sense. Sure I felt guilty asking her to hold the string to my kite while I blew across the country, but no one was more suited to keeping me grounded.

"Look, I picked you as my point person because you can handle it if something goes wrong. My sisters would freak out."

"I'd freak out too. I'm a lawyer, not an android!"

Calmly, I unscrewed the cap on the bottle of Parmesan, dumped the cheese on the table, and began to rake through the flakes with my fingertips.

Lisa grabbed my wrist. "What are you doing?"

I shrugged. "Making a mess."

"Are you crazy?" She grabbed the bottle and swept every flake back inside.

"See?" I leaned back, satisfied. "People count on you to clean up their messes."

Lisa grinned. "You knew I'd go nuts until I cleaned that up."

"I've been in your apartment. Do you still make people wear paper booties?"

"This isn't about me." She called the waiter over. "Bring us your most expensive cabernet and give my crazy aunt the check." She grinned. "It's the price for my silence."

I smiled. There was nothing but love at this table.

"Do you know what my dad used to call me?" I asked.

"I don't know, maybe *Barbara*?"

I rolled my eyes and tapped the side of my head with a bread stick. "He called me *luftmensch*, a person with her head in the clouds."

Lisa laughed. "Are you sure he wasn't just calling you an airhead?"

The waiter arrived with the wine and poured a glass for each of us.

"Here's to your imagination." Lisa lifted her glass. "May it *not* get you killed."

I clinked her glass. "My dad knew I was a dreamer, and he appreciated my wild side. But lately, all I've been reaching for is a way out of this quicksand. Understand?"

"I think so. You think by buying a bike from a guy in Buffalo named Dave—"

"Guys," I corrected her. "There are two guys, both named Dave, and they're picking me up at the airport. One owns the bike—he offered me a room in his house for a few days—the other is familiar with selling things on eBay."

"You're *staying* with one of them? Can't you just get strangled in a hotel room like a normal idiot? And why are you sticking around for a few days? I mean, how long does it take to give someone a bunch of money and let them murder you?"

"Will you take this seriously? I have to stay long enough to get acclimated to a bigger bike. And as far as staying with one of them, I don't know, it just feels right."

"Great, so you're flying to Buffalo to meet *two* guys named Dave, staying with one of them for a few days to learn how to ride a more dangerous bike than the one you have, and if one of the Daves doesn't murder you, you're going to ride thirty-five hundred miles across the country *by yourself* with practically no riding experience. Does that about cover it?"

"It could be a few more miles, but yeah, that pretty much covers it."

"Fine, I have one question: Why are you knowingly putting yourself in danger?"

It was a fair question, and I wanted to get the answer right.

"I don't know. Maybe I want to feel something again . . . even if it's fear."

Lisa nodded thoughtfully. "Okay, I get that. I get the challenge of the ride. I get pushing the boundaries—I get *all* that. What I don't get is how you can fly across the country and meet two complete strangers, then go back with one of them to his house!"

"Trust," I said simply. "Let me tell you a little story."

Lisa leaned forward, feigning interest. "Go ahead, Aesop. I'm listening."

"God, you're a tough audience." I poured the last of the wine into both of our glasses and then I told her the story of my sensei in Santa Fe.

"Back in the eighties, I was trying to find myself and—"

"Again?" Lisa smirked. "Maybe you should wear an ankle bracelet?"

"Can I please tell the story?"

She waved me on.

"Anyway, I was waitressing in Santa Fe, and every night after my shift I'd walk my dog. One time, right after I got home, the phone rang, and it was this guy who said he liked my dog, and the way I dressed. It was creepy, so I immediately called the police."

"Smart move." Lisa pointed her fork at me. "But I'll bet they said they couldn't do anything until a real threat was made. Am I right?"

"Wow, you know your stuff. Anyway, the next night I didn't have to go to work, so I walked my dog a little earlier, and the second I walked in the door—"

"He called *again*?"

I nodded. "He asked me why I hadn't gone to work. I told him it was none of his business and to leave me alone. Then I called the police and asked if they could at least patrol the area. They said they would, but the next night the guy called *again*."

"Okay, so his calling has escalated a little, but he hasn't actually *done* anything yet, right?"

"I think harassment is doing something." I shook my head. "Man, I don't know how you defend jerks like him. Anyway, this time he asked if I wanted him to walk *with* me. He said he wanted to protect me, and I told him that I'd called the police and *they* were going to protect me."

"Okay, now I just need you to tell me he left you alone."

"He *didn't*. The next day, I saw a wire dangling from my roof. I checked where I kept a spare key and it was gone, so I ran inside to call the police, but the line was dead."

"Wow, you must have freaked."

"I sure did. I ran to my neighbors' to call the police and—"

"Why didn't you just call them on your cell phone?"

"It was the *eighties*, remember? My cell phone wasn't glued to my hand until I was at least forty-five. Anyway, the police told me I should leave immediately. So I packed up and moved in with a friend that same night."

"Scary," Lisa said. "But what does this have to do with your motorcycle trip?"

"Well, after that, I realized how vulnerable I was. So I took a self-defense class from a six-degree black belt. We had life-size dummies to knee in the crotch and gouge in the eyes. It was actually a lot of fun."

"Fun?" Lisa looked skeptical. "I wonder if I should try one of those classes."

"You should. There is no greater feeling than kneeing a guy in the balls. Anyway, for the last class, our sensei hired someone to dress up in a padded suit to attack us. We beat the guy into a fetal position and were feeling pretty confident, until our sensei gave us our final lesson. 'Everything I've taught you is useless,' he said. 'Your attacker will be stronger than you. He'll have the advantage of surprise, and he might even have a weapon. But *you* have something that can disarm anyone. You have a concealed weapon sharper than any knife, more powerful than any gun— your *gut*. Listen to it. If you feel that you shouldn't go out one night, don't go. If you feel that walking down a certain street is dangerous, go another way. On the other hand—'"

"Okay, I see where you're going with this. You never got any bad vibes from the Daves. Your *gut* told you so." She rolled her eyes. "Give me a break."

"Look, it's not just something I sense about the Daves. It's something else my sensei said. I was just about to tell you when you cut me off."

"Fine. What else did your sensei say besides you wasted your money?"

"He said, 'On the other hand, if you're *too* careful, you'll never leave the house. You might live to be a hundred, but you'll never really *live*.'"

Nine

The Split

——————

There is nothing worse than doubt, except waking alone in the middle of the night with it. I hadn't slept soundly since the day I was laid off, the day when the person I knew myself to be stopped existing. Other selves slipped away soon after, and by the time my mother died, and I lost the little girl who had been her daughter, I no longer slept because I was tired, but as a means of escape.

As a coping mechanism, I split in two. Not two halves of a whole person, but two people going separate ways. One remained in the minds of those back in California who believed I was a crazy aunt, a wild friend, a sister gone awry. She was the person who would eventually call from the road to hear a familiar voice and remember she belonged to someone. She felt hunger, exhaustion, pain, and fear.

But the woman wearing a black Harley-Davidson leather jacket with zip-in lining and zip-off sleeves, the one who strode toward the taxi in front of her house on Sunday morning, May 21, 2006, had no feelings at all. She fell into the cab's backseat wearing black Levi's and black steel-toed boots with polyurethane shin protectors. She carried a black motorcycle T-bag over each shoulder, and a full-face helmet under her arm. She was more comfortable in what she wore than in her own skin, and she answered the driver's questions with clipped one- or two-word answers.

I liked this person who had risen within me, this person who was strong enough and tough enough and who had come to save me. Without her this trip would not be possible, and with her I might survive.

The driver looked me up and down. "Who are you? Johnny Cash?"

"Very funny," I said.

"I take it you're headed to the airport. Which terminal?"

"United." I suppressed a smile. "Terminal 6."

He glanced in the rearview mirror. "So you ride, huh?"

I darted a look at his reflection. *No, I just lug around a three-pound helmet wherever I go.* "Yup," I said, stone-faced.

"I've got a Ducati Monster rusting in my garage. What do you ride?"

"Sportster 1200," I lied. Tomorrow it would be the truth.

"You headed to Oklahoma? Nice rally on Route 66 this time of year."

"No, Buffalo."

He shrugged. "Figured by the way you're decked out you'd be following your bike to a rally somewhere."

"Nope."

"There's a great ride in Niagara Falls this July. It's only an hour from Buffalo."

I made a mental note to ask the Daves about the Falls. Maybe I could go there before heading west.

"Me, I've done lots of rallies—Sturgis, Cannonball, the Florida Biketoberfest." He glanced in the rearview mirror again. "But the ride I always wanted to do was the Devil's Highway loop—just never had the guts."

"Where's that?" I wrote *Devil's Highway* on the back of my boarding pass.

"Through the Navajo Nation, from Gallup to Shiprock. It's a real biker's ride."

"Challenging, huh?"

"Yup, four hundred fifty switchbacks, and supposedly cursed. Used to be Route 666 until the religious nuts got it rechristened to Route 491."

I couldn't help myself. "Cursed?"

"Could be. There've been more deaths there than any road in New Mexico."

At the terminal, I had an hour before my flight, so I slipped the Harley-Davidson Sportster Manual from my bag, hoping to be semi-fluent in Harley by the time I got across the country.

Before I bought my bike, I was told to make sure it was the new rubber-mounted model, said to have less vibration than previous Sportsters. Now I was reading that the 2004 I'd purchased produced less oil seepage and was fitted with three dog-bone stabilizer links. This, I figured, meant that my bike would provide a confident ride with less shaking, minimal weeping, and more stability than generations of bikes before.

But now what I really wanted to know was if my Sportster had been modified and tuned for maximum performance as described in chapter two. Did it have standard Thunderstorm heads or the more efficient "hungry-for-air" ones? Did it have proper "squish clearance" and enough "meat" for the combustion chamber? More important, was it fitted with a "Big Sucker" air cleaner kit and "Screamin' Eagle" performance parts? I had no clue what most of this meant, but I loved the strangeness of it all.

"The Daves will explain everything." I glanced around. Had I said that out loud? Quickly, I tucked the manual into my bag and boarded the plane.

It was when I walked over the threshold of the Boeing 747 that I expected to feel something—fear maybe, possibly excitement. But the biker woman I had become, the one boarding United Flight 958, felt nothing except the wheels tucking under the plane. I had no concern that the two men I was going to meet were strangers, or that the asphalt in my future could rise up and bite me as suddenly as a snake. Nothing fazed me now because finally I was able to sleep again. What had happened in my life was no longer of any consequence.

And so, when the plane landed in Buffalo at 9:12 that evening, I disembarked with the unconscious bravado I needed and the undeniable fear I wished I could have left in California. I was a woman of two minds walking down the Jetway, two halves of a whole decidedly at war. One half was numb and wanted to stay anonymous, to travel alone on my quest for inner peace; the other half was a jumble of raw emotions, and wanted to shout in the middle of the terminal, *Hey, look at me! I'm a biker chick!* Both halves of this oddball walked right up to the two men named Dave who were easy to recognize.

"I'll be the one who looks like a concert roadie in a Rolling Stones T-shirt," one of the Daves told me when I called the night before. "And you can't miss my buddy. He's got shaggy blond hair and never stops smiling. Okay, that's what *we* look like. So how are we going to recognize *you*?"

"I'll be the one who looks like she doesn't belong there."

"I don't follow?" He cleared his throat, then chuckled nervously. "Oh, I get it. This is a big deal for a lady—hell, it'd be a big deal for anyone. I know I'd never let my wife—if I still had one—pull a stunt like this. Anyway, Dave and I are real excited you're coming, and your room's all ready."

"Oh, about that. I was thinking maybe I should stay in a—"

"Nonsense. Dave and I will be at the bottom of the escalator at baggage claim."

I was about to tell him that my plane wasn't coming directly from Los Angeles, that it was routing through Chicago, when I heard a *click* and a dial tone. It was then that I got my first false impression of Rolling Stone Dave. I thought he was a man of few words, but as it turned out, this guy could talk.

As promised, there he was in his Rolling Stones *Sticky Fingers* long-sleeved tee, his eyebrows raised in amusement, a wild grin spreading from cheek to ruddy cheek. Tall and thin, he ran his fingers through his thinning grayish hair, and he looked as thrilled and nervous as the man next to him looked relaxed and easygoing. They seemed like each other's sidekick, both loyal and playful, except one looked like an aging gaunt hippie and the other like a golden retriever pup. As I walked up to them, I felt instantly at ease, settling right into the biker chick I had become.

"Dave?" I offered my hand to each of the men. "And Dave? I'm—"

"We know who you are!" they chorused. "Welcome to Buffalo!"

Shaggy Blond threw me a lopsided smile. "Well, aren't you a sight." He took my helmet and one of my bags. "I think Dave and I are more excited than you."

Rolling Stone threw an arm over my shoulder. "You are *too* skinny, girl! Whaddya say we grab us some crab legs and steak?"

"Sounds great. All I've had is a bag of peanuts and two Scotches."

"I love this girl!" He grabbed my other bag. "Don't you just *love* her, Dave?"

Shaggy Blond nodded. "She's a keeper, all right."

They whisked me out of the airport, threw my bags into a rusty pickup, and nestled me in between them in the front cab. Ten minutes later, we were at Fat Cat Jack's.

"Dave!" everyone shouted as soon as we came through the swinging double doors. We sat down and a pitcher of beer and three frosted mugs appeared on the table.

I looked at the waitress; she was more wrinkled than my neighbor's bloodhound. "I don't suppose you have a glass of chardonnay, do you?"

"Not a good one," she said, slinging a grin across her face. "You must be the nutcase from California these two lugs have been babbling about all week."

Rolling Stone Dave's face fell. "Yup, she's the one who's gonna take Maggie's bike off my hands. Barbara, meet Gertie, one of Buffalo's finest."

"Oh, you old goat!" Gertie cried. "When are you gonna get over that gal?"

Shaggy Blond Dave popped me in the side. "Maggie is Dave's ex-wife. She just left him, and he's still a tad raw."

"*Raw?* The man is stone-cold sad!" Gertie turned on her heels. "Back in a sec with that chard."

An hour later the Daves were into their second pitcher and I'd had three glasses of something white. The food, however, was amazing. The crab legs were big as mutton chops, the steak was marinated in bourbon, and the cheesecake was New York's finest.

"How about I follow you in a cab?" I said. "I don't think I can squeeze between you anymore."

"Not to worry, my wife's picking me up." Shaggy Blond Dave nursed the last of his beer. "Her shift is over in about fifteen minutes."

"Where does she work?"

"At the T-shirt factory. Just like half the town."

I thought he said, "The calf has drowned," and by the time I realized what he had said, I had to admit the wine and the Scotch were doing a tango in my head. I stood up to leave and almost fell over.

Rolling Stone Dave grabbed my arm. "You're probably exhausted." He tossed four crumbled twenties on the table. "It's on me, Dave. I'm gonna take this girl home."

Shaggy Blond Dave was on his feet and pumping my hand. "Nice to meet you, fellow Harley rider. You're gonna *love* your bike." He finally let go of my hand before it came off. "Now get some rest. Tomorrow Dave and I will have you popping wheelies."

On the way to his house, Rolling Stone Dave assured me that his daughter's old room had a comfortable mattress and a color TV. "Darlene's off at college now. She won't mind if you just throw all her stuffed animals in the closet." He laughed. "I swear I don't know how she sleeps with all those eyes staring at her."

I smiled weakly.

"And you can stay as long as you need to get comfortable on the bike."

"Actually, I was thinking about leaving tomorrow."

He pulled over and stared at me. "Have you ever ridden a hog?"

I shook my head. "Uh, no, a couple of horses and a mule once."

"Don't you be making jokes. A Harley is a whole different kind of animal. You just wait till you throw your leg over her. *Then* you can decide when you're gonna leave."

As it turns out, I wound up staying for three days. That's how long it took to adjust to so much horsepower between my legs. I also spent a lot of time playing psychotherapist to brokenhearted Dave. I got an earful about his ex on the first night, talking with him about her until after midnight. All the while, he never once asked me about my love life—maybe it was clear I didn't have one—and every time I brought up the bike, he seemed reluctant to talk about it. The motorcycle was clearly bound up with the memory of his marriage, the last vestige of happy times with Maggie, and perhaps one of the only ways he could maintain a connection with her. Still, it was getting late, I was barely conscious, and I'd yet to see a drop of shiny teal.

When he offered me a nightcap of whiskey-laced tea, I declined politely, then carefully broached the subject again. "Listen, I'm sure my bike is as beautiful as the pictures, but do you think I could see it before I go to bed?"

"Yup, she's a sight to see!" Dave slumped back in his easy chair. "But it's too dark in the garage right now."

"No lights, huh?"

"I need to replace the bulb."

"How about a flashlight? I just want to catch a glimpse of her chrome."

"She's under a tarp. You'll see her first thing in the morning, I promise."

I was beginning to worry that my niece was right. Maybe the bike was some kind of lure. Why hadn't I listened to her and at least stayed somewhere else? Was there even a lock on my bedroom door?

"Well, Dave, I can barely keep my eyes open." I got up and started to head toward his daughter's room. "See you in the—"

"Wait! Don't you want to meet Cosmo?"

"Cosmo? You named my bike after George Jetson's boss?"

He laughed. "You know, you're funny. Maggie didn't have a sense of humor." He walked over to something on a side table covered with a sheet, whisked it off like a magician, and shouted, "Voilà!"

"Hello, Dave!" a beautiful cockatoo squawked. "Gimme a cracker?"

"Hello, Cosmo," I said. "Can you say Barbara?"

"Hello, asshole!"

"Cute bird," I said. "Should I change my name to Dave or asshole?"

"Damn thing was Maggie's " He threw the cover back over the bird. "I ought to have it stuffed."

"Go to hell!" cried Cosmo. "Hello, Dave!"

"Shut up!" yelled Dave.

I walked into Darlene's bedroom. "Good night, everybody."

"Stupid bird," muttered Dave.

Thankfully, the door had a lock.

The next morning, I heard Dave whistling and felt it was safe to come out. He was in the kitchen, and as soon as he heard me, he yelled, "I've got hot coffee on the stove and a motorcycle in the garage! Come and get 'em!"

I had barely gotten a sip of coffee past my lips before Dave practically pushed me down the back steps that led to the garage. "Ta-da!" he cried, whipping off the tarp to reveal a motorcycle far more beautiful than I'd imagined. "Go on and sit on her. It's time to let this baby go."

I climbed aboard, and even in my pajamas, I felt powerful.

Dave was grinning like a proud father. "She purrs like a cougar. If she doesn't make you tremble when you take her for a spin, I'll buy her right back."

Later that morning, I not only trembled, I almost swallowed my heart after riding only half a block. When I sputtered to a stop in front of Dave, I nearly burst into tears.

"She's got some muscles, doesn't she?" He stepped back from my green face. "You're not gonna puke, are you?"

I patted the tank. "No, I'm fine."

He patted my back. "You'll get her under control."

I shut off the ignition and the quiet was so distinct I heard a spider dangle from the tree above us.

"Religious, isn't it?" He threw an arm around me and walked me back into the house. "Let's go have a little breakfast, and I'll take you over for a tour of the factory. Then after lunch, Dave and I want to take you shopping."

The New Buffalo T-Shirt Factory was like a city unto itself. Hundreds of machines, all operating at once, cut reams of cloth, spray-painted designs, and dried the ink. Then they pressed, folded, and boxed tens of thousands of shirts to be shipped to rock concerts all over the world. It was the noisiest place I've ever been, and I finally understood why the Daves shouted all the time.

Rolling Stone Dave was a quality control inspector, weaving in and out of bellowing machines while he eyeballed everybody's work. He was on duty for a few hours, so he handed me over to Shaggy Blond Dave, the plant's computer geek and chief mechanic, to conduct my tour. Halfway through, he stopped in front of a mammoth contraption with huge spinning blades and held up nine fingers.

"This old girl bit off my pinkie!" he yelled over the hiss of a steam iron. "A buddy of mine found it on the floor. We kept it on ice until an ER doc sewed it back on, but it didn't take." He shrugged like he couldn't care less. "Now it just droops like a limp—" He caught himself and chuckled with embarrassment.

Back at Fat Cat Jack's for lunch, both Daves regaled me with stories of their numerous accidents at the plant and the dozens of motorcycle trips they'd taken. Neither of them had done the Devil's Highway loop.

"And don't you dare try it!" Shaggy Blond Dave wagged his droopy pinkie at me. "Not without one of us along!"

Rolling Stone Dave frowned at his burger. "Damn, I wish I could go with you."

"Me too." Shaggy Blond Dave took a piece of paper from his pocket and pushed it toward me. "But since we can't go, we're gonna make damned sure you're road ready."

I looked at a checklist of gear they wanted me to take. "I can't lug all this shit."

"Well, I guess you're not going then," said Rolling Stone Dave. "If you think I'm letting you off my property without everything on that list, you are sadly mistaken."

Three hundred dollars later, I'd bought an orange-and-black Harley-Davidson rain suit I figured I could always wear on Halloween, a bike cover that folded down to the size of a change purse, another can of pepper spray, and a key chain that squirted Mace. In addition to all that, Rolling Stone Dave supplied me with hours of road sense and two of his own turtlenecks.

"That way I'll always have your back covered," he said, his eyes glistening.

Shaggy Blond Dave bought me an H.O.G. (Harley Owners Group) membership—the bikers' equivalent to AAA—and slapped his Swiss Army pocketknife in my hand "'cause every rider should have one."

Both Daves filled me with bikers' tips that they'd gathered from years of experience, from how to lift your bike if it tips over—which I still can't do—to warning me to always unlock the fork "so as not to wrench your shoulder out of its socket." Then, the night before I left, Rolling Stone Dave sat me down for our last biker-to-biker talk.

"I'm gonna give you forty years and a million miles of experience," he said. "Whatever you think you know, well, you can just forget it."

As he went on, only a sliver of me listened. I had given this trip a lot of thought before I left Los Angeles, and I wanted to make it my own. Still, I let him ramble on. He was a nice guy, and when I pulled out of his garage the next day, I swear I saw a tear in his eye, which was more emotion than either of my parents showed when I left for college.

I took off at nine-thirty a.m. on the dot, wanting to track not only the days but also the hours I was on the road. Against Dave's advice, I decided to go east to New York City, and if things had gone according to plan, I would have rolled into Manhattan at three-thirty, checked into my prepaid hotel, showered, and been at the theater by eight. I had lots of plans for this trip, most of which fell flat. But as Rolling Stone Dave had tried to tell me the night before, it's impossible to foresee what's going to happen on a motorcycle trip, and you're lucky if it's just your plans that fall flat.

"Motorcycling is like life," he warned me. "There's nothing solid about it. Sometimes not even the asphalt under your tires."

Ten

You Can't Map Out Your Life

When I was growing up, I had big plans, most of them made with my neighbor and best friend, Cindy. We'd sit astride our sawhorses in tiny leather saddles her father had hand-tooled in his workshop, and we'd ride along the open range, which was her backyard, mapping out our lives. I was seven, and she was six. I was going to be a reporter, and she wanted to be an artist. We'd marry guys like our dads, have a boy and a girl who'd marry each other, and somehow, we'd all be neighbors forever.

What we didn't foresee was that Cindy's older brother, Matt, was going to die of melanoma before his twenty-first birthday, and in an instant, our own teenage lives would be rerouted. Her parents would forget they still had a child. Cindy would do lots of drugs, nearly overdose, and because I was slightly older, her parents would blame me.

For the next two years, they wouldn't allow us to see each other, and in time, Cindy and I drifted apart like lifeboats floating away from a shipwreck, except I sailed off to college and she remained at sea.

While I became a free spirit, slipping in and out of jobs, relationships, and cities like mercury, Cindy stayed planted in El Paso like a tree root.

She married a great guy, but it ended in divorce, leaving her alone and depressed. I had an affair with a woman twice my age, then went back to men and fell for my optometrist. He was a wonderful musician, who fell for me too, but no matter how hard I tried, my body simply rejected sweet Andrew, and he wrote an angry song about our relationship that I will forever cherish. Neither Cindy nor I had any children, and nearly every-thing we had predicted about the future didn't pan out.

As for my sexuality, unlike most of my gay friends, who claim they knew their preference in childhood, I never had a clue. In the nature ver-sus nurture controversy, I've never known where to plant myself, but I would have liked to have seen where I might be today had I avoided one terrible detour I took in college.

I'd chosen a small university in Missouri known for its journalism program. It was at the foot of the Ozark Mountains, and when my parents dropped me off, neither they nor I realized we were in Ku Klux Klan ter-ritory. We never imagined that many of my classmates had never seen a Jew, and that one of the girls in my dorm would actually ask to see the bumps on my head where my horns were supposed to be. This was not the friendly Midwest where innocent Dorothy and her Auntie Em lived.

So I chose my friends carefully, and did as my parents asked—I dated only Jewish boys. But free for the first time to question authority, I soon began going to parties at non-Jewish fraternities, and within a few months, I fell in love with a blond-haired, blue-eyed Baptist named Kyle, whose frat brothers saw me as a novelty.

One day I went to visit him and found a trail of pennies leading from the front stoop up the stairs to his room. I knocked on the door, and his roommate answered.

"Oh, I didn't know *Jew* were coming over," he said. "Your boyfriend is in the kitchen. Just follow the money downstairs."

I found Kyle playing poker with three frat brothers. The minute they saw me, they burst out laughing, and I burst into tears.

Kyle pulled me into the hallway. "Come on, it was funny."

"It was humiliating!" I cried. "And sick!"

He stroked my cheek and grinned. "Come on now. *Jew* can't still be mad."

"You're *not* funny." I tried to suppress a smile. He was so handsome. "I know I shouldn't let them get to me."

"That's my girl," he said. "But I will tell them to lay off."

Weeks went by and nothing happened. Then one night, six of Kyle's frat brothers strode into my dorm and kidnapped me. They carried me on their shoulders as they stormed across campus, and though I was scared, I tried to laugh, until they threw me into a Dumpster, poured molasses on my head, and left me in the alley behind my dorm.

Kyle thought that was funny too.

"It's the equivalent of tarring and feathering!" I cried. "They'll lynch me next time!"

He shrugged. "It was a prank. It's what frat brothers do."

I searched his eyes for the boy I loved. "Please tell me you didn't know about it."

"You're lucky I found out. They were going to haul you off into the woods. I talked them into leaving you on campus."

I couldn't believe what I was hearing. "Why didn't you try to stop them? I could have been killed!"

"They're my brothers. Do you know what kind of hell my life would be? They'd never let me forget it."

I knew how important it was to fit in. One of a small number of Jews in my grade school, I had been told I was going to hell so many times I often wondered if it could be true. I felt different from everyone in El Paso, different from my family. I don't think my sisters experienced anti-Semitism the way I did, perhaps because they were members of Jewish youth groups, and among the more popular kids. But I was shy and kept more to myself. I couldn't wait to grow up and get out of El Paso, where I wouldn't be the youngest Schoichet daughter with so much to live up to.

So I threw my arms around Kyle and thanked him for saving my life; then, unbelievably, I let him convince me not to tell anyone.

"If you get my brothers in trouble, you'll get me in trouble," he said. "Besides, you won me over, you'll win them over too."

But a week later, they upped the ante.

Kyle and I were going to a movie playing near his frat house, and though I hated being around his brothers, we agreed to meet there.

"Just stand up to the big apes," he told me. "They'll respect you for it."

I didn't want to taunt those guys, but I wouldn't be bullied either, so when I went to the frat house, I wore my lucky necklace—a tiny gold חי I'd gotten for my bat mitzvah—proudly on the outside of my sweater.

When I got there, the front door was open so I went up the stairs. But as I headed down the hall to Kyle's room, I had a bad feeling. I hadn't learned to listen to my gut the way my sensei in Santa Fe would teach me years later; I hadn't learned to mistrust. So I ignored the drops of red paint on the carpet and dismissed the red handprint smeared on the wall. And then I got to Kyle's door.

There, dripping down the wood, was a crudely painted swastika. I stifled a scream and turned to run, but halfway down the staircase my anger kicked in, and I went back and banged on Kyle's door. "Your frat brothers have gone too far!"

Slowly the door opened. Someone grabbed my hand and yanked me into the room. It was dark, but I could see a circle of guys in their underwear sitting around a candle.

"Come in, *Jew.*" It might have been Kyle who spoke, but the pillowcases over everyone's heads made it hard to recognize a voice. "Come join the party."

I tried to bolt from the room but someone blocked me, then everyone began to chant, "Stop dating our fraternity brother, *Jew*."

"Kyle?" I whispered into the darkness.

"Stop dating our fraternity brother, *Jew*."

I hit someone in the chest. I grabbed someone's hair, I scratched someone's face, I was trying to get to the door, but only my memory left the room.

Years later, I remember going up that spiral staircase, but I don't recall going down. I know the movie Kyle and I had planned to see was *The Sting*, and I know I wore my gold ♰ to the frat house, but when I awoke in my own bed the next day my necklace was gone.

"You can't just remap your life without consequences," my guidance counselor told me when I wanted to transfer without telling her why. "You'll lose credits."

We worked out a way for me to cram the next three years into two so I could graduate early, and I never went back to see her. I stuffed the memory of what had happened deep inside. I let nurture take over nature, or maybe I let nature emerge. Regardless, I didn't date a man again for ten years. Nurture or nature—does it really matter how you wind up where you are as long as when you get there you feel safe?

For the rest of my undergraduate education, I was like a puzzle missing a part of the sky. I acted as though it didn't matter that a part of my life had suddenly gone missing, and I smoked a lot of pot. After graduation I drifted through a year of meaningless jobs, so I decided to go for my master's. It was 1980, the year John Lennon released his album *Double Fantasy*, and wrote, "Life is what happens to you while you're busy making other plans." It was a bad year for him, but a great one for me. He was gunned down by Mark David Chapman, and my graduate professor kissed me. In an instant I was in love.

After a few months, she was horrified by what she'd done. "Go back to men," she said gently on the last night we slept together. "It's an easier life."

I cried like an addict in withdrawal.

"Use this experience," she coaxed me, and then broke into a wise grin. "If nothing else, use it to fuel the fantasies of your future husband."

We went back to being teacher and student, and I went back to a celibacy made miserable by watching her in class.

Years later, after having my heart broken by both men and women alike, I finally met a woman at a party and fell reluctantly in love. Slowly the naïve girl who'd been silenced in that frat house found a new voice. I called everyone I knew to tell them I was a lesbian.

"No you're not," my mother said flatly. "Tomorrow you'll call to say you're a vegetarian."

"Listen to her!" my father bellowed on the extension line. "It's not meat she's giving up!"

Harriet was tentative. "Maybe you just haven't found the right guy?"

Sandra was blunt. "I always knew you liked girls."

Naomi asked the only question that mattered. "Are you happy?"

But I couldn't answer the question because I didn't know. The only thing I did know was that I seemed to like poisoned apples, and I'd bite into anything that quieted my insecurities and put my restlessness to bed.

Who knew I'd be covering my head with a helmet, not a veil? Who knew I'd be more comfortable wearing leather, not lace? So what if I didn't wind up walking down the aisle on my daddy's arm? Burle had been a wonderful guide through the aisles of the Harley-Davidson store in Los Angeles, and two guys named Dave proved to be the finest of fatherly figures to usher me out of Buffalo and toward the adventure of my life.

Eleven

Road Whimsy, Fatigue, and Surprise

quarter of a century after my sexual preference did a one-eighty, I made another plan that got rerouted—it was a fifteen-page TripTik designed by Lester Himple at the AAA in Los Angeles. Rolling Stone Dave looked at the collection of maps with scorn, but ninety-one-year-old Lester, who had meticulously outlined every mile of what was supposed to be a ten-day trek, was thrilled with his directions. In fact, he would have had a stroke if he knew how far I would veer off course. Lester was a man of commitment, and even more so, a man running from guilt.

"I was married to the same woman for sixty-three years, and I'd still be married to that she-devil if she hadn't died on me." Lester banged his wrinkled hand on his desk. "Yup, my Maryann was stunning. Her beauty could stop your heart just as much as her sting. But I couldn't leave her."

"Good God, I've left women because they snored."

Lester's green irises brightened. "Really?" He stroked his stubble and studied me. "Well, maybe girls like you operate differently. Hell, I would if I were of a different persuasion. But in my day, a man married a woman and stuck by her, even if she turned into someone else."

He threw a dart at a laminated map behind me. I turned around to see that he'd missed the United States, Canada, and Europe, landing somewhere in the Atlantic. "Truth is, Maryann was stuck in my route for a reason, but I took a detour once, and we never quite found each other again."

I shrugged. "You had an affair. It happens."

He touched his neck. "So you can see the albatross." He leaned toward me and I smelled the bourbon he'd had for breakfast. "Ironic I work here, isn't it?"

I leaned away from him. "Why's that?"

"Because I strayed off course! I got lost, don't you see? Now I help others stay on track. I give them direction. I—"

"Lester, *I* need direction. Do you think you can help me?"

"Yes, yes, of course I can." He clapped his hands together as if breaking a spell. "Now, let's get you from where you are to where you want to be. Where is that exactly?"

Carefully I guided Lester back to the task at hand, and for the next hour, we mapped out the perfect marriage between the road and me. At several points, he got so emotional he had to stop and blow his nose. "You'll call from the road to let me know you're all right, won't you?" he asked.

"Of course I will," I lied.

"I'd love that. I help plan trips for people, but I don't go anywhere."

As he slid his Magic Marker along highways and through towns, Lester lived the trip through me, and after a while, I found myself doing the same. I too wanted to ride along with this daring woman who couldn't possibly be me. I too was curious as to who she was and why she was doing this. And more than anything, I found myself hoping that she would be my friend when the trip was over.

"Okay, the least complicated route would be to head directly west from Buffalo, except you'd wind up in Lake Erie." He drew a tiny buffalo trotting into Ohio. "So I'll send you to Columbus. That'd be a good place to spend your first night—in a city named after the man who discovered America!"

I looked at the map. "Cool, then I won't be far from Chicago. One of my sisters lives there. I could stay with her."

Lester drew a bear cub over Chicago. "She as pretty as you?"

I laughed, but I couldn't help but feel a jab in my heart. "She's a rock star."

His mouth dropped open. "Really? Have I heard of her?"

"No, Lester. I mean she's gorgeous."

He must have realized by how I said it that I didn't think the same of myself. "Do you know that you remind me of Marilyn Monroe?" He smiled. "Her and Judy Garland."

"What? Strung out and suicidal?"

"No, sweet and sad."

My hands began to tremble.

"Sorry, hit a nerve, huh?"

"Kind of. How about you get me from Chicago back to Los Angeles?"

"How much time you got?"

"I'm not on anyone's schedule. Take me wherever you want."

His eyes twinkled. "Oh, how I wish I could . . . But I digress." He went back to his maps. "Now let's see. This route might have you zigzagging a bit, but I really think you ought to buzz through Oklahoma City to see this museum." He handed me a brochure with a cowboy on it. "Every decent American should see this place and I want you to promise me you'll go."

I gave him a salute. "Consider it done, sir."

"Okay, now logically you should go through Texas after that, but since you're obviously in need of cheering up, I want to take you through a place that'll make you feel downright grand—Mount Rushmore!"

"Lester, I need to go west eventually. South Dakota is way up north."

"True, but that way you can take the Beartooth Highway." He looked wistful. "I've always wanted to see the Big Blue. That's what they call the sky in Montana."

"Great," I said, realizing I'd never get out of Lester's office unless I let him take me wherever he wanted. "Where's next?"

"Next you should dip south to get your Annie Oakley back."

"My Annie Oakley?"

"Your feistiness. Something knocked it right out of you, didn't it?"

My chin wobbled.

"Another nerve, huh?" He drew a tiny rifle in a rectangle state. "Cody, Wyoming—that's where Annie Oakley starred in Buffalo Bill's Wild West Show. Did you know she could split a playing card in midair and put five holes in it before it hit the ground?"

"I did not know that."

"*And* she was only five feet tall! That's why her buddy Sitting Bull used to call her Little Sure Shot. She met him in—"

"Excuse me, but why do you know so much about Annie Oakley?"

Lester studied his fingernails. "Remember that detour I took? Well, it was with a woman who looked a lot like Annie Oakley." He slammed his hand on the desk. "Well, I'll be damned if you don't look like her too!"

"I thought I looked like a drug addict."

He took out his wallet to show me a photo of a woman who looked nothing like me. I soon learned he had a daughter with her who was about to make him a grandfather. When he wanted me to guess if it was a boy or a girl, I looked at my watch.

"Sorry." He slipped the sonogram back into his wallet. "I do get carried away."

He picked up his Magic Marker and quickly got me through Utah, Nevada, and into California. When he finished, he drew a Hollywood sign over Los Angeles, then dug a silver dollar out of his pocket and laid it in front of me.

"My granddad gave me this a million years ago. It was supposed to bring me luck." He shrugged. "Maybe it'll work for you."

I started to take the coin, then pushed it back to Lester. "Don't you want to keep it? I mean, your grandfather gave it to you."

"I'm twice as old as he was back then." He slid the coin across the table. "Now take it before I have a stroke."

I slipped the coin into my pocket. "Thanks. Maybe it will bring me luck."

"Luck, schmuck!" he said. "I'll be happy if it brings you back alive."

While Lester's plan had me weaving all over the country, it didn't take into consideration any kind of weather conditions. After all, we were on the West Coast and both of us were wearing shorts. But when I sat with Rolling Stone Dave in Buffalo, he had to light a fire while he trashed the TripTik Lester had so lovingly prepared for me.

"Hand over that stupid set of maps you got from Triple A-Hole." He pointed to the TripTik I had in my lap. "I haven't even seen the damn thing and I know I can map out a better way."

I handed over Lester's handiwork and watched while Rolling Stone Dave shook his head and guffawed at it.

"This guy drew you a map made for a Popsicle, not a person!" he yelled. "The only thing this is good for is kindling." He held my maps over the fire. "I'll dismantle the motorcycle before I'll let you take this route."

I grabbed the TripTik. "Fine, which way would *you* have me go?"

A thoroughly prepared H.O.G., he laid his very own *Harley Owners Group Touring Handbook* across the coffee table. "I'd go straight south to Graceland by way of the Great Smoky Mountains." He ran his finger along the yellow Magic Marker he'd already traced on one of the maps. "From there, I'd head west till I saw palm trees and movie stars."

"I'll think about it."

He handed me the touring book. "That's yours to keep. Now sit back and listen. I've got a few things to tell you about life on a motorcycle."

I propped my feet on the coffee table and leaned back on the couch. "Lay it on me, Rolling Stone."

"Number one: *never* book a hotel in advance."

"Why? That's one reason I brought my laptop. Hotels.com lets you see pictures before you book a place so you don't wind up in a dump."

"When you've been on a motorcycle all day you could sleep on porcupine quills. What I'm saying is you've got to be able to change your mind." He pushed his easy chair back and gazed at the ceiling. "Look, you can try to follow every line you've drawn on your map, but road whimsy will get you every time."

"What the hell does that mean?"

"It's like this—you'll be riding along and you'll see a sign that looks interesting, and before you know it—*bam!*—road whimsy hits you. So off you go somewhere you'd never explore in a car and—*boom!*—you never make it to where you planned. Got it?"

"*Bing, bang, boom.* Got it."

"And then there's highway fatigue."

"Right, I could get tired. In bicycling, it's called bonking."

"In motorcycling, it's called dying." He glared at me. "Let me put it this way—you'll wake up planning to do three hundred miles, but your body can only do a hundred. And what if your body says it can ride even farther, but your mind says no." He tapped his temple. "Takes a lot of concentration to ride a motorcycle. You'll see—after trying to pick out every rut and avoid every granny, you'll be wiped out."

I laughed. "You mean *cranny*, not granny."

"No, I mean *granny*. Old people behind the wheel are worse than serial killers. Their blind spots have blind spots!"

"Okay, whimsy, fatigue, and grandmothers. I'll watch out for them."

"You think this is all a big joke. Just wait till you have your first surprise."

"What? A clown's gonna jump out from behind a billboard?"

"No, but a deer might." He didn't crack a smile. "Hell, you have no idea what you're in for. Blown tires, traffic jams, oil slicks, all kinds of shit strewn across the road."

Mattresses, I thought, the image of Carla on life-support popping into my head.

"Then there are the *good* surprises." His voice went soft. "Unbelievable sunsets, roadside stands full of amazing junk, and times when there's not a soul on the road but you. My point is that the landscape looks different on a motorcycle. You're not just riding *through* it; you're a *part* of it. Understand?"

"Not exactly, but hopefully I will someday." I yawned. "Sorry, I'm a little tired."

"I'll let you go to bed after this one last piece of advice. Don't ever tell anybody where you're headed. A girl traveling alone doesn't want to be followed. Enough said?"

"Enough said. And, listen, I'm sorry if I sounded like a smart-ass. I really do appreciate all your advice."

"No problem," he said, waving over his shoulder as he headed out of the room. "And I'm sorry if I sounded like an old fart." He turned around and winked. "I'm just looking out for you, kiddo."

That night I had a real gut check, and I admit I stayed up late surfing the Web for ways to get out of my trip. Turns out there are 4,220,000 hits on Google for motorcycle shippers and 10,700 for falsifying odometers. But after clicking on a few sites and reading about the cost, the fines, and the possible prison sentences, an old proverb I once heard calmed me down: "You don't drown by falling in the water. You drown by never getting out."

I shoved my TripTik in my pack and began to ink out a new route in my *H.O.G. Touring Handbook*. If going west wouldn't work weather-wise, I'd jog east to Manhattan, see a few plays, then head south to Florida, where it would be warm enough to go west toward Graceland. After that, I would let road whimsy be my guide.

Sure of my new plans, I got online and made my first mistake. I booked a hotel room in one of the many places I would never reach.

Twelve

Questioning Authority

<hr/>

I *had to drop* LSD only once to know that Timothy Leary was right about questioning authority. Said to have taken acid more than three hundred times, Leary was a clinical psychology professor at Harvard during the sixties until he was fired by the university for advocating psychedelic drug use as a means of mind expansion. He was also known for being part of John Lennon and Yoko Ono's famous bed-in, for inspiring the Beatles song "Come Together," and for coining the phrase "Turn on, tune in, drop out." Though I was never really a part of that antiestablishment generation, I did feel that my three-week motorcycle trek was a rebellion of sorts, a way of thumbing my nose at grief, and turning up the volume to my all-but-silenced life.

Now on the open road, I thought about that ten-hour acid trip I took in the early eighties. I was twenty-six and teaching creative writing at Stephens College, too immature to be a professor and a complete idiot for doing drugs around my students. I was supposed to be an authority figure, and there I was in a bar, talking with a man I believed to be Satan, watching a rainbow shoot out of my index finger, and hearing the sun come up. I was lucky I didn't get fired.

I've matured since then, and gained a whole new perspective on authority figures. Some—like politicians—need to be questioned if only to keep them in line, and some—like revolutionary thinkers—deserve respect while they go about changing the world. I didn't really consider Rolling Stone Dave to be an authority figure of any kind, but seventy-five miles outside of his garage, I knew he was an authority on motorcycles whose expertise I should never have questioned. Though he'd warned me against making a hotel reservation in advance, I'd wanted something concrete for my free spirit to rely on once I arrived in Manhattan. More than anything, I wanted a shower before I headed to Broadway. But after only thirty minutes on the freeway, my free spirit was freezing, and I was rethinking my entire wardrobe. I needed a Patagonia or a Timberland, and like a frostbitten skier, I began searching for the next city as though an avalanche were nipping at my tires.

An hour later, Rochester, New York, became my promised land. I zipped off at the first exit and hustled into a gas station. It smelled like motor oil and bleach, and no one was there. I saw a pot of coffee brewing behind the counter, and thought maybe I should just pour a cup over my hands. Instead I yelled, "Hey!" toward the back office. "Is anyone here? I'm looking for a store that sells warm clothing. Maybe a ski shop or something?"

Loose as a strand of spaghetti, the attendant finally ambled out, running his fingers through his oily hair. It dripped down the sides of his head like marinara sauce, and I surmised that's how he got his nickname *Red*, which was stitched on the pocket of his overalls.

"Sorry, I don't know anywhere offhand." He ducked under the counter and came up with a tattered old phone book. "Maybe this piece of shit can help you."

"Wow, I've almost forgotten how to use one of these things." I peeled off my gloves and began thumbing through what was left of the yellow pages. Most of them were ripped out, crumpled up, or doodled on. "This is ridiculous. Is there a mall nearby?"

The kid scratched a splatter of freckles on his nose and shrugged. "So you ride, huh? Wish I had a bike."

I wanted to kill him. I took off my helmet. "How about a Kmart or a Walmart?"

"I *knew* you were a woman!"

"Yes, I ride a motorcycle and I'm a woman—a *freezing* woman with a Harley."

"Actually, I guessed you were female when I saw you struggling with your kickstand. That's a big bike for a lady."

"Look, I'm turning into a Popsicle." I showed him my hands. "You own a coat, don't you? Where did you buy it?"

He whistled at my purple fingers. "Wow, you're turning my favorite flavor. How long have you been on the road?"

I was going to carve him up with Shaggy Blond Dave's pocketknife if he didn't start coughing up information. "About four hours. I left before dawn."

He swallowed the lie easily. "No wonder you're cold. You need to get to Extreme Biker. They sell heated gloves and the best leather in the state. They even sell lingerie."

"Seriously?" I felt a twinge of excitement. "You think they have thermal socks?"

"Hell, it wouldn't surprise me if they had thermal panties."

"Sold!" I cried. "How do I get there?"

"It's just down the road." He grabbed a Hershey's bar from the candy rack and drew me a map on the inside of the wrapper. It was a straight line with three *X*s.

"We're here." He pointed to the first *X*. "Extreme Biker and Physical Graffiti are here, and here." He pointed to the last two *X*s almost on top of each other. "Physical Graffiti is probably the best tattoo parlor in the country—maybe in the *world*."

"I can't miss that. About how many miles away am I?"

"Miles? We're talking blocks. You could walk there."

I tucked my Hershey's bar map in my front pocket. "Thanks, I think I'll ride."

"Suit yourself. I could spit shine your bike while you get a flower or something on your butt." His cheeks reddened. "Every biker's gotta have a tat or two."

I thought of the tiny heart my ex had under her left breast and felt a longing I thought I had trashed with all of her photos. "I'm not really a tattoo kind of biker."

"They do piercing too. They'll punch a hole just about anywhere."

"I don't have time for excruciating pain. I want to be in Manhattan before dark."

He stared at me. "You do know that's over three hundred miles from here, don't you?"

"Yeah, I figure if I just bundle up a little, I can make it."

He puffed out his cheeks like Louis Armstrong and let out a rush of air that smelled like Budweiser. "You're one tough lady!" He offered me a square of chocolate.

"Thanks, nothing like a hunk of Hershey's before noon." I reached out for the candy and noticed a tremor in my hand I hoped he didn't see. "What do I owe you?"

"Nothing. Just promise you'll stop by Physical Graffiti and say hello to Squish and Maxwell. The tats on their arms are awesome." He rolled up his sleeve and made a muscle. It popped up bare as a baby's butt. "See? We're not so different."

"Oh, yeah? How do you figure?"

"Bare skin. I'm not into excruciating pain either."

I walked away shaking my head. I had to stop judging people so quickly. Red wasn't just a gas station attendant, that's who he was today. Tomorrow this stringy piece of pasta who pumped gas and rarely took a shower might invent something that people couldn't live without. And next week, long after he'd left my consciousness, he might meet the love of his life, a dark-haired beauty with a tiny heart under her left breast.

Extreme Biker was different from your average motorcycle shop. It didn't have wall-to-wall posters of naked women straddling motorcycles, licking chrome, and kissing other naked women; and there were no dreadlocks of cycle parts dangling from the ceiling. What it did have was more cowhide than a Texas cattle ranch. I bought some heated gloves, two sets of thermal underwear, a padded leather vest, and several pairs of very unusual panties from a salesgirl named Cherry. She was about a foot shorter than me and looked like she had a porcupine on her head.

I handed her my credit card. "Love your hair. Does everyone want to touch it?"

She blew a pink bubble in my face, then looked at me as though acknowledging my presence was painful. "Not really."

I hated her attitude and decided that the minute she turned her back I would give her spikes a quick brush whether she liked it or not.

"That'll be $214.74." She handed me a receipt along with an Extreme Biker handkerchief. "I threw that in for spending over two hundred dollars."

"Gee, thanks." I pointed to some key chains behind her. "Can I see the skull-shaped one?"

She turned around and I went in for a quick stroke.

"I wouldn't do that if I were you," she said, her back still toward me. "I'd have to hurt you."

I declined the key chain, and then locked myself in a dressing room to put on another layer of clothing before heading over to the tattoo and piercing parlor next door. While I'd told Red I had no interest in getting ink burned into my flesh, the truth was I always wished I'd had the guts to get a little something only a select few could see. But peering through the window of Physical Graffiti at dozens of gruesome yet gorgeous tattoos all over the walls, I decided I should wait to see if I made it back to Los Angeles alive. Then I'd have plenty of time to sear my skin with something commemorative of the trip.

I was musing at the shop's slogans: Think Before You Ink and The Ultimate Prick, when a bald man with silver studs embedded in his head waved me in. I was afraid he'd chase me down, so I did as I was told.

"Ya think I was gonna bite ya?" He tugged on his goatee, a black curtain of hair that looked like Hitler's mustache had fallen on his chin. "I'm just here for a quick nose ring. You getting a tat or a poke?"

"Nothing today." I looked at two other guys covered in more ink than *The New York Times*. "Would either of you be Squish or a Maxwell?"

"Sorry, I'm Cronk." The larger of the two gigantic men offered me a hairy hand the size of a roast. "S and M are on a break."

I shook the roast. "A gas station attendant down the road sent me to say hi."

"Red?" The pierced guy sneered. "I hate that jerk. He comes in here like a walking asshole and just stands around talking. Never once has he gotten even an itty-bitty titty pierced!" His eyes fell on my chest. "I don't suppose you've ever considered . . ." He raised his eyebrows, so laden with metal they actually clinked. "The piercer here is amazing. You'll never feel a thing."

"Yeah, especially if I don't get anything done." I whipped my helmet out from under my arm and onto my head so fast I bent an ear in half. "Maybe next time."

The other tattooed mountain grinned. "Come on. There's always time for a tat. How about a skull or your astrological sign? Let's see, you're probably a . . ."

I didn't stick around to see if he guessed I was a Leo. Instead I threw down my visor and was out of the shop, back on my bike, and swinging onto the highway in seconds.

In minutes I was already a nice shade of indigo. The Daves had bundled me up, but they hadn't considered the difference between a man's resistance to the elements and a woman's. I could *walk* around in northeastern weather, but not fly in the face of it at seventy miles per hour. So while I hadn't experienced road whimsy or even a modicum of fatigue, the windchill factor was definitely my first surprise. I managed to withstand another twenty minutes before I hustled off the highway, made a U-turn, and headed back to Rochester to rethink my route. In an instant, I nixed my plans to make it to Manhattan, lost my hotel deposit, and decided that Rolling Stone Dave was not to be questioned.

Later, after mailing off half of what I'd packed to make room for my new wardrobe, I found a liquor store, where I bought a bottle of wine and got directions to the nearest motel. The old man behind the counter wore an eye patch and looked like he'd been sailing around the world chasing a whale.

"You look like you need some whiskey." He glanced at my wine. "Not this shit."

I danced from boot to boot. My hands were warm from the heated gloves, but the rest of my body was ice. "That wasn't a compliment, was it?"

He shrugged. "Just an observation. Whiskey packs some heat, that's all."

"I think the wine will do me. Any chance there's a decent motel around here?"

He rang up my chardonnay, slipped it into a paper sack like he was hiding it, and handed it over. "You want a map or should I just point you in the right direction?"

"I've grown pretty fond of maps."

"Fine, I'll do both." He licked his finger and dragged a wet *X* through the dust on the counter. "We're here." He tapped the *X*, then spun around and pointed to the wall behind him. "About a half-block that way is a Motel 6." He handed me a coupon for Domino's. "It's not the best you'll ever eat, but they deliver to your room."

Outside, while tucking the bottle of wine into my pack, I had the distinct feeling the old man lived at that Motel 6 and I had to suppress the urge to go back inside and ask him. As I settled into my saddle, I wondered what difference it would have made to me. Would I have tapped on his door later that night to ask him if he wanted to play cards?

I powered up my bike and about thirty seconds later shut it down in front of the Motel 6, one of many I'd stay at over the next twenty-one days. On my way into the office, I powered on my cell phone for the first time since I'd left Los Angeles and called Domino's to order a pepperoni and mushroom pizza. It would be one of many identical pizzas I'd eat, all bought with coupons. I quickly learned that at the end of every day, I was happy if a motel was clean and had Internet and television. Dinner would soon become inconsequential. As long as I had some wine to wash it down, my evening meal was nothing more than fuel for the next day.

It hadn't happened yet, but soon I would regard my body as though it too were a motorcycle. When I stopped for gas, I pumped snacks into my mouth. When I checked my oil, I quenched my thirst. I rubbed medicated cream into my stiff joints every morning, and at the end of every day my legs were so rubbery I weaved around people as though I was still in traffic. I scrubbed bug juice off my leathers as often as I scraped it off my windshield. And every night, as I rested in my hotel, my Harley cooled down in the parking lot. Though I was slower to start in the morning, I quickly matched my bike's rhythm, and there were moments when we both entered the landscape and seeped into the horizon like paint on canvas. Soon the adrenaline of acceleration rushed into my veins and my body, like my bike, felt feverish until I gave it more speed.

But on this first night on the road, I didn't identify with my motorcycle at all. I felt like I barely had the power to walk. In fact I felt just one shade livelier than the motel clerk who dragged himself out of the office when I slapped my glove on his reception bell. He looked me up and down as though perhaps I could make his night more interesting, then asked, "How can I help you?"

I thought of everyone who had recently asked me that same question. If only the answer had been so simple. "I just need a room, thanks."

He bent over his computer, then looked up. "I've got 113. It's kind of a lucky room. Last person there found a gold tooth."

"Is 118 available?"

"Why? You superstitious?"

"No, just partial to that number."

I was upset with my agitation. The need to try to get a room with eighteen in it was absurd. The number had been my father's, and now, like his temper, I couldn't shake it.

He used to wind his watch eighteen times, bet on eighteen at the roulette table, give donations to charities in multiples of eighteen, and write birthday checks with an extra eighteen cents tacked on. I knew the tiny gold חי I'd lost at the frat house corresponded with the number eighteen in Hebrew, and my father often reminded me when he made a toast that *la-hai-yim* meant "to life." He was a man who celebrated his heritage, who never forgot where he came from, and who often reminded me how lucky he was to have escaped persecution for such a good life in America.

"When your grandfather and I left Russia we took nothing with us but luck," he always told me. "I was just a six-year-old boy, but I remember the terror of those soldiers coming into our house. They took everything. They even yanked the boots off my feet." He shook his head and then tapped his temple. "But my father was smart. He took me—his oldest son— and we got out. We worked harder than you'll ever know, and years later, the rest of the family was finally able to come here." He'd wave his arm wherever he was, as if the living room or the den or everything outside of the car was the whole of America. "I am indeed a very fortunate man."

Probably because he didn't know what to say when we were alone— driving to the drugstore or coming home from Sunday school—I heard his story of escape during the Bolshevik Revolution numerous times. Always I listened as if I'd never heard it before, and I didn't have to pretend to be in awe because I was.

"We wrapped our feet in burlap sacks and walked across a frozen river," he told me. "Then we stowed away on a herring boat, and the smell of the fish and the rocking waves made me sick to my stomach. I was scared to death, and my father wrapped his big arms around me. Do you remember how tall your grandfather was?"

I nodded that of course I remembered him. I was nine when he died from a massive stroke, but who could forget my giant grandpa Louis, who had to duck to get through doorjambs and lifted me on his shoulders so I could touch the sky.

My father's eyes would tear up when he talked about his father, and often when he did, he'd show me his signet ring. "Your grandfather wore a ring like this, but when the soldiers stormed our house . . ."

Sometimes my dad had to stop in the middle of remembering, leaving me to imagine the rest. Did they pull off his ring? Did they ransack his house and point a gun to his head? I was fascinated by the story, having felt no more fear in my little-girl life than the trauma of changing schools. And so every time my father showed me his ring, I would kiss his engraved initials with reverence and think of the little boy he had once been watching soldiers raid his house.

"Maybe one day, you'll have this ring—you already have my initials. But for now, always wear your *hai*." He winked and pointed to my necklace. "It will bring you luck . . . especially if you bet on eighteen."

I'd been dipped in religion, minted a Jew every Saturday in synagogue. I knew the Judaic symbols, and understood that my gold חי was something like my friend Cindy's gold cross. Hers was a symbol of suffering, a reminder to live a good life, and mine was much the same. But now I couldn't look at a חי without feeling queasy. The symbol reminded me of that awful time at the frat house, and I was glad that my father was absentminded enough not to notice when I was no longer wearing it.

Today I get my luck from that signet ring my dad always wore. He was right, it did become mine, and on the day I left for Buffalo, I dropped it into my jeans pocket to take a little bit of my father's good fortune and courage with me. Throughout the plane ride, I ran my fingers over our shared initials, and when I paid for my Harley, I tacked on an extra eighteen cents just like he would have done. I decided I would carry the ring in my pocket every day of my ride so that when I felt my nerve about to slip, I could touch it to give me strength. If ever I grew sick with fear, I knew it would be his ring that could settle me, and each evening I knew it was my dad's good fortune—the luck that he and his father had brought with them out of Russia—that had helped me get to my destination in one piece.

Now, looking at the clerk as he searched for his available rooms, I felt silly to think that fortune could come from a piece of metal, and good luck from a number, but I was glad when he found room 118 to be free.

"Why, this must be your lucky day." He looked up from his computer and smiled. "I thought the gentleman in that room was still here, but he checked out this morning."

I was calmed and irritated, relieved and shackled by a number. "Well, aren't I the lucky one?" I couldn't keep from sneering at myself.

The clerk frowned as he pushed the key across the counter without a word.

I tried to smile but couldn't. "Listen, I ordered a pizza. Could you—"

"I'll see that it gets to your room."

I started to leave, then turned around. "I appreciate your switching rooms for me. Eighteen was my dad's lucky number. Now it's mine."

He shrugged. "I understand. We all had fathers."

Once in my room, I headed to the shower, stripping off my gear behind me. When I got out, I had to laugh. It looked like a gladiator had melted in a trail from the door to the bathroom. Free of grit, I flopped on the bed and finally called my niece, whom I'd promised to contact when I got to Buffalo. Thankfully, I got her machine so I wouldn't have to lie to her directly. "Sorry I haven't called, but—"

Suddenly she picked up. "Where in the hell have you been?"

"It's nice to hear your voice too."

"I've been calling you for days! Didn't you get any of my messages?"

The truth was, I had powered off my cell phone on the runway in Los Angeles.

"For God's sake, Lisa. I left my phone on the plane and just got it back."

She sighed, clearly reluctant to accept my lie. "No landlines in New York?"

"I can't even remember my own number let alone someone else's."

"Fine, just tell me how you are. How's the bike? *Was* there a bike?"

I laughed. "I'm fine, and yes, there was a bike. It's beautiful."

"Congratulations. And the Daves?"

"They were perfect gentlemen."

She sighed. "God, I hate you sometimes. I was ready to call the FBI."

"Sorry, I'll try to stay in better touch. I might even call my sisters soon."

"Good, I'm running out of diversions. So tell me about the trip."

I launched into a pack of lies, starting with how easily I had acclimated to the bike and ending with how I met a woman during intermission at *Les Misérables*.

"That's wonderful! Do you think you'll see her again?"

"Doubtful. She was from Kansas. The Midwest and I don't see eye to eye."

There was a knock at my door and I ushered in a beanpole of a boy holding my pizza. "I gotta go. My dinner is here. I ordered ravioli from a cute little Italian bistro."

"That's funny, I thought I just heard someone yell 'Domino's.'"

"It was Domi-*nick's*." I winked at the beanpole, who shrugged like he couldn't give a shit.

"Where exactly are you, anyway?"

"A little hotel in downtown Manhattan. It's kind of shabby chic, but—"

"Funny, I haven't heard any street noise. Not even a siren."

"What are you, a detective?"

The kid smirked. Fucking eighteen-year-old. I gave him a twenty and waved him out of the room.

"Okay, I'm having pizza in a little hotel in Brooklyn."

"Brooklyn?"

I heard Lisa through the phone and the pizza guy through the door. "Yeah, I thought the motorcycle would be safer parked in the suburbs. Listen, I hate cold pizza."

"Fine, I'll let you go. I just need to know you're okay."

"I'm okay, just hungry."

"You're a lunatic."

"You're a lawyer."

"Damn right I am. I'm the lawyer who has the only copy of your will."

I grinned. "Are you threatening me?"

"Yup. If you don't make it home in one piece, I'll forget I said I'd pull the plug."

"I'll have you disbarred."

"Not if you're a vegetable."

We both laughed and hung up, me promising to call more often; she not believing a word I said.

Thirteen

Coffee and Sympathy

—

I **woke up the** next morning pinned to the mattress as though a sumo wrestler had died on top of me. My *H.O.G. Touring Handbook* was draped over my chest like a shroud and an alarm I must have set before passing out was ringing. Mental fatigue had clearly struck during the night, but it wasn't as powerful as the physical fatigue that fastened me to the bed like an insect to Styrofoam.

Had I ridden my motorcycle or dragged it?

Convinced a body part would snap off if I moved to silence my alarm, I bumped the nightstand with my shoulder and knocked the clock to the floor. It kept ringing, but I rolled over and fell back asleep. An hour later, I dressed in as much clothing as I could wear and still swing a leg over my bike, then hobbled to the office for directions to Starbucks. The clerk looked like the guy who had checked me in except he was someone else.

"We've got one." He scratched his head. "But I don't know where it is."

"Great. Do you have any aspirin? There's an axe in my forehead."

He took a step back and raised his hands as though I'd whipped out an assault rifle. What in the hell was wrong with this guy? Did he think I was just another grumpy middle-aged woman on the edge of doing something crazy? Couldn't he see that stuffing cellulite into leather and wearing a helmet all day could make *anyone* a little out of sorts?

I flashed him the same mischievous grin I'd had when I was a five-year-old outlaw with a six-shooter on each hip, then I raised my finger pistol at the man's starched shirt and whispered, *"Kapow!"*

He smiled weakly and lowered his hands. "Sorry, I'm not allowed to dispense drugs, but I'll draw you a map to The Frog Pond. There's an egg dish there that should suit you. It's called The Hangover."

I took the paper-towel map he handed me and looked at him in disbelief. "Just down the road from Thelma's Mastectomy Boutique? You're kidding, right?"

"Nope, they sell specialty bras, wigs, you get the idea. Not many towns have a shop like it."

"Kind of a niche place, huh?"

"I've never been in there, but I hear one of the owners is a registered nurse and the other one made corsets. I pass by the place whenever I go get my teeth cleaned."

Unable to help myself, I did what I always do when someone mentions teeth—I thought of Grandma Rose, who didn't have any. She lived with us during my six-shooter phase, and each night, after I draped my gun belt over my bedpost, I went down the hall, to where she would pop out her teeth and plop them in a glass of water on her nightstand.

"Anchors away!" she'd spit at me, handing over a denture-cleaning tablet.

Proud to be her assistant, I'd drop the chalky tablet into the water and lean toward the glass to feel the bubbles on my face.

"Watch out for piranhas!" she'd slur as the fizz swarmed her teeth.

She died shortly after I stopped wearing weapons on my hips. Everyone in my family but me went to her funeral—I was too young, so I stayed home with Juana. We took turns dropping denture tablets into the toilet and pretended we had no teeth. I think Grandma Rose used to wear a corset too.

Now standing in front of this Motel 6 clerk, my head splitting, I drew my lips over my teeth and slurred, "Funny you should mention teeth cleaning. Forgot my choppers back in Los Angeles."

He looked at me like I was crazy and didn't even crack a smile, so I raised an imaginary Uzi and blew him away. Then, feeling like a freak, I stuffed my paper-towel map into my pocket and left.

Who was I? A geek who accidentally woke up in leather, or someone who deserved to wear it? I looked back through the window at the clerk's blank face, and stared until I saw him blink, then I strode toward my Harley. How stunning was this bike—*my* bike—and how cool was I to be riding it? I swung into the saddle and fired her up. Today I would be a bank robber throwing Ben Franklins to the wind. Tomorrow I would be simply the wind. I nodded to the clerk, hoisted my bike up with authority... and tipped over.

Pinned underneath a quarter-ton of Harley, I struggled out of my helmet and craned my neck to see the clerk standing stone-faced at the door. I gave him a thumbs-up to let him know I wasn't in need of a paramedic, just someone who could bench-press a motorcycle. Still, he didn't make a move. It was some kind of standoff, and we both knew who would win. Finally, I gave him what he wanted. I screamed for help. And he gave me what *he* wanted, a ghoulish smile with his lips pulled over his teeth.

"Clever!" I called out as he sauntered toward me.

He burst out laughing and then finally managed to ask if I was okay.

"I'd be better without a motorcycle on top of me."

"Let me see what I can do." He gave it a try, but my Harley wouldn't budge. "I'd better get help. I don't want to lift this thing, then drop it on you."

"No, that would be bad. Go get help. I'll just pretend I'm a pancake."

He jogged over to room 114 and knocked on the door. After about a year it opened and the clerk stepped back like he'd discovered a dead body. Soon I recognized the disheveled old man—the guy from the liquor store, probably reeking of a few pints.

The clerk walked back and squatted next to me. "Well, get comfortable. Old sourpuss over there usually doesn't get up till noon."

"You've got to be kidding. Isn't there somebody else who can help?"

"Relax, wild thing. The old man is just showering off his beer. In the meantime, I'm going back to the office. Can I get you anything? Maybe a glass of water?"

"A mojito would be nice." I laid my head on the asphalt. "Maybe a pillow?"

He came back with a bottle of water and a camera, and then he started snapping pictures. "You ever read *Gulliver's Travels*?" He pointed to some ants heading toward a hamburger wrapper wedged under my thigh. "I think they're carrying ropes."

I glanced at the approaching army. "Help?"

"Let me get a picture first. Say Lilliput!"

He took shots from different angles, and then stomped the tiny lynch mob to death. "One more thing." He let his camera dangle from a cord around his neck and then pointed an imaginary rifle at my head. *"Kapow!"* he said, blowing smoke off the barrel.

"Bite me!"

"Let's not get testy." He wagged a finger. "You'll look great over my fireplace."

I was about to chew off my leg and kill him, when the old man showed up.

"Jeez Louise, you look like you could use a shot of whiskey!" He knelt down beside me so the clerk could snap a photo. "You want a copy for your scrapbook?"

"Are you guys through? I've got a country to cross."

They finally began to lift the bike, and a lot of swearing later I was free.

I scrambled to my feet. "Glad you boys enjoyed that."

The old man looked me up and down. "Seriously, you okay?"

"Oh, she's a tough customer." The clerk patted my shoulder. "Went down like a drunk. It was like watching someone demonstrate how to fall."

He was right. The bike hadn't so much hit me as I'd tucked myself underneath it. Most of the weight landed on the foot peg and balanced there. "Yeah, I should make a video." I felt a throb in my ankle and patted my boot. "Thank God for polyurethane."

The old man inspected the bike. "Everything looks okay except for this bum peg."

I looked where he pointed. The peg was pushed off at an angle like a broken nose.

The clerk giggled. "Lucky you weren't speeding."

I dusted off some asphalt embedded in my chaps, put on my helmet, and swung back on the bike.

"Want us to hold you upright until you're off?" the old man yelled over my engine.

I threw down my visor as an answer, then idled away using my feet like training wheels. There was no use in trying to look cool. These guys knew better, and I was happy just to see them recede in my rearview mirror.

Since The Frog Pond wasn't far away, I couldn't work up much speed, which was fine by me. I needed to shake off my fear, so I just cruised along, squeezing my thighs around my tank. Soon, I felt comfortable enough to take a hand off one of my grips to give my bike a reassuring pat, and I swear it purred an apology.

We were going to be okay, my Harley and me, as long as I remembered who was boss. Already I could feel the heat from the slash cut drag pipe radiating through my boot, and I knew that if I dared to touch a part of this machine I wasn't supposed to, I'd feel a sting as nasty as any human's slap. Knowing my motorcycle's power more and more each day, I realized as I drew near the diner that it wasn't up to me, but to my Harley, if I got there.

The Frog Pond turned out to be way too commercial, and packed, but I spotted a little place not far away, and it was just my style—empty and retro. In fact, when I pushed my way through the screen door I felt like I'd just stepped right into the 1950s. The Formica counters, the leatherette booths, and the linoleum floor looked like part of a movie set, and the waitress, Maxine, looked like a fossil from my cartoon days. Except for her platinum-blond beehive, she was Olive Oyl's doppelgänger, and I liked her on the spot.

"Hope you can find a seat." She waved a crossword puzzle at all the unoccupied tables. "We're kind of busy, but I think I can squeeze you in."

I chose the only booth that didn't have stuffing coming out of it, laid my gear next to me, and looked at the menu.

"You want two sunny-side ups, hash browns, bacon, and biscuits." She slapped her crossword on the counter. "Right?"

"What are you, a psychic?"

"No, just been in business longer than Jesus." She appeared before me with a mug of steaming coffee and disappeared into the kitchen. "Be back in seven."

I looked at my watch, and sure enough, in seven minutes, my breakfast was in front of me. The coffee was the worst I'd tasted yet, but the biscuits were hands-down heavenly. I think they were laced with some kind of liquor, maybe even absinthe.

I held one aloft to Maxine. "Are these legal?"

"No; the cops will be here any minute to haul us both away."

"Seriously, they're amazing. You should sell them."

"I just sold one to you."

"No, I mean *market* them. You know, like Mrs. Fields or Sara Lee?"

She pitchforked her pencil into her hair as if she was killing something inside and stomped over. "I know what you're talking about." She waved her arm around the room. "You think all this just appeared on its own? No, ma'am, it did not. Old Maxine work-her-fingers-to-the-bone Tattle built this shit hole."

"Sorry, I just thought—"

"I know what you *thought*, but I've got news for you." She poked her chest. "Good old Maxine about-to-change-her-name-back-to-Ebony created this dump all by herself—and she's proud of it."

"You're changing your name to Ebony?"

"I said *back* to Ebony. It's my maiden name. Doesn't *anyone* listen anymore?" She stomped behind the counter, grabbed her crossword puzzle like it was trying to get away, then carefully laid it down. "Look, I'm a little on edge. My excuse of a husband just left me. I know I should be happy as a pig in shit, but I'm not." She looked at my coffee cup. "That's gotta be ice cold. Let me warm it up."

She came at me with her black ball of steaming swill and it took everything in me not to recoil. I covered the rim. "Thanks. I'm good."

She rolled her eyes. "Look, doll, I just serve it, I don't drink it. I'm a teetotaler myself—no coffee, no booze."

I laid three fives on the table. "I'm sorry you're going through so much."

"Yeah, right." She palmed the bills. "Change?"

"Keep it." I started to gather my gear.

"Do you know there are lots of famous people who don't drink alcohol?"

She was trying to be friendly, but I didn't want to get into a conversation, so I worked as fast as I could to get bundled up. "I'll bet there are, but—"

"Donald Trump, Stephen King, and Adolf Hitler—all teetotalers."

The hairs on the back of my neck did a goose step. "Any *nice* people?"

She laughed. "Maybe that's why I'm so mean. Guess a glass of wine now and then couldn't hurt."

"Might take the edge off." I headed for the door. "Listen, I'm going to get pretty mean myself if I don't have some coffee soon."

She gestured toward my full coffee mug. "Whaddya call that? Orange juice?"

"Uh, more like brown juice. Listen, I don't mean to be rude, but—"

"Well, ya coulda fooled me!" She tossed me a grin. "Sugar, you'd have to insult something I give a damn about."

"Okay, then how about telling me where the nearest Starbucks is."

"Never been to one." She made a capital T with her fingers. "*Tea*, remember?"

I tapped my temple. "See, my memory's going without my coffee." I wasn't about to tell her Starbucks also served tea. She might whip off her apron and try to join me. I put on my helmet and got one foot out the door.

"Where ya off to next?"

I lifted my visor. "Starbucks and then south."

"South *where*?"

Since I hadn't left New York yet, the only place I knew I was going was out of the state. I shrugged. "Hell if I know."

Maxine shrugged back. "I've been there."

I nodded and walked away. There was so much raw emotion in her shrug, and I identified with Maxine more than I wanted to admit. She had no idea how she had landed where she had, and neither did I. It might have been good to talk for a while, but I couldn't afford another day of going nowhere.

I walked outside into the crisp morning air and breathed in the freedom of day two, and then I went riding through Rochester looking for a Starbucks. It was fun checking out the town and looking at the reflection in store windows of this cool biker chick who couldn't possibly be me. I could have watched her astride her Harley for hours, but I knew my caffeine withdrawal would soon crush my will to live, so I began tapping on car windows at every light to ask for directions. Most people stared straight ahead until finally an old man, with snowy tufts in his ears, rolled down his window.

"I'm looking for a Starbucks. Do you know where—"

"Star-*whats?*" he yelled.

I was in trouble. "You know, the coffee place?"

He gave me directions to The Frog Pond, so I gave up and circled back to the Motel 6 for a few cups. I didn't care if the clerk and the old man gave me shit, and I didn't care if the coffee looked like it had just rinsed a dirty plate. At least, like dishwater, it was free.

I finally got out of Rochester by ten-thirty and knew I was in trouble by eleven. Between the heavy idle of my bike and my full stomach, I had to go to the bathroom just a few miles out of town. Later on in my trip, I would talk myself out of frequent stops, but now, even though I was dressed like the Michelin Man, I was willing to struggle out of my gear and squeeze into a stall.

Bladder and bowel control are definitely developed skills for any biker on a cross-country venture. The vibration of the road is killer, but add the thrill of acceleration and you could suddenly have cause for concern. I've certainly found myself in tough situations before, with long lines, facilities shut down for cleaning, or for the use of paying customers only, but when you've raced to the wrong bathroom on a motorcycle, and you've got only seconds to explain your needs, well, let's just say, I'd have screamed that I was wired with explosives if it cleared my path to a stall.

Though I never made any threats to get my way, I did become quite adept at playful deceit while I was on the road, taking on personas simply because it was fun to be someone else for a little while. This kind of trickery was often useful too. It got me into places I wanted to go, got me sympathy when I needed it most, and got me out of situations that made me uncomfortable.

At the Trout House in Gatlinburg, Tennessee, I found a fish bone in my salad and held it up to the waitress. "I've seen people come through my ER with everything from a penny to a bullet stuck in their throats. Something as small as this can kill you."

She treated me to a slice of key lime pie.

In Nashville, I got a free shot of Scotch when I convinced a bartender I was a descendant of Johnnie Walker. And in Memphis, I was seated immediately at a crowded restaurant where Elvis ate barbecue pizza when I told the maître d' I was hypoglycemic.

If I had been my normal self and not this entity on a motorcycle even *I* didn't recognize sometimes, I'd have been mortified by my behavior. I was usually the kind of person who told waiters they forgot to charge me for something. Ordinarily I was painfully honest, leaving notes on parked cars that I *might* have scratched by tapping a bumper. I couldn't sleep if I told someone I had other plans when I didn't, I couldn't enjoy playing hooky if I called in sick, and I couldn't keep the change if I got too much. But now I was dreaming up identities to get room upgrades and telling cute hotel clerks I was a retired firefighter or a film producer just so I could flirt with them. Making up stories about myself amused me when nothing was amusing at all. It made me feel unusual, extraordinary, and a cut above normal when not a single thing in my life felt usual, ordinary, or the least bit normal anymore.

Fourteen

A Hole in the Road

———

When I left Maxine's, all I knew was that I was going toward
warm weather, and not being much of a geography student, I thought
that Florida wouldn't be out of my way. About two hours outside of Rochester, I decided to consult my *H.O.G. Touring Handbook* and liberate my
knees. Locked into position, they were headed for a meltdown, so just
before I hit the New York–Pennsylvania border, I pulled onto the shoulder to give them some relief. I'd just peeled off my helmet and hadn't even
gotten my butt out of the saddle, when suddenly I wasn't alone.

I didn't know it at the time, but Harley riders won't let another Harley rider sit by the side of the road unattended for long. Similarly, if you're
cruising down the highway, brother and sister hogs demand your attention. Once spotted, you'll get a signal, usually a sweep of the hand across
the leg, a sign you must then acknowledge by doing the same. At first I
was afraid to let go of a handgrip long enough to do an appropriate down-
low sweep, but after a while, my pride in being a sister in that exclusive
siblinghood gave me the courage to do a proper wave—low and slow, just
shy of the thigh. In fact, I began gesturing like this to every biker I saw,

which is taboo in the Harley world. To hog riders, people who ride an inferior bike are themselves inferior, and not worthy of a wave. Like it or not, I was part of the motorcycle elite.

But despite their outward snobbery, I'm pretty sure Harley riders felt the same affinity I did with anyone who chose two wheels over four, and I doubt even the snootiest hog would pass a crotch rocket or a dirt bike if the rider was in need. Anyone on a motorcycle was, after all, not in a car, and that stood for something. Hog riders themselves, however, had to rely on one another. Out of gas, broken down, or bleeding, a Harley rider might as well settle in until a fellow hog arrived. Most people can't fix Harleys, and everyone else is just afraid.

I wasn't thinking about any of this when I pulled over. I wasn't thinking about how important electric windows and door locks are. I was merely thinking about my knees, until a legion of bikers—all of them on Harleys—pulled up behind me.

Choking on exhaust fumes, I flashed back to Bart Mange's warning about women alone on the road, and I began to scan the sea of leather for a female face. No woman would stand by while I was being dismembered, and if nothing else, maybe I would pass out before the torture began. I was already going deaf.

I had just lapsed into a fit of coughing when a guy who looked prehistoric walked up to me and drew his finger across his windpipe. Naturally, I figured this meant he was going to slit my throat, but suddenly, as if God had commanded it, everyone cut their engines, silence fell upon the earth, and the air became less toxic.

Big as a hairy armoire, the caveman before me unstrapped his brain bucket and tossed it to a guy behind him. Then he tossed me a wink that I actually felt hit me square in the eye. "Something wrong with your Sportster, sugar?"

Still straddling my saddle, I patted my gas tank. "No, she's fine. Just giving my knees a break." I glanced at my helmet on my lap, longing for it to be on my head. "You wouldn't know how many hours it is to Florida, would you?"

"Hours? You mean *days*, pumpkin." He scratched his beard and then his crotch. "Jacksonville would be your closest city, and that's two days riding sunup to sundown."

Several smaller but just as hairy cavemen nodded, and then one lit up a joint the size of a cucumber and passed it around. I figured when it got to me I'd know whether or not I was going to be executed, and if I was, I'd take a hit before I died.

While all this raced through my head, I spotted a woman in the crowd. Skinny as a licorice stick with stringy black hair, she sidled up to the Goliath in front of me. Clearly the Bonnie to his Clyde, and maybe a year older than jailbait, she was so thin that she was either anorexic or a cokehead, and I figured she'd be of little help if her pals decided to attack. In fact, I felt like helping *her*—feeding her at least—so when I thought it was safe to reach in my pack I planned to give her all my PowerBars to keep her alive.

For now, I just sat there watching her whisper into a Brillo pad of hair on the caveman's cheek. There had to be an ear in there, and suddenly, I wished it were my ear she was whispering into. Was it a contact high from the reefer, or did I actually think this skeleton was sexy?

"Good idea!" The caveman slapped the girl's nonexistent butt as she walked back to her Electra Glide. Then he turned to me. "My old lady thinks you should ride with us. We're not going to Florida, but we can see you through the Carolinas."

"I appreciate the offer, but—"

"But what? You have a death wish?"

"Uh, no. I didn't know Florida was so far south. I need to head west right away. My husband is expecting me in LA by the end of the week." I smiled weakly. "Yup, Florida is definitely on the chopping block."

"Whack!" The caveman sliced the air between us. "I like your style, Sportster." He grinned and I counted three gold teeth. "But you're not much of a liar."

"Okay, we're not actually married. I keep thinking he's going to ask me, but—"

"Not buying it, Pinocchio." He made a circular motion over his head and instantly the air filled with the sound and smell of revving Harleys. "The natives are restless and so am I!" Then waving over his shoulder, he strode to his Road King, flipped on some Led Zeppelin, and sprayed me with gravel.

"Take care, Geppetto!" I screamed, knowing there was no way he could hear me. "It's my party and I'll lie if I want to!"

At the sound of the last backfire, I took in a deep breath of the polar opposite of fear. Though the exhilaration of staring death in the face had made me forget about my knees, I stretched them anyway, then unpacked my *H.O.G. Touring Handbook*. I had hoped that the caveman was just pulling my chaps about Florida, but he was right.

"Who wants to set foot in a state that elected George W.?" I screeched into my helmet as I lurched back onto the road. *"Flamingo schlamingo!"*

As I rode along, wincing every time I shifted gears, I begged for no more fatigue—mental or physical—and I prayed for no more surprises. I willed away the chill in my bones, the ache in my joints, the ruts in the road, and I waited, no I *yearned*, for whimsy to enter the picture and make my next destination clear.

Then just across the Pennsylvania state line, it did.

I had stopped for the third time to get some circulation into my back, butt, neck, and knees when I found myself pulling up to a shack that was posing as a diner. Someone had written *A Hole in the Road* on the wood part of a screen door, and because the screen was mostly ripped off, I poked my head through the opening, and looked around.

"Well, are you coming in," someone snarled, "or should I throw you a menu?"

I walked inside, slid out of my helmet and into a booth. A waitress with mousy hair and dull eyes slapped a filthy plastic menu on the laminated tabletop and walked away. The two suctioned together, and I didn't try to pry them apart. I just sat there, thinking about absolutely nothing.

In truth, I was actually thinking about how thinking about nothing was unusually hard for me. Just *trying* to meditate gave me anxiety. Generally I was the Woody Allen of unwinding, but just over a day into my motorcycle trip I'd become a guru at zoning out. And the irony of it was that while my body was tenser than ever from vibrating in the saddle, my mind was never more serene than when it was careening through scenery.

And so there I was, my black-leathered butt sitting on red leatherette, reflecting like a good little *luftmensch*, when I heard the hollow slap of the screen door I'd just come through. I shifted my gaze from the tabletop to a little girl walking into the diner with her nose stuck in *Gone with the Wind*. I had read the novel when I was about her age and had gotten so consumed by the story that I used to check the weather reports in Atlanta. Even more vivid was my memory of the film, especially the Battle of Gettysburg, when a boy walked among the rows of casualties playing a fife and weeping.

I looked at the girl's narrow back hunched over the counter, and then I did something I hate when someone does it to me—I bothered her.

"Good book, isn't it?"

"Uh-huh," she said, not turning around.

"Aren't you supposed to be in school?"

"Uh-huh," she said, then twirling around. "Aren't you supposed to be working?"

"Touché." I pointed my chin at her book. "I read that when I was your age."

"This is my second time."

I shrugged. "I only read it once. Too many books, too little time."

She mirrored my shrug, maybe in solidarity, maybe mocking me. "It's my favorite book. Did you see the movie?"

I grinned. "Three times."

"Did you ever meet Clark Gable?"

My jaw fell. "I'm not *that* old!"

"I know. I was just kidding." She waited a moment, then stuck her finger down her throat. "Ashley Wilkes makes me gag."

It was a peace offering and I took it. "Yeah, what did Scarlett ever see in him?" I studied her. "You kind of look like a Scarlett. What's your name?"

She grinned. "Actually, *Gone with the Wind* was my mom's favorite book, but she named me after the wrong character—Melanie. *Ugh.*"

"My name is Barbara and my middle name is Mae. Pretty bad, huh?"

She giggled. "You a hillbilly?"

"Luckily everyone just calls me Barb."

"My name doesn't shorten to anything good. Mellie rhymes with too many stupid words. Mel just sucks."

We bonded for a moment over the loathing of our names. Then she asked me where I was headed, and did I like riding a motorcycle.

"I don't know," I said, answering both questions at the same time.

"Well, if you've never been to Gettysburg, you ought to go there. The battlefields will blow your mind."

"My mind could use a little blowing. How far is it from here?"

"Only four hours if you speed a little. I've been there a million times." She rolled her eyes. "All the teachers around here think they've come up with the perfect field trip. When we studied the presidents, we went there. When we studied the Civil War, we went there. If I see another cannon, I'm gonna puke."

"I grew up in El Paso, Texas. We did field trips to Las Cruces."

"What's in Las Cruces?"

"The jail cell where Billy the Kid slept."

"Cool."

Done with me, she went back to her book and a slice of pie now in front of her.

"He was sentenced to hang for killing Sheriff William Brady of Lincoln County, New Mexico, but Pat Garrett gunned him down when he tried to escape."

She didn't turn around.

I motioned for the waitress. "I'll have a cup of coffee and a piece of that pie my friend over there is having."

Melanie's back tensed as the waitress glared at her. "She been bothering you?"

"No, I think I've been bothering her."

She sloshed coffee into an empty cup already on my table. "Well, good. She's my daughter. Missed the bus *again*." She stomped behind the counter, lifted the bell of glass covering the pie, and cut me a slice.

I decided that I'd tell the next person who asked my name that I was Sylvia Plath, and then I dug into the pie as though I would die without it.

The waitress sighed, took off her apron, and wiped her brow with it. "Her damn father wrecked the car, or I'd have driven her to school. Worthless bastard." She looked up at the pancake batter splattered on the ceiling. "Dear Lord, take him *puhleese!*"

I shoveled another forkful of pie. "What is this, rhubarb? It's amazing."

She glared at me. "Do you like men?"

I covered the gape in my mouth with a napkin.

She grabbed a flyswatter and murdered something on the counter. "I hate them!"

I wanted to grab Melanie and run.

"I swear, if another swinging dick tries to touch me, I'll poison his coffee."

I laid a ten-dollar bill on the table and got up. "This ought to cover my check. I want to get to Gettysburg before dark." I headed for the door and was just about to step out when I turned and called to Melanie, "By the way, Margaret Mitchell was a one-book wonder. Whatever you do, don't read the sequel some hack tried to write. It's called—"

"*Scarlett* by Alexandra Ripley." Melanie showed me the book in her backpack. "You're right, it sucks. I'm gonna read it again anyway."

Her mother stood there with her arms folded. "If it sucks, why read it twice?"

"I bought it with my allowance. How else am I going to get my money's worth?"

I laughed. "You've got a smart girl there. Can I take her with me?"

As I walked out to my bike, neither Melanie nor her mother knew I was serious. But that fireball of a little girl was going to be fine. She had a mind of her own and would leave as soon as she saved enough money for a ticket to anywhere.

For me, books had been a way to get out of El Paso, the middle of nowhere as far as I was concerned. I started with horse books, *Black Gold*, *Black Beauty*, and *Misty of Chincoteague*. Then I got into dog books, *Big Red*, *Old Yeller*, and *The Call of the Wild*. All those animal books, especially *The Incredible Journey*, brought me out of El Paso and into the world of instinct and survival, truly a foreign place for the fourth daughter of Ben and Florence Schoichet.

I had everything a kid could want—all the hand-me-down clothes and toys of my sisters, *new* clothes and toys as well, and never the ache of hunger or the fear of abuse. It was just that *love* stuff my parents seemed to have a problem with, that enthusiasm and celebration one sees in parents' gazes as they raise their child, not the stalwart obligation I saw in my mom's and dad's eyes. Just once I wanted to see my mother nudge someone at the playground and say, "That's my child," instead of always checking her watch. If just *one* of my parents could have built a single sand castle at the beach or tossed me around in the waves . . . If only they could have put their books down for a minute while we were on vacation and let me bury them in the sand, then maybe I wouldn't be having such a hard time with this adult orphan stuff. Maybe I wouldn't still be craving my parents' affection the way a freezing person craves warmth. Was that why I seemed to be longing for both my parents now more than ever, now that each of their fires was out and could never be rekindled?

In college, I read all the American and English literature I was supposed to, and of course I loved it all, but it was the Russian classics I was drawn to most—Tolstoy's *War and Peace*, Dostoyevsky's *Crime and Punishment*, and Solzhenitsyn's *The Gulag Archipelago*. Reading those books helped me to understand the inbred toughness of my father, born on the border of the Black Sea, fleeing his country in the aftermath of the Bolshevik Revolution. He never got his high school diploma, and my mother left college after a year, but they instilled the love of reading in all their daughters, and I remember seeing stacks of books on their nightstand, just like novels have always piled up by my bed. Be it the latest from Margaret Atwood or Toni Morrison, or something fun like Yann Martel's *Life of Pi*, I was always lost in a book . . . until I just stopped—stopped dead in the middle of Jonathan Safran Foer's *Extremely Loud and Incredibly Close*, published a month before my mother died.

I'd gotten the novel a week before that five a.m. call, and I was totally immersed in the mind of that nine-year-old boy who lost his father in 9/11. I was spellbound by the child's search through the boroughs of New York to find a lock that fit a key his father had left behind. But then that call came, and suddenly I couldn't concentrate on anything more than a paragraph or two. I just couldn't get back into the mind of a child trying to solve a mystery that would link him to his dead parent when I was never going to be able to figure out my buttoned-up mother, my old-world father, or, most important, the reason I still felt so compelled to discover exactly who they were.

Fifteen

The Ghosts of Gettysburg

B*y the time* I rolled into Gettysburg, my knees felt like rigid jelly, and I knew I had a bad case of what Rolling Stone Dave called "highway legs." Since I hadn't taken Burle's advice to bring along some knee braces, I decided to get foot pegs installed on the front of my bike. Both Daves had suggested I do that before I left Buffalo, but it was on my third full day under their tutelage and by then I was only half-listening.

"Riding a long distance is like running for office." Rolling Stone Dave reclined in his easy chair and put his feet up on imaginary pegs. "You have to keep readjusting your position to make any headway."

Shaggy Blond Dave balled his hands into fists and put them on either side of his neck. "They look like Frankenstein bolts. I'd think about installing a crash bar too."

I was half-asleep, but that woke me up. "Please don't say crash. Contrary to popular belief, I do *not* have a death wish."

"Hell, call it a candy bar!" His face grew red. "Just install one for *my* sake, okay?"

I pretty much had to agree to anything either Dave told me because if

I didn't, they would tag-team me into submission. I flashed both guys a grin. "Frankenstein pegs and a candy bar. I'll install them the next chance I get."

Both Daves nodded and chorused, "Better to slide on chrome than bone."

I have to admit that half the time I didn't understand what either Dave was talking about, but I did know that a foot peg had spared me pain in the Motel 6 parking lot. So my first stop in Gettysburg was at Battlefield Harley-Davidson to install highway pegs and a crash bar. I also decided to have my bike thoroughly checked out. Up until now, I had relied completely on Dave and Dave's word that my Sportster was in perfect running order. It was time to have a professional tell me the same.

Battlefield's was closing when I rolled in, but a guy who looked like a barrel with a baseball cap assured me I'd be first in line the next day. "Harley dealers give road warriors top priority. Tell 'em Junior sent you. They'll fix you right up."

Sure enough, the next morning I was serviced right away, and Junior even gave me a lift into town so I could see the sights while they worked on my bike. If only he'd held on to my credit card. I went crazy over all the Civil War memorabilia, and by the time I left town I'd bought an authentic 1842 musket.

The salesman at the Union Drummer Boy gave his mustache a twirl and sized me up immediately. "That musket probably freed some slaves." He gave me a wink and sealed the deal. "You could strap it on your bike as a symbol of independence."

I held the cold twelve pounds of metal. It was nearly five feet long, almost as tall as the young soldier I imagined had carried it. Cool as it might have looked on the back of my Harley, I'm sure it would have made me tip over. Besides, it probably wasn't legal to travel with an exposed weapon, even if it hadn't been fired for more than a century.

"I can ship her to Los Angeles for a small fortune." He grinned because he wasn't kidding. "She'll be there waiting for you the second you walk through your door."

And indeed he was right. Lynn, my friend who was staying with my dogs while I roamed the country like a madwoman, called me a week later.

"Your coffin has arrived."

"It's a Civil War musket," I said. "Made in Harpers Ferry."

"Well, it looks like a cannon. I swear, this box takes up half the living room."

We chatted for a moment about the dogs and the house, but when she asked me about the trip, I told her I had to go. How could I describe the scenery I was riding through when I didn't see it, I *felt* it? How could I tell her about the people I'd met when each disappeared into the next? The places and faces that populated the road were souvenirs, seconds in my present that were neither the future nor the past.

Now, as I held this Civil War musket, I had no idea why I was buying it, but I would be glad one day that I had. A week, a month, or a year after this trip, I would pick it up and feel the weight of the fallen soldier who had once held it, and then I would recall the thrill of what happened while I was standing on the battlefields at sunset on the evening I drove into town.

I'd arrived in Gettysburg dead on my feet and starving—pretty much the way I arrived almost anywhere after a long day on the road—but upon the insistence of Achnir and Amrita, the East Indian owners of my motel, I immediately got back on my bike and quickly rode out to see the eternal flame that commemorates where Abraham Lincoln delivered the Gettysburg Address. I was told I had to get there before sundown.

"You *must* experience the battlefields at twilight." Achnir leaned over the counter and stared deep into my eyes. "Something magical always happens at that time."

I shook my head. "Not tonight. I'm too exhausted for magic."

He wagged a finger at my nose. "My name means 'spiritual teacher.' I know what I'm talking about. Twilight is the time of learning. You must find the strength to go."

His wife, Amrita, wagged a finger at him. "Stop that, Achnir. You are no more of a spiritual teacher than our cat. The girl said she is tired. If she wants to miss the most magnificent experience of her life, she is entitled to."

"Go," he said to me. "You will not be sorry."

"Stay," she said to me. "I've made some chicken tikka and fresh naan."

Amrita's voice reminded me of honeysuckles, which made sense since her name meant "full of nectar," but the look she threw Achnir was anything but sweet. I was just about to thank her and go to my room for a shower when things started to get ugly.

Achnir banged his fist on the counter. "She can eat your tikka when she returns!"

Amrita glared at him. "She can eat my tikka when she *likes*."

I had already paid for the night, and the idea of homemade Indian food sounded wonderful, but I decided I should find another place before they got a divorce.

Achnir saw my discomfort and apologized. "My only goal is to be a good host."

"My husband is a passionate man." Amrita tenderly smoothed a piece of hair on his bald spot. "He is right. Now is the time to see the battlefields. The tourists will be gone, and you will have an especially pleasing ride on your motorbike."

And so, wiped out as I was, I climbed back on my Harley and headed out to the battlefields with about thirty minutes of daylight left. It was worth it.

To my amazement, not a living soul was there, and so I ambled around, reading plaques on cannons and statues. I learned that the United States suffered more casualties during the Civil War than in any other conflict from the Revolutionary War to Vietnam, and I felt humbled by the death still lingering in the air.

As the sun went down, I could feel the hundreds of thousands of souls around me and I knew I stood where the ground had once been littered with bodies. The air was electric with their energy, making the hair on the back of my neck bristle with respect.

And then two astonishing things happened.

Achnir and Amrita were not surprised when I burst into their lobby, my mind reeling from the first thing, my heart racing from the second.

"It was amazing. I was in an empty battlefield at a place called Cemetery Ridge—not a building was within miles—and suddenly I smelled freshly baked bread!"

Both Achnir and Amrita sat there smiling serenely.

"Many have told me about smelling bread at the Farnsworth House, but never on the battlefields." Achnir stroked his chin. "Jennie Wade's ghost must be restless."

Amrita pointed to her temple. "I heard Jennie took a bullet to the brain. Apparently she refused to stop baking even after the battle broke out." She squeezed Achnir's hand. "I would have climbed right into my oven!"

Achnir kissed her cheek. "Not you, my darling. You would have been one of those ridiculous women who disguised themselves as a man to join the fight."

Amrita raised an eyebrow. "Ridiculous, were they?"

"I only meant they were crazy to fight when they didn't have to." Achnir looked to me for help. "Would you have dressed up like a man to go to war?"

I thought of the tuxedo with tails I'd worn to a lesbian tea dance and grinned. "Hell no. I'd dive into my closet and hide behind my petticoats."

Amrita smiled politely at me, then snarled at Achnir, "The girl is probably starving. How about some chicken tikka?"

She whirled into the kitchen, and Achnir stood there with reddened cheeks. "We have free Wi-Fi. You can go online to read about the women who fought in the battle."

Amrita, who had the hearing of a dolphin, slammed a pot in the kitchen. "Yes, go read about the hundreds of women who died in the war—all of them stark raving mad!"

Later in my room, munching on the best tikka and naan I've ever had, I clicked on several articles about women who actually chose to go to battle, and I wondered why anyone would cross-dress to dive into carnage. Some of them, I reasoned, had no choice. If their husbands, fathers, brothers, and uncles were off fighting, who was left to support them? There wasn't a welfare system or food stamps, and most women weren't educated enough to work. Why not pencil in a mustache and don a pair of pants if it meant getting fed every day?

I shut down my computer and took a swig of Scotch from a flask my neighbor Frank had given me for one of those "gotta have a snort nights." I had finally decided to call my sisters for the first time and tell them what was going on. If my journey so far wasn't snort-worthy, what I had just experienced was. My sisters wouldn't believe that I'd smelled freshly baked bread on Cemetery Ridge—it would only make them think I was nuts—but I *had* to tell them about the other thing that had happened that evening on the battlefields. It was something they would want to know.

The sun was dropping behind the hills in the distance, and the twilight that had splayed light on the battlefield was quickly disappearing. I'd been wandering in the fields, trying to shake off a terrible loneliness, and along the way I'd seen dozens of holes—probably filled with snakes—pitting the ground. Now, with only a sliver of light on the horizon, I could barely see anything, and when the sun dropped from the sky, it left me in almost complete darkness. For a moment, I stood there trying to stay calm and letting my eyes adjust. I didn't know what I was about to step on, or *whom*, and my mind reeled with images of reptiles and dead soldiers.

I kept telling myself that this was not a cemetery, that although the battles were fought on this ground, and people died here, their bodies were buried somewhere else. And the holes were probably made by cute little gophers—and they don't bite, do they?

All the creepiness made me want to yell something irreverent to lighten my dark mood. It had to be something truly disrespectful of the dead, something that would make me feel more devilish than forlorn, more like a brazen rebel than the forsaken little girl I'd become. And then suddenly, just as I was about to let loose with an impudent cry, I felt an arm slip around my waist . . . and then another.

Certain some kids had come to vandalize the monument but decided to scare the hell out of me instead, I whirled around to defend myself, but no one was there. I took off for my motorcycle, not caring if I stepped on a snake or a dead body as long as I didn't feel whatever it was that had just touched me. But then I stopped short. Something had brushed my cheek, something that didn't scare me, but soothed me. I breathed in a hint of lavender, and in an instant, I knew what I'd felt was my mother's hand.

"Hi, Mom," I whispered into the darkness, standing as still as I could for fear she would leave.

Then, suddenly, one of the arms that had slipped around my waist before was there again. It held on to me now, but I felt no fear. I took in a whiff of cigar smoke, and I knew whose embrace I was in.

"Hi, Daddy." I dug into my pocket to touch his gold ring.

For what seemed an hour but was probably seconds, I stood there in awe of what was happening. Then a strong silent wind pressed against me and my parents were gone.

I walked back to my bike, my skin electric with their presence, and when I swung into the saddle, I realized I'd never driven at night, but I wasn't afraid. I fired up my engine, flipped on my headlight, and calmly drove back to my motel. All the way, I was blinking back tears and laughing. My parents had come to fight off my sadness, to chase off my fear, and to stop their little hoodlum from disturbing the dead.

"Well, that confirms it," Sandra said. "You're crazy."

I had dialed Naomi first because she could make conference calls and would get my other two sisters on the line. Naomi was also the most likely to believe what had happened.

"I knew Mom and Dad were together! Did they say anything to you?"

"They're dead, Naomi," Sandra said. "They can't talk."

"They showed up, didn't they?" Naomi said indignantly. "Did you tell them about your trip?"

"All I said was hi."

"Hi?" Sandra laughed. "Our parents came back from the dead and you said *hi?*"

"She was in shock!" Naomi shouted. "I wouldn't have been able to speak at all."

It was wonderful to hear my sisters argue and to finally be able to tell them about my trip. We talked for over an hour, and I told them all about my motorcycle class, about the Harley I bought on eBay, about the Daves in Buffalo. I spoke at a furious pace, as if my sisters were ghosts like my parents, and they too would disappear.

"You're *where*?" Harriet kept saying. "You bought a *what*?"

I was laughing and crying at the same time, pacing around the motel room with my cell phone pressed to my ear, slugging Scotch, and talking as fast as an auctioneer. We were all babbling over one another, and as much as I'd just been enveloped by death on the battlefield, I was now overwhelmed by their liveliness. I couldn't have been happier to be called crazy by Sandra. I was absolutely starving for each of Harriet's gasps, and I drank Naomi's veiled envy like an elixir. But more than anything, I was ecstatic that each of them kept asking how I was, and I felt comfort knowing that now they would be out there worrying about me. While it was true I was no one's little girl anymore, I was relieved, overwhelmed, and unbelievably grateful I was still their little sister.

Sixteen

Payback

I *had a hard* time getting out of Gettysburg, and it started with something that happened the last time I saw my mom alive. That was when she instilled in me the idea of payback, or as it's more commonly known, guilt. On the morning I left, it was definitely she who made me head back to the motel when I was already twenty miles away. I'd forgotten to do something that no one but my mom would have noticed. Since she was dead I thought I could get away with it, but after a few miles, she popped into my brain, and there she stayed until I finally turned around—all because I hadn't left a tip for the maid.

When I rode up, Amrita was outside shaking a blanket. At first she didn't look happy to see me. In fact, as soon as I unstrapped my helmet, she wagged a finger at me.

"I cannot believe you left without saying goodbye. Do you think I make my tikka for just anyone?" Finally, she allowed herself a smile. "Okay, what did you forget?"

"I forgot to tip the maid."

She burst out laughing. "Well, you're looking at her, so just keep your money."

I reached into my pocket for some cash. "I won't leave until you take it."

"And why is that? I found no animal sacrifices, no poetry scribbled on the walls."

"No, of course I left the room in good condition. I need to leave a tip because my mother can't anymore."

Amrita frowned. "Your mother . . . she's no longer here?"

I could still feel her touch on my cheek, but I shook my head. "She died almost a year ago. We weren't that close, but she's in my bloodstream, you know?"

Amrita folded the blanket into a neat rectangle. "My mother is gone as well. May God forgive me, but I'm sorry that any of her blood flows in my veins."

I staggered back as if her sourness had slapped me.

"Forgive my harsh words. I see your pain is fresh." She smiled, but her lip curled in bitterness. "Let's just say my mother did me a favor. Her callous heart drove me out of India to America, but I guess I took more of her venom with me than I thought."

It was odd how upset I got with Amrita or anyone who talked badly about a parent. It's not that mine were the paradigm of what a mother and father should be, but I would have given anything to have either of them alive so I could rail at them openly. "Listen, I just want to leave a tip and be on my way."

Amrita frowned as though she had been a bad girl. Then, to my embarrassment, my eyes welled up with tears.

"Oh, my goodness." She threw her arms around me like the mother neither of us had. "Let's go inside. I'm going to fix you a proper Indian breakfast and you are going to tell me why you drove all the way back here to give me a tip I will not take."

And so, while drinking espressos and eating *malpua*, Indian pancakes alive with cardamom, saffron, and pistachios, I told Amrita about my mother's obsession.

"A few months before my mom died, she and I shared a hotel room at a friend's wedding, and when we were checking out, I noticed a fifty-dollar bill on the nightstand. I thought she'd left it by mistake, so I picked it up and she nearly bit my head off."

Amrita's mouth dropped open. "My goodness, your mother was very serious about her tips, and generous too."

"She was definitely a generous person," I said. "I'd seen her leave tips before but never quite that much. So I asked her about it, and she explained that she felt responsible for getting a maid in trouble once when her bracelet went missing."

"The maid stole it?"

"No, and my mom never accused anyone. It was a terrible misunderstanding."

Amrita grinned. "My mother would have had the girl shot."

I threw her a look. "Anyway, weeks after my mom had reported the bracelet missing, the hotel sent her a check for five hundred dollars along with a note saying the maid had been fired."

"So the girl *did* take it."

"No, my mom found the bracelet in her suitcase a week later. All she could figure was she must have swept it off the nightstand and it fell into her bag. Anyway, she returned the check and begged the hotel to rehire the maid, but the girl was long gone."

Amrita sighed. "Such a sad story, but you make it sweet. Your mother used to leave tips, and now you keep up the tradition to honor her."

"Something like that. She left a tenth of what the bracelet was worth, kind of like a tithe." I reached into my pocket. "So will you please accept the money?"

Amrita smiled and offered me her palm.

I slapped a five-dollar bill into her hand. "On behalf of my mother, I thank you."

Amrita looked at the money and I could tell she was disappointed.

I shrugged. "There are a *lot* of motels between here and Los Angeles. I'd go broke if I left more than a tithe of her tithe."

Grinning, Amrita tucked the money into her bra. "Come, I'll walk you out."

But as I gathered my gear, I suddenly had an overwhelming urge to take a nap. Seeing my eyes droop, Amrita told me to sit down.

"*Malpua* can be like a sedative. Relax, I'll make you an espresso for the road."

I drank my espresso beneath a huge elm tree next to my Harley. Often the bike seemed to be waiting for me, faithful as a horse that didn't need to be tethered. As I lay there, using my helmet as a pillow, I could feel heat still rising from the drag pipes, and I heard tiny *ping*s coming from the engine as it cooled down. Like heartbeats, the *ping*s eased off as the bike settled, but as it did, I grew restless. I longed for that prickle of expectation in my fingertips when I turned on the ignition, and I couldn't wait for my senses to snap into focus as soon as I was in motion. The acute concentration I felt on my Harley was impossible to replicate in stillness, less possible to achieve in a car. On my bike I felt every particle of the wind, saw every granule in the asphalt. Motionless, my attention wandered, as it could behind the safety of four walls, as it often did balanced on four tires. There was no zoning out on two wheels, no air bag between my body and impact. If I wanted a snack or needed coffee, there was no staving off hunger or fatigue, no free hand to hold a sandwich or a cup, and no way to pass either through my visor.

As I lay there under the elm, everything about my motorcycle, about this ride, about this contest with grief, was intriguing. I had no idea what was ahead of me, I just hoped I would see it before it took me down. Rolling Stone Dave had told me that anything unexpected could do it . . . like the small piece of luggage he claimed almost killed him.

"I'm telling you, it was like a bomb full of clothes exploded on the highway," he said, sucking down his fourth beer on my second night in Buffalo. "Socks, shorts, shirts, and shoes—everything was spread everywhere." He lifted his baseball cap and resettled it on his head. "It was a mangled pair of jeans that nearly did me in. When I finally got around them, I pulled over to the side of the road and nearly got sick."

"Wow."

"Yeah, wow. I remember thinking, that's a nice pair of Levi's I just ran over. Weird how we think about stuff like that." He pointed his beer bottle at me. "Dave and I will make sure you leave with all your gear tied down properly, but you're gonna have to learn to do it yourself. Just remember—tie down your shit like it's trying to get away."

I tapped the side of my head. "Duly noted. Tie things down like a man."

He leaned over and tapped my knee. "Well, duly note this. The bike I sold you got me through that mess. Damn good bike you're getting."

Now, under the shade of a Pennsylvania elm, I looked at my damn good bike. "Remember your old pal Dave?" I stroked the foot peg.

The bike pinged.

I wanted to lounge around all day talking to my Harley, and for the life of me I couldn't see why not. What was driving me back to Los Angeles anyway?

I drained the rest of my espresso, scrambled to my feet, and jogged inside to say goodbye to Amrita. She looked up from where she sat at her computer and smiled. "Off to leave more tips across the country?"

"Yup. Say goodbye to Achnir." I looked around. "By the way, where is he?"

She rolled her eyes. "He took the red-eye to Las Vegas last night."

"Really?"

"Yes, he's a professional poker player. He just called. He's already up a couple of grand."

"Wow, who'd a thunk it?"

"I know. He doesn't look the part. It's probably why he's successful. Anyway, I told him that you had come back and why, and he said I should give *you* a tip in return."

She put two quarters on the counter and pushed them toward me.

"Fifty cents?"

"Achnir said to give you 10 percent back for good luck."

I slipped the coins into my pocket and felt around for my dad's ring and Lester's coin. "I wonder why everyone seems to think I need luck."

Amrita raised an eyebrow. "Perhaps because you ride a motorcycle."

As I rode away from the motel, I wondered what it was that drew me to risk. Why had I run with the bulls in Pamplona? Why was sex more thrilling if I thought I might get caught? When it came to motorcycling, I knew it was the sensation of straddling danger and power. Feeling defenseless and impervious in the same second was fascinating.

I loved how each day I gained mastery over my fear, and the more strength I commanded, the more I wanted to flex my street muscles. I'd seen other bikers do this by zigzagging through traffic or challenging cars at stoplights to be the first off the line. But me, I expressed my prowess by cranking my speed to a hundred at least once a day. It was my way of blowing away terror. It was how I faced down semis, and in the end, I realized that roaring by with a show of confidence was more important than actually having it.

The first time I hit a hundred, I half-expected to explode from the pressure of the wind, or at least hear a sonic boom. Instead I heard a siren. Officer Michael Patrick Fitzgerald of the Pennsylvania State Police snagged me like a trout with his radar gun and pulled me over just before I crossed the state line.

I watched him stroll up to me grinning like the killjoy he was. "Going pretty fast there, ain't ya?" He whacked his thigh with his ticket book. "All right, let me see 'em."

I put my hands in the air.

"No, you knucklehead. Your motorcycle license and registration." He sighed and pointed to my helmet. "And take that thing off."

I fumbled with my chinstrap and released a horrible case of helmet hair.

"Well, look what I've pulled over!" He grinned like Jack Nicholson. "I thought I was dealing with a Hells Angel the way you were flying."

I tried to look sincere. "Would you believe I've never sped like that before?"

"Nope."

"Would you believe I'll never do it again?"

"Nope." He let out a low whistle and eyed my bike like it had cleavage. "If I had a beauty like this, I'd open her up too." He turned and swaggered back to his cruiser. "And you didn't hear me say that."

"Hear what?" I called after him. "By the way, how fast did you clock me?"

"One oh three."

"Cool," I whispered under my breath.

After a few minutes he was back beside me shaking his head. "I had my dispatch run a check on you. I can't believe you just got your license."

"That's correct, sir." I beamed. "And I've never gotten a ticket."

"Not for riding a motorcycle. You're Mario Andretti in a car—three tickets and two wrecks. Are you trying to kill yourself?"

I had to think about that. I didn't have a death wish, but I didn't have a life wish either. I swallowed hard. "No, I'm not trying to kill myself. I think I'm trying to live."

He scratched his head. "What am I going to do with you?"

"How about a warning? I think I've gotten this speeding thing out of my system."

"Yeah, right." The radio in his cruiser signaled him to pick up. "Hang on."

He headed back to his car and reached in for his handset. I watched him talk back and forth to his dispatch, and then he strolled back to me. "Okay, listen up." He tapped the helmet on my lap. "I want you to put this on and follow me."

He headed for his cruiser; I put on my helmet and followed him to his patrol car.

"No, sweetheart." He stopped dead and spun around. "Follow me on your *bike*."

"Right. My bad." I tried to look cool as I walked back to my Harley, threw my leg over the saddle, and waited. After a moment, he fired up his cruiser and I gunned my bike. Then off we went, he knowing where I was headed, me figuring it was for trouble.

"Fuck, fuck, fuck!" I yelled, clouding up my visor as I focused on the backend of his black-and-white. "I am such a fucking idiot!"

Ten minutes later, I stopped swearing at myself and settled into the ride. It was a sexy strip of highway, and with a cop in front of me, I didn't have to worry about one sneaking up behind. But twenty minutes later I was getting upset. We were headed back where I'd just come from. At this rate, I'd never get across the Mason-Dixon line.

After another ten miles, Officer Mike finally pulled onto the shoulder. I parked behind his dust, and realized why we were there. Sirens, screeching tires, slamming doors, and shouting people converged and erupted around me. I sat frozen in my saddle and watched two paramedics huddled over a man lying in the middle of the road. A puddle of dark blood seeped out of him like motor oil.

Officer Mike bolted past me. "Stay put!" He raced to an elderly woman sitting in the dirt. He squatted before her and was saying something, but she just stared past him like a broken doll. After a few minutes a paramedic took over, and Officer Mike walked back to where I sat feeling like I might throw up.

"I'm sorry." He wiped his face with his sleeve. "I didn't realize it was this bad."

"What happened?" I pointed to the old woman. "Is she all right?"

"She's pretty shook up. Nothing broken as far as I can tell. Her husband wasn't so lucky. Steering wheel crushed into him. I'm not sure he's gonna make it."

"Oh, my God." I looked around but didn't see another car. "What did they hit?"

He walked to the front end of the wreck, motioning for me to follow. I swung off my bike, and my knees almost buckled. A washing machine was smashed into where the car's motor had been. The engine was now in the backseat.

Officer Mike pointed up the road to an old truck. "That fellow up there was hauling appliances and didn't tie them down properly."

"Son of a bitch," I whispered.

"I shouldn't have brought you here. My dispatch said it was a car versus a box. I didn't think to ask what was *in* the box."

Two paramedics were lifting the old man into the ambulance. His wife, now out of her haze, was being helped inside to be by her husband.

Officer Mike looked at his boots. "I was going to teach you a lesson, but you didn't need to see this."

I watched the ambulance disappear down the road and then saw the tow truck lifting the wrecked car. It looked like a gored bull dripping fluids. "Yeah, I did."

Officer Mike wrote me a ticket, tore it out of his book, and ripped out his copy. "You were lucky I stopped you today. Lucky you didn't kill yourself or someone else." He handed me both copies of the ticket along with my license and registration. "Okay, there's no record of our little encounter, but I hope you'll remember it."

"I will." I shoved everything in my pack. "I can't believe you just did that."

"I've been waiting for the right person to pay back. Looks like you're the one."

"What do you mean?"

"Remember when I said if I had a bike like yours, I'd open it up too?"

I grinned. "No, I didn't hear anything like that."

He slapped his leg with his ticket book. "Now is *not* the time to be a smart-ass."

"Fine, yes, I remember."

"Well, I did have a bike like yours, and I got pulled over for being an idiot, just like you." He shook his head. "Man, I was a good-for-nothing punk back then. I didn't give a damn about myself or anyone, and this cop handed me the luckiest day of my life."

"Because he stopped you from hurting yourself?"

"Well, that too. What I was talking about is he wrote me up and gave me both copies of the ticket like I just did. And that's when I decided what to do with my life."

"What? Become a cop?"

He lifted his mirrored sunglasses. "No, I decided to give a shit about something. How about you, Speedy Gonzales? Do you give a shit about *anything*?"

I thought about that for a moment and realized that what I cared about most was staying upright . . . and I wasn't too sure about that. If dying instantly in a fiery crash wouldn't hurt anyone else—especially my sisters—and if my dogs were cared for, I saw no reason to return home.

"Sure I do." I looked him straight in the eyes. "I care about lots of things."

He swept his arm around. The tow truck and ambulance were gone, the glass had been cleared, and cars were already whizzing by with blood and brake fluid on their tires. "You going to remember all this tomorrow when you're cranking it up to a hundred?"

I looked around at the nothingness that was left behind. "Of course I will."

He grinned. "Of course you will, what? Crank it up to a hundred again or remember all you just saw?"

I started to speak but he shut me down. "Too late. Give me your driver's license."

"Aw, come on. I've learned my lesson."

He pointed to my tank bag. "Your driver's license *pronto!*"

I did as I was told. "You're not going to give me another ticket, are you?"

He didn't say anything. He just stared at my license for a moment, then looked at me. "How in the hell do you pronounce your last name?"

"Schoichet—*Shock-it.* It's Russian. I'm not sure how my ancestors used to pronounce it, but we sort of clear our throat and sneeze it out."

"Russian, huh? I figured you weren't Irish."

I was starting to get antsy. "Look, if you're going to give me a ticket, go ahead."

"Does Schoichet mean anything? My name means son of a man named Gerald."

I sighed. "It comes from the Hebrew word *sho-hait,* which means slaughterer."

"No kidding?"

"Yeah, I like to think my ancestors were kosher butchers, not mass murderers."

"Interesting." He studied my license again. "And tell me this—what is a fifty-year-old woman doing out here alone on a motorcycle?"

I suppressed a grin and finally told the truth. "Not giving a shit about anything."

"Not even that old man and his wife?"

I thought about that and my eyes went glassy.

"Okay, you've had enough." He gave me back my license. "You're free to go."

I watched him swagger to his police car and drive off. Then I swung into my saddle and sat there, letting the breeze waft through my hair. I didn't feel like putting on my helmet or taking off into that nothingness. I didn't feel like thinking about Officer Mike, that old man, or his wife. I simply didn't *feel* . . . and I wasn't sure I was able to.

And that's when my wall of sarcasm began to crack, and the heat of a deep sorrow bubbled feverishly within me. I wanted to cry, to feel hot tears running down my cheeks. I wanted to beat down my cool exterior, to feel something—*anything*—even if it was stone-cold sadness. But here it was, not even thirty minutes since the ambulance took the old couple away, and already I didn't care about either one of them.

Seventeen

Is Virginia Really for Lovers?

I **still took my** speed over a hundred every day even after my encounter with Officer Mike. I don't think a motorcycle or a car is going to kill me. I'm probably going to wind up being an old lady who everyone can't believe is still alive. I'll be the reincarnation of Georgia O'Keeffe out in the middle of nowhere on a ranch in New Mexico. I'll surround myself with animals and art, and the person living closest to me won't be within walking distance.

I sat in my saddle for a long time, taking in the deep green ridges and valleys of the Pennsylvania–Virginia border. When I finally took off, mindful that Officer Mike was probably tucked behind a billboard, I kept my speed at a thoughtful cruise.

In truth, the old man and his wife were already out of my consciousness, but the word *old* was not. When Officer Mike looked at my license, it wasn't my gender but my age that had him wondering why I was out there. If I'd been younger, he'd have seen me as an Amelia Earhart on a motorcycle, a Thelma or a Louise on a joyride. But he didn't even consider that I might be on an adventure. No, he saw me for who I was—a fifty-year-old woman lost in flight.

I looked at the horizon over the tips of my boots and thought about Amelia evaporating into the sky. Then I saw the sun directly overhead and realized that my day was also evaporating and I was still in Pennsylvania. I pulled off at a town called State Line to top off my tank and see how far I could get before sundown. Once I began my trek through a sliver of Maryland (about thirteen miles), and after I rode through twenty-five miles of West Virginia, which separated from the Confederacy to become a Union state in 1861, I would officially be in Virginia, one of the eleven states that formed the pro-slavery South during the Civil War. It was mind-boggling to think that after riding only about *forty* miles, I could go from Yankee territory to a place where being a rebel used to mean you were willing to die for the freedom to enslave others. After my college experience in Missouri, I figured it was time to start swallowing my political views.

My goal that morning had been to make it to Gatlinburg on the Pigeon River in the heart of the Great Smoky Mountains. It was more than five hundred miles from Gettysburg, doable by car but risky by motorcycle. Still, I thought with my new highway pegs, I could handle it— until Officer Mike and a washing machine ate half my day. Now I was going to have to stop in Roanoke, Virginia, which I began to think wasn't such a bad idea. I needed to dance, to remind myself that being fifty didn't mean I was dead, and with each passing billboard, I wondered if Virginia's state motto was right. Was Virginia *really* for lovers? If there was a decent gay bar there, I aimed to find out.

For the next three hours, I buzzed down Interstate 81, watching the insects of the Appalachian Mountains splat against my windshield and worrying about locusts. I'd overheard someone at the gas station talking about the infestation that hit the Blue Ridge mountains in 1995, and though the cicada, as the locals called them, had a seventeen-year cycle, it would be just my luck for them to return early. Grasshoppers, locusts, dragonflies, and ticks bred like crazy in the fir trees that lined the highway, and though I loved the shimmering blue sheen of their pine-scented needles, I wanted out of there fast.

At the first Roanoke exit where I saw a Motel 6, I zipped off the ramp, parked my bike, and hobbled to the office. A grizzly old woman who looked like a garden gnome greeted me. "You need some help, hon? 'Cause if you do, I—"

But before she could finish, I broke into a terrible coughing fit.

"Lord, you *do* need help!" She ran off and returned with a Styrofoam cup filled with something purple.

"Thanks, I'll pass. My throat's just dry from the road."

In truth, I'd swallowed a bug the size of a Volkswagen. I'd lifted my visor a split second to scratch my nose and the creature dive-bombed into my esophagus. I almost did a wheelie but stayed grounded, glad a truck hadn't kicked up a pebble and taken out my eye. That's what happened to Cyclops Jack, one of the Harley guys who "joined me" when I pulled over on the New York–Pennsylvania border more than four hundred miles before. I'd been studying his eye patch, wondering why a lot of bikers looked like pirates, when he decided to regale me, in gory detail, with the story of how he got his nickname.

"Popped out like an ice cube." He lifted the black patch and showed me the jagged scar above his cheekbone. "Lost more than an eye that day. Lost my nerve too."

"But you got it back," I said, trying to be friendly so he wouldn't kill me. "I can't believe you still ride."

"Who said I got it back?" He grinned. "I'm scared shitless every day."

"Oh, come on." I studied his rugged face. "You're kidding me."

He crossed his heart and hoped to die. "What's wrong with being a little scared? It just might save you one day."

"Oh, come on." The old woman now before me pushed the Styrofoam cup toward my face. "What are you scared of? It's Kool-Aid, not poison." She crossed her heart and hoped to die.

I could still feel the scrape of the wings on the back of my throat. She didn't look like a cult leader, so I drained the cup and the winged roadkill washed away. "Thanks, I think that hit the spot."

"Well, thank you for not dying. I don't have the insurance to cover it. I also don't have a room. That's what I was about to say when you started hacking up the road." She eyed me up and down. "Looks like you need a decent bed and some nice linens anyway."

I tried to straighten up. "How'd you guess?"

"I used to ride, honey. Been on the road awhile, haven't you?"

"Jeez, this is only my third day. Do I look that bad?"

"Just a little crooked. How far you fixing to go?"

When I told her she guffawed and the toothpick in her mouth flew out.

"What's so funny?" I was slightly insulted, though I knew why she was laughing. If I looked this bad already, I'd need a body bag by the time I hit the West Coast.

"Nothing, honey. It's just that you look more like a passenger than a rider. Those tough-looking women holding on to the handlebars, well, they look *different.*"

She meant dykey, and instantly I felt pleased to have escaped the label. My inner homophobia was always squaring off with my outward gay pride, and I just wished no one gave a shit . . . especially me.

I winced, and the Motel 6 lady heaved a sigh. "Oh, dear, I've hurt your feelings, haven't I?"

I rubbed my arm. "I'm just a little sore."

"Yup, you need a feather bed, but you won't find one here. Your best bet is in Salem. My friend has a lovely B and B off the Lynchburg Turnpike. I'll give her a call."

True to the hospitality I found throughout the South, my new geriatric friend secured me a room at the Brugh Inn, and drew me a map on a napkin. "The road there curls around like a Slinky, but you'll find it." She smiled warmly. "It was built in 1907. That's when Katharine Hepburn and Frida Kahlo were born—damn I loved those two!"

Wondering what that had to do with anything, I ambled back to my bike like John Wayne, who was also born in that year, then once I was back on the road, my mind turned to the irony of a town called Salem off a turnpike named Lynchburg. But that whole witch thing happened in 1692 in Massachusetts. This was Salem, Virginia, with no murders recorded since 1998. Not so in Roanoke, as I found out later that evening.

On the advice of my B and B host, I doubled back to Roanoke to check out Awful Arthur's. There I watched the Detroit Pistons play the Miami Heat at the bar where I ate awfully good crab legs and eyed a woman with a buzz cut. She was sitting two stools over in a cloud of cigarette smoke as she drank a mug—not a glass—of bourbon.

She glanced over and winked. Then before I knew it, she moved to the bar stool next to me. "Not from around here, are you?"

"No, I'm not." I wiped a beard of butter off my face. "How'd you know?"

She pointed to the ashtray nearest me. "That's empty. Let me guess, California?"

"Wow, you're good."

"Not really." She pointed to my pack on the floor. "All your info is right there."

I squinted down at my bag, and saw nothing but the fuzzy edges of my ID tag.

"Twenty-twenty." She pointed two fingers from her eyes to mine. "I get a bead on things." She offered her hand. "Nice to meet you, Barbara. I'm Sandy, like the beach."

"I suppose you read my name on the tag, too?"

"Yup. How do you pronounce that last name of yours—looks Greek to me."

"*Shock-it*, and it is Greek. It means killer."

"No kidding?"

"Yeah, I'd watch your back around me."

Sandy laughed and nearly coughed up a lung.

I looked around the place. A butt was burning in each ashtray. "Does *everyone* around here smoke?"

"You're in tobacco country. Virginia isn't for lovers; it's for lung cancer."

"Um, you wouldn't happen to know of any gay bars around here, would you?"

She grinned. "I thought you'd never ask. The Backstreet Café is a couple of blocks away. Gulp down your girlie drink, and let's get outta here."

I sipped my wine like a lady, paid my bill, and followed Sandy, like the beach, outside. She nearly swooned when she saw my Harley.

"Sweet Jesus." She stroked my tank like she probably stroked half the women in Roanoke. "We'd better take my truck. Your bike will be safer here."

"It's nice out. Why don't we walk?"

"Um, you don't want to be walking around *here* to a bar like *that* with a person who looks like *me*. Virginia is selective about who people should love."

So I slid into Sandy's pickup, and on the way over, she filled me in on the bar's history. It seems that on September 22, 2000, a guy named Ronald Edward Gay was driven to the breaking point by his last name. He announced he wanted to "waste some faggots," so he walked into the bar and opened fire.

"When it was all over, one person was dead, six were wounded, and

Ronald's last name was *still* Gay." Sandy lit up her hundredth cigarette. "Idiot could have gotten his name changed, but no, he had to lose his fucking mind."

"How about I buy you another mug of bourbon back at Awful Arthur's?"

"Don't worry about that bastard. He's rotting through *four* life sentences. Besides, last I heard his name isn't Gay anymore. Now everyone just calls him *Bitch*."

She laughed so hard her Camel fell in her lap, but I barely cracked a smile. She'd parked in front of a row of abandoned buildings. In the middle was a tiny establishment with no name on the outside and a neon sign that flashed. WE'RE STILL OPEN.

"Where is everybody?" I looked up and down the desolated street. "It's kind of creepy around here."

Sandy jumped out of her pickup. "Someone was murdered here, remember?"

I stayed in the truck.

"Come on, what do you ride—a Harley or a bicycle?"

I smiled weakly. "The Harley's just for show, I ride a Schwinn."

"Jeez, this is probably the safest bar in town now."

"Yeah, right," I said. "Why is everything around it boarded up?"

"Can you spell *recession*? Move it, ya big baby."

I decided she was right. The bar was probably like the house hit by an airplane in *The World According to Garp*. What was the likelihood of another disaster striking it?

Sandy swung open the wooden door, and I laid my eyes on true emptiness. No one was there but a skinny bartender sucking a beer bottle and playing a video game.

"Beam or Turkey?" he called over as we headed toward the pool table.

"Turkey!" Sandy called back.

"And you?" he yelled at me.

"What kind of chardonnay do you have?"

"White!" he yelled. "And we're out!"

I ordered orange juice, and then I watched Sandy sweep the table.

"Wanna play for a tank of gas?" she asked, corralling the balls for another game.

"No thanks, I just look stupid. I don't think I hit a ball more than twice. Besides, I'm leaving early in the morning for the Great Smoky Mountains National Park."

Sandy grunted. "*Touristville*—I hope you've got a hotel already."

"I never book ahead. I like to be free to change my mind."

"Well, I hope your mind is okay with sleeping outdoors. Tourists run around like roaches there. I swear one will crawl up your leg."

I shuddered at the thought and waved to the bartender for the tab.

"It's on the house!" he called. "It was nice to have the company."

Sandy and I walked out, and I whispered, "Wow, is it always so dead in there?"

"Well, it's true, you're not the only one who got spooked by that shooting."

"So why aren't you afraid?"

She padded her right boot and grinned. "I carry a gun."

And with that, what little comfort I felt around Sandy sifted away. I managed to chitchat with her until she got me back to my Harley, and I rode away from Awful Arthur's to my room at the Brugh Inn. There, settled in one of the most comfortable beds I've ever slept in, I drifted off into what I thought was a relaxing sleep, until I woke up the next morning tangled up in blue sheets, as restless as if I'd never closed my eyes.

Eighteen

Uncle Buck and the
Hungry Mother

Usually *after surfing* the Internet and consulting my *H.O.G. Touring Handbook*, I had an idea of where I wanted to go the next day. Sometimes I left without a clue, so I'd just ride till I exhausted myself. But when I woke up in my little B and B in Salem, VA, I knew that my next destination was simply to get to where I hadn't gotten to the day before. And so, after a plateful of flapjacks and bacon, I sat fat and happy on my Harley with hardly a wince of pain, glad to hit the highway and feeling that perhaps the siege that grief had launched against me was losing its stronghold.

It was probably just the highway pegs, because in the days to come, my readiness for the road and my ability to buoy my mental stamina still came into question each morning. As much as I might have felt like my body was a machine, the truth was I had no inner gauge to predict how far I could go, no dipstick to check if my spirit had gone dry. Too often I found myself lying in bed taking my biking temperature, asking myself if I was too weak to ride or just sick of movement. It reminded me of how my mother used to test my readiness for school if I claimed to be ill. The difference was that she was able to see right through me with her cheek, soft as a peach as it swept across my brow.

But with no mother to rouse me from bed and no companion off whom to bounce my disposition, I had to rely on myself to determine if I was road ready. It was tricky. If I fooled my body into thinking it had enough juice to go a few more miles, I might end up in the middle of nowhere, too exhausted to hold up my bike. If I convinced myself I was unfit to ride, I might wake up in the middle of the afternoon, drunk on TV. The only thing I knew for sure was that, according to Uncle Buck, I couldn't allow myself to land in limbo. "Never," he said, "give yourself the luxury of twenty more minutes."

A cowboy crossed with a lumberjack, Uncle Buck had a bushy red beard and legs that stayed bowed even after he climbed off his Gold Wing. He rode up while I was lounging by Hungry Mother Lake, one of my road whimsy stops on the way to Gatlinburg. Full of agitation, Buck wanted to talk to me whether I wanted to or not, and being polite, and a little scared, I let him lecture me about biking for a good half-hour before he finally roared off. I disliked him on sight, and I don't remember much else about his personality except for one thing—he never sat down or shut up.

"Twenty more minutes will turn your cozy bed into quicksand." He paced in front of me like a pompous professor. "Fact is, twenty more minutes is *never* twenty more minutes." He stopped and looked down at me. "I see you understand what I'm saying."

"I do?" I pushed my back up against the tree. "Not really. I was just looking out at this lake and wondering why I was here when I got kind of tired and—"

"Then you *do* get me. When you're tired, you get off the goddamn highway before it hypnotizes you. *Never* try to squeeze in another twenty more minutes. Got it?"

I think I actually had dozed off, because for a second I thought I was back in Bart Mange's classroom. "Got it," I mumbled. "Nineteen minutes—max."

"You think you're so smart?" He hovered over me until his belt buckle was inches from my face. It was shaped like a Brahman bull and large enough to be used as a weapon. "Well, answer me this—have you ever wrestled a steer?"

"Have I ever wrestled a *what*?" I started to look for an escape route, and then I got mad. "What's wrong with you? Do I remind you of someone who cut off your testicles?"

I was sorry the second I said it, not because the man might have hauled off and smacked me, but because his whole body slumped like a doll with its stuffing pulled out. "I'm sorry. That just kind of came out."

"No, I'm the one who's sorry," he said. "It's just that leaning up against that tree, well, you reminded me of someone I once knew."

"Who? Rip Van Winkle?"

"Ha, you're a funny one." He frowned, reached inside his shirt, and drew out a necklace with a tiny silver bird dangling from it. "See that? That's my albatross."

"Sorry, I make jokes when I'm nervous." I could see he was serious, and that I was in for a long story. I started to get up. "Listen, I should get back on the road."

"Wait a sec or two." He held up two fingers, and guessing he wasn't throwing me a peace sign, I plopped back down.

"Okay, I have a couple of things to say. One—the person you reminded me of was a buddy I used to ride with. He dozed off on his bike and almost got killed."

"Holy shit," I said. "I'm sorry."

"And two—it was *my* fault. He said he was tired, but I wanted to get to the next exit. Hell, it was only twenty minutes away."

"He *lived* though." My stomach turned like a dog trying to settle. "Didn't he?"

"Oh, he's alive all right. Even jokes about it—says trying to hold up his bike was like wrestling a steer backward from the ground up." He shook his head. "Man, I never forgave myself."

With his story off his chest, Uncle Buck reached down and patted my shoulder. "Don't worry. I can tell you're gonna be fine out there."

"Oh, yeah? What makes you think so?"

"Well, you might be crazier than shit riding out here all by yourself, but from the looks of it, you've got a pretty clear head on your shoulders." He grinned. "You stopped for a rest, didn't ya?"

The man clearly didn't know me. I'd been in a fog for at least nine months, and up until about an hour before I got to the lake, my mind had been so preoccupied I had barely seen any of the landscape around me. But not long after I rode away from Virginia with my sights on Tennessee, I actually experienced a respite of clarity, enough so that I could finally see the gorgeous panorama around me.

How could I not? I was on the Blue Ridge Parkway with the Appalachians rising in the distance. Massive hunks of topaz dusted with jade, they swept into imposing peaks topped by misty crowns of sapphire. Like royalty, the mountains commanded my respect—just as the road itself did.

Wide and easy to ride one minute, the parkway would suddenly shrink to barely a single lane. It was an unpredictable piece of road—sometimes stretching before me in a cruise-worthy straightaway, other times whipping into a curl like a wood shaving. It was one of my teaching roads, making me aware I could wipe out if I went too fast, and demanding that I downshift swiftly or risk stalling out. Unable to pick up any pace, I knew I needed the interstate to get to Gatlinburg before dark, so I winged out onto the freeway paralleling the parkway . . . and flew.

Zipping along at sixty, I was thinking about taking it up to a hundred when I glimpsed a roadside sign that took me off in a direction I never intended to go—HUNGRY MOTHER STATE PARK. Though the sign had been like any other highway marker, it might as well have been invisible. Like a siren, it called to me, and I didn't have to turn my motorcycle toward the off-ramp; the bike just went there on its own.

After several miles under a canopy of trees, I came upon a huge lake, gorgeous but populated with noisy teenagers. I was ready to leave the second I got there, but I was exhausted from the unpredictable road earlier, and I wanted to take a moment or two to close my eyes. I swung off my bike and found a shady spot, and using a tree as a backrest and my helmet as an ottoman, I gazed out on the water. During one of the serene moments when someone wasn't buzzing by on water skis, I got to thinking about the last couple of weeks before my mom died. There were red flags everywhere before her cancer diagnosis—her ankles were swelling, she was always exhausted, and worst of all she'd almost completely stopped eating. Worried, I'd begun calling her almost every day to coax her into having a solid meal.

"You and your sisters are driving me crazy!" She banged a pan against something. "You hear that? I'm making myself a scrambled egg. Are you happy now?"

"We're just worried about you, Mom. Have you seen a doctor?"

"I'm fine, damn it. Besides, I could lose a few pounds."

I could picture her beating an egg to death, slamming the shells into the trash, stomping around her kitchen like the five-foot-two giant she was. "Come on, Mom. If I was starving myself, you'd bug me to see a doctor, wouldn't you?"

"I'm your mother. I'm supposed to nag you." She took in a deep breath. "Look, I appreciate your concern, but I'm telling you right now if you and your sisters don't stop pestering me, I'll stop answering the phone."

"Fine. Seen any good movies lately?"

She chuckled. "That's my girl."

We talked a few more minutes about which celebrity would die next and who of her friends had collapsed recently. Then we hung up and I called Naomi. I didn't know it at the time, but she already had plans to fly in to El Paso the next week. Together, Naomi and Harriet were going to take our mother to see a doctor, and a few days after that, I would get a call from them with our other sister Sandra conferenced in. This was six days before my mom would die, two days before she was officially diagnosed with the cancer that would kill her.

"Dr. Zelnich saw something on an X-ray," Harriet began. "It's probably a tumor, but we're not sure. We want a second opinion."

"Oh, my God," Sandra whispered.

"But I just talked to her," I said. "She was as feisty as ever."

"She probably didn't want to scare you because we don't know anything for sure yet," Naomi said. "Anyway, apparently Dr. Zelnich saw some kind of a—"

"A shadow," I said quietly. "Something shaped like a kidney bean, right?"

"That's exactly what he saw. How did you know?"

"I had a dream last night."

"A dream?" Sandra asked. "You *dreamed* that Mom had a tumor?"

"Not exactly." I got a chill, remembering how when my father had died I'd actually *felt* him pass through me like a gust of wind. "I dreamed that Mom and I went out to a restaurant, and had ordered something—I don't remember what—but when the waiter set Mom's plate in front of her, there was nothing there but a huge kidney bean.

"'This isn't what I ordered,' she said. 'Take it away.' But the waiter just shook his head and Mom got really upset. 'Take it away!' she screamed.

"The poor guy just stood there. 'I'm sorry,' he said. 'I wish I could.'"

Naomi sighed. "Wow, dreams are so amazing."

"So what was on your plate?" Harriet asked.

"Actually nothing, and when Mom saw the empty plate, she was really happy. 'Yours looks wonderful,' she said, and then she started to cry. 'Now I want you to promise me you'll enjoy every bite.'"

"I just love dreams." Naomi sighed again. "But we need to talk about Mom. I have a friend who got us in to see a specialist in Houston. Harriet and I are flying there with Mom tomorrow."

"Tomorrow?" Sandra gasped. "Is it that serious?"

"It might be," Harriet said, her voice cracking. "We need to find out for sure."

"But she was eating normally at Nancy's wedding," I said. "I mean, she couldn't stop raving about the buffet."

Harriet sighed. "That was a month ago. She's hardly eaten anything for a week."

"She likes eggs," I whispered. "Someone should make her some eggs."

Suddenly we all began talking at once, until Harriet spoke above us. "Either Naomi or I will call you from Houston when we know more."

And two days later I did get a call, but it was from my mom.

"Well, I was hoping it was gas, but it's cancer." She chuckled. "Guess I'll be seeing your dad sooner than I thought."

"I can't believe you're making jokes, Mom."

"Okay, Barbara, I want you to listen to this."

I waited a moment but didn't hear anything. "Listen to what?"

"I was wringing my hands. See what good it did?"

I felt like hanging up on her. "I'll call you back. I'm making a plane reservation."

"Quit being so dramatic. I'm an old lady. I'm supposed to die."

"But Mom."

"Don't *Mom* me. They gave me six months, maybe a year. Hell, I bet I make it past *that*. Besides, I promise to haunt you for eternity, okay?"

She had me laughing before we hung up, and she died the following Monday.

Now, after the bluster of Uncle Buck, I was enjoying the serenity of his absence and staring out at the lake. It was clear why I'd been drawn here, but I was still curious about how the park got its peculiar name. I figured I would Google it later, and in Uncle Buck's honor, I decided to take a proper nap. I was just about to doze off when I heard someone walk up and clear his throat to get my attention.

"Excuse me. Would you mind if I have a look at your bike?"

I glanced up to see a young black man with wire-rimmed glasses and a frosting of gray in his hair. "Sure, but be careful of the pipes. They're probably still hot."

He stroked the saddle and frowned. "My wife won't let me have one."

I wanted to say my mother would have died if she knew I had one, but I just smiled. "Yeah, I understand."

We both fell silent, watching a moment of tranquillity on the lake, and then he asked if I knew how the park got its name.

"No, I was going to Google it later. Do you know?"

"Actually, I read about it on Wikipedia." He squatted next to me and began drawing in the dirt with a stick. "It seems a woman and her little girl were captured by Indians around here. When they escaped, they wandered around in the wilderness, eating berries until the mom collapsed from exhaustion."

I glanced down at the guy's drawing expecting to see a map, but instead I saw what looked like a hamburger on a sesame seed bun. "Sad story."

"It gets worse. The kid ran off for help, and when she found someone, all she could say was 'hungry mother.'" He drew a glass with a straw next to the burger. "Poor thing led a search party back to her mom, but the woman had already starved to death."

I pointed to the side of fries he'd drawn. "I'll bet you're kind of hungry yourself."

"Oh, that's what my kids had for lunch." He laughed and dragged the stick through his sketch. "When you have three little ones, you go to McDonald's a *lot*."

I strapped on my helmet, a surefire conversation ender. "Thanks for the history lesson, but I have to go. I want to get to Smoky Mountains National Park before dark."

"We just left there." He made a sour face. "Talk about a tourist trap."

"Well, I'm gonna check it out anyway."

He stuck out his hand. "The name's Marcus. And you are?"

"Sylvia Plath."

He looked puzzled. "You know, that name rings a bell."

I grinned. "It's kind of a common name."

I fired up my engine, flipped down my visor, and gave Marcus a thumbs-up. Then I watched him watching me with envy in my rearview mirror.

Nineteen

Catch and Release

———◆———

Although my Harley was intimidating, it had a built-in feature that offered me a chance to get out of trouble—a reserve tank. Like most human beings, I had one too, but the amount of energy I had left was never as predictable. In fact, my Sportster had a fairly specific distance it could go once the reserve tank kicked in, and I knew that if the main tank went dry, I could get to a gas station as long as it was within twenty-five miles.

"Not every bike has one of these save-your-ass backup tanks," Bart Mange had pointed out. "But you damn well better find out if yours does."

And so one of the first things I asked Rolling Stone Dave when he was showing me my Sportster was if it had a reserve tank, and if so, how it worked.

"I see you've done your homework." He put a hand on my shoulder, pushed me gently into a squat, and pointed to a red lever below my Harley's crankcase. "Give her a flip if the gas light comes on and you'll have twenty-five miles to go before you crap out. Unless you're a complete idiot, you won't get stranded." He patted my Sportster's saddle like a proud papa. "I double-checked every inch of this goddamn bike."

Now, far from the Daves and within thirty miles of Gatlinburg, an amber light blinked on by the fuel gauge, and I was lucky I noticed it. Thoughts of hungry mothers and the beauty of the Appalachians had distracted me. I quickly pulled over and flipped on the reserve. If Rolling Stone Dave was right, I'd make it to within five miles of town—a long walk, but doable. Downing a Chocolate Brownie PowerBar and my last bottle of water, I swung back on the bike and steeled myself for a nerve-racking ride.

"Idiot, idiot, idiot!" I yelled into my helmet. "What a fucking idiot!"

Twelve miles later, I was bargaining with God. "I won't say 'fuck' for a week if I don't run out of gas. I'll give up wine for a day if the station has beef jerky and Evian."

But if anyone knew I could stretch the truth, it was God, so I threw in another promise. "Okay, fine!" I yelled. "I will *never* lie again!"

And then, God actually believed me. A sign appeared that said a gas station was at the next exit, five miles away. I checked my odometer. I might just make it.

Four miles, three, two, one, and . . . the odometer clicked to zero. With the gas station in sight my bike began to buck.

"Come on!" I screamed. "We're almost there!"

The bike sputtered but kept going.

"You can do it!" I cried. "I know you can!"

And just as I turned into the station my engine died, leaving me with enough forward motion to roll up to the pump. I took off my helmet and was about to kiss the reserve tank when I realized I would burn my lips off, so I gave the bike a pat with my gloved hand and dug out my credit card. It was cause for a celebration, and after I'd bought my Harley all the gas it could take, I was going to buy myself the best bottle of wine I could find. But the one-pump station had a store no bigger than a jail cell, and the guy who ran it didn't stock wine or take credit cards. I walked back to my bike for some cash, and slipped a fifty out of my tank bag.

The old man, who looked like Rumpelstiltskin, shook his head when I returned. "You should never leave your bag behind. Mine just attaches with magnets, and unless yours is fastened on with superglue or cement, you're just asking to get it stolen."

"Wow, I didn't think how easy it would be to lift. Thanks."

"No problem, the advice is free, the gas is five bucks a gallon."

"You're kidding."

"Have you seen a gas station lately? I'd say no by the fumes you rolled in on."

"Fine. Gouge me." I looked behind him at every cigarette brand imaginable, and a display of candy so extensive, just looking at it could give you diabetes. "I'll take a bag of grass, some Skittles, and a Snickers."

"Sorry, my pot supplier didn't show." He broke into a grin, ducked beneath the counter, and came up with a mason jar full of auburn liquid. "This is better."

"That isn't moonshine, is it?"

"Yup—190-proof. I made it myself."

"Isn't that illegal? And more to the point, how much do you want for it?"

"For you, twenty bucks." He winked at me. "For anyone else, twenty bucks."

I bought a jar along with the candy, some Gatorade, and a can of cashews. The Gatorade and half the Snickers was gone before I got my change.

"Now don't you be chugging my hooch like you did that Gatorcrap." He stuck an *Apple Cider* label on the bottle. "And try not to kiss the floor tonight."

Gassed up and high on sugar, I arrived in Gatlinburg by five-thirty, but all the tourists had gotten there before me. Every sign read no vacancy.

Finally I came upon a Comfort Inn that didn't have a sign at all, so I parked and went in. But before I even hit the reception bell, someone yelled, "Sorry, we're full!"

"How do you know I'm not the president of the United States?" I called back.

A burly red-faced man walked out. "Last time I checked George Bush was a guy."

"But if I *was* Bush, you'd have a room. Well, guess what—he's not coming."

The man scratched his beard. "Okay, I confess. Our maid didn't show up and I didn't want another room to clean. But for you, Mr. President, I'll make an exception."

"Thanks, the secret service men can sleep in the limo."

He ignored me and looked at his computer. "I have a nice room with a terrace overlooking the Little Pigeon River, but I'll need a hundred twenty for it. Do we have a deal, George?"

I checked in before he raised the price and went off to wind down. That meant stripping off my layers and channel-surfing for news. The collapse of the Twin Towers had forever spooked me, so I couldn't relax until I found out if the world was in the same condition I'd left it in that morning. Thankfully, the only world-shattering news I found was that Barry Bonds had broken Babe Ruth's record by hitting his 715th homer. The TV showed the sell-out crowd in a collective jaw drop, and even though baseball bored me, I celebrated anyway with a shot of moonshine on my terrace.

But the instant I hit the lounge chair, I knew I'd be ordering in that night. There was no way I was budging from that balcony, and I thought I might even sleep there. The sound of the rushing water and the serenity of the fisherman I saw on the riverbank below gave me all I needed for the rest of the day. In fact, I even forgot to order in.

As the sun went down, I sipped my moonshine, popped cashews, and watched the fisherman's every move. Time and again, he baited his hook, cast his line, and reeled in nothing. I called him Ahab, and every time he drew back his rod, I reeled back in my chair, threw a cashew in my mouth, and washed it down with rotgut. My heart skipped across the water every time he released his line, and sank when his hook came in empty. After a while, I grew agitated, almost angry with him for not succeeding. I wanted—no, I *needed*—him to prove something elusive could be caught.

In my mind's eye the slithery creature became everything that had gotten away from me, and I became both the fish and the one who wanted to capture it. What was the bait *I* was afraid of taking? I popped another cashew, took another swig. Getting close to someone? Getting hurt? I thought of my ex and shuddered. Vivacious creatures like her always reeled me in, attracted me like north-pole magnets to their opposite south. But always, I grew afraid of our differences and tried to conform, unaware that by doing so our magnetism would fail.

I took a gulp of moonshine to wash away my ex . . . and then it happened. All at once the fisherman leaned back, pulled hard, then released a few feet of line. He let it run for a moment, then jerked his wrist and pulled back again. Over and over his rod arched and bowed as he pulled and released, held on and let go.

I was on my feet now, leaning over the rail and cheering him on, but I was three stories above him, and the roar of the river below drowned me out. Truth be told, I don't think he'd have heard me if I were standing right next to him; that's how focused he was. Then with a violent splash the fish broke the surface and the man hoisted its wriggling body in the air. It twisted and resisted for a few seconds and then suddenly lay twitching in a net the man seemed to produce from nowhere.

I pumped my fist in the air. I clapped and whistled like a lunatic, until finally, for the first time, the man looked up. He flashed a triumphant smile, unhooked the fish with a deft sleight of hand, and threw it back in the water.

"Oh, my God!" I cried. *"No!"*

I flung myself into my lounge chair and sat there. Then I jumped to my feet, threw on my sneakers, and stumbled down to the riverbank as the man was packing up his gear.

"Wait up!" I called. "Please, I have to know why you did that?"

"Did what?" he asked. "Go fishing?"

"No, throw that fish back. It wasn't a sardine. It was a *big* fish."

"I know. Minnow or marlin, I always throw them back."

"But why put yourself—hell, why put the *fish*—through that trauma?"

"Trauma? Honey, I enjoyed every minute of that. And the fish? Well, sure, it might have been scared when it took the bait, but I'd say it's pretty happy now."

I looked at the man like he was crazy. "But you worked at it so hard."

"Look, I wasn't going after anything I needed to have. Besides, I captured it anyway." He tapped his head. "Right here." He tapped his heart. "And here, too."

I climbed back up the riverbank, walked into my motel room, and turned on my computer. Then with the push of a button, I deleted every picture I'd taken since I left Los Angeles. I would not take another photograph for the remainder of the trip. I would capture every experience and release it to the safe insecurity of my memory.

The next morning I didn't need an alarm to get up. I awoke in my lounge chair with a knife in my forehead that did the trick. I stumbled into the bathroom and looked in the mirror. The woman I saw wasn't anyone I wanted to know.

"Hey, genius." I tapped my head. "How ya gonna stuff this into a helmet?"

I knew the answer would come with coffee, so I left, not bothering to comb my hair or change my clothes. Removing the blade from my forehead was my first goal.

As I meandered through the crowded town, I recalled what I'd done the night before. Sometime between obliterating all references to my trip and passing out, I'd Googled the Great Smoky Mountains National Park and learned that ten million people visit every year. Maybe my hangover was making me see double, but I swear all of them were in Gatlinburg that day.

Behind all the hotels, souvenir shops, and restaurants were parking lots full of buses, cars, and motorhomes, and as I walked along looking for breakfast, families of every kind swarmed around me. There were bickering couples with herds of kids, most obese or anorexic. There were wiped-out single moms corralling brats and clueless divorced dads with whiny toddlers. There were interracial couples with biracial babies, Muslims, Jews, Christians, and Hare Krishnas, religious groups of every ilk, and members of the YMCA, the DNC, the NRA, and the GOP. Lesbian couples with sperm-donor infants and gay men with surrogate twins walked among heterosexuals, bisexuals, and transsexuals, all flirting, fighting, or getting ready to have sex. And just about everyone was eating something fattening while talking about where they were going to eat next.

I took refuge inside the Pancake Pantry, an asylum of hungry tourists devouring every kind of pancake known to man. I ordered poached eggs, dry toast, and coffee.

"Aw, come on!" The waitress glanced at the floor-to-ceiling menu on the wall. "We've got fifty kinds of flapjacks, omelets with all kinds of garbage stuffed in them, and waffles up the wazoo." She yawned. "Your order is putting me to sleep."

I looked up at her, hoping to prove that what I had ordered was all I could handle, and she took a step back as if blood had actually seeped from my eyes.

"Okay, so you had a rough night. But you're getting pancakes instead of toast whether you like it or not."

"Please, I just want to die."

"Look, I'll make it easy. I'll give you two choices—laced with chocolate chips or smothered in apple compote. Choose or I'll bring you both."

I shook my head and was about to snarl something when the family that was squished into the booth next to me exploded.

"You had him yesterday!" A tow-headed boy grabbed a stuffed bear dressed like a park ranger from his sticky sister, and raced away. "You can't even *touch* him today!"

The girl erupted into high-pitched wails. She'd have broken a window if her father hadn't leapt from his seat and dragged his son and the bear back to the table.

"If this thing didn't cost more than a car payment, I'd cut it in half!" He yanked the bear from his son's arms and flung it across the room, grazing my waitress's head.

She walked off in a huff, muttering something under her breath to the mother, who was retrieving the bear from a puddle of syrup. I thought they were going to get into a fistfight, but my waitress ducked into the kitchen.

Holding the bear upside down by its paw, the mother walked by me with such a beleaguered look I offered her a comforting smile.

"Who do you think you are?" she snarled at me. "Dr. Spock?"

I thought about telling her that I was a child psychologist, but I quickly glanced away instead. She looked certifiable, her husband looked homicidal, and her children looked like Hitler Youth. It was best to keep my distance. When my breakfast came, I ate quickly and got the hell out of there.

Back on the sidewalk, I felt my eggs churning in my stomach like wet socks and if that didn't make me sick, the smell of Coppertone was about to. Touristville, my ass. Gatlinburg was a petri dish of consumerism, a conglomeration of life-forms with leathery, burned skin and money flying from their hands. As diverse as everyone was under their floppy hats and fezzes, in their sundresses or saris, Birkenstocks or cowboy boots, they were all starting to look the same, and I swear, a Martian could have walked by me unnoticed if he wore a polo shirt and Ray-Bans.

Feeling spacey myself, I ducked into a shadowy little shop to have my tarot cards read by a wrinkly woman with squinty eyes and dark skin. Her name was Madame Zabrina and she looked like a caricature of a Gypsy. Her shop smelled like dust and peppermint oil, and there was velvet everywhere—maroon velvet drapes, a red velvet couch, and garish velvet paintings of celebrities all over the walls.

I sat down opposite Madame Zabrina, who held a scrappy-looking Siamese with a loud purr that reminded me of my Harley's growl. I reached over to pet the cat as Madame Zabrina shuffled the cards and growled herself: "Lay your money on the table. I'm tired of working for free."

I put a twenty on the table and the bill was down her blouse in seconds. Then she offered me the deck to cut, and fanned out the cards like a blackjack dealer. "Pick five, and think about what you want to know." She folded her hands. "Try to be specific."

I tried to sort out all the questions I had, but they were crisscrossing in my head like a traffic jam. Of course I wanted to know about my love life, if I was going to get a job, if my mom was with my dad, but weird questions started pushing their way in, too, like should I get Lasik surgery or a facelift with my inheritance, or should I call up my niece and have her put Lynn in my will so she'd have money to care for my dogs in case I didn't make it back?

While all this was racing through my brain, Madame Zabrina arranged my five cards faceup in a cross. Then, with a velvet Elvis pouting over one shoulder and a velvet Jesus praying over the other, she looked up and smiled tenderly at me.

"I see you have been very confused recently." She touched each card. "Perhaps you are very sad?" She looked deep into my eyes as she placed her palm over one card in particular—the Chariot. "A great deal has happened to you . . . A great deal lies ahead."

I almost laughed out loud, but my kinder self sat there quietly and let her ramble on about a long journey I was taking, about how that journey was difficult, yes, but definitely worth making. It could have been a reading for Garth Brooks, Gloria Steinem, or Gandhi. I told myself that at least the woman wasn't begging on the street, that she was providing some kind of entertainment, and perhaps giving hope to those who needed it. Then my sarcastic self and my kind self stood up, not able to sit for any more bullshit.

"My goodness that was amazing," I said, and then I noticed she still had her hand over that one card. I pointed to it. "What are you keeping from me? Is there something significant about that card?"

"Oh, that's the Chariot." She quickly pushed all the cards into a pile and scooped them up. "It just stands for being on the road. You always wear a helmet, don't you?"

I was wearing shorts and flip-flops. "What makes you think I ride a motorcycle?"

She shrugged. "Lucky guess."

"No, really, how did you know?"

She grinned. "Your reading is over, my dear. If you'd like to ask any specific questions, I'll need another twenty."

I bought a souvenir pack of cards and walked out with the strange feeling Madame Zabrina was keeping something from me. Why did she ask if I always wore a helmet? A shiver ran through me, and then I smiled.

She'd probably seen me walking into the Comfort Inn when I first arrived in town. It was the last time I'd been in my gear and the only time she could have seen that I ride. I got a little queasy and decided that maybe I'd take the day off and just go hiking.

But as I squeezed my way through the tourist-filled sidewalk, I decided that if the town was this packed, the trails would be too, so I went back to my hotel to rest before I checked out. I still had some moonshine to shake off before I felt safe on the road, and I was sure that was why I felt queasy.

Flopping on the bed, I stared at the ceiling, regretting the twenty dollars I'd just thrown away, regretting that I hadn't had anything but cashews and rotgut for dinner, and waiting to regret deleting all evidence of my trip. But instead I felt relief and a glimmer of clarity. I didn't need the physical proof of an event to have it live inside me just as the fisherman didn't need a trout to remember he'd caught it. As this simple insight peeked through my hangover, I started to feel ready to log a few miles, but when I swung my legs off the bed, my equilibrium stayed on the mattress. Balancing on two wheels was not an option for at least another hour, and since Nashville, my next destination, was only three hours away, I figured I could loaf around awhile.

I called the front desk and asked for a late checkout, then went back to staring at the ceiling and the tiny white balls of spray paint that clung to it. They reminded me of the sugarcoated cottage cheese my aunt Connie put into her blintzes. She was famous for those blintzes and for never being without her Nikon. No one could have a conversation in peace without Aunt Connie interrupting to snap some memories.

More concerned with creating proof of an event than actually enjoying it, Aunt Connie lived in a cluttered apartment stacked with photo albums, boxes of party favors, embossed napkins, and programs from plays and funerals. Whenever I'd go to visit her, all she wanted to do was drag out mementos and relive the times she had archived for others but had missed herself. Though it was nice to get a packet of photos now and then, they always wound up stashed with other things I never looked at, like the huge portrait of my father that once hung in my childhood home. When my mom died and my sisters and I went through her belongings, I wound up with Dad, and since I didn't want him staring at me all the time, I slid him under the bed in my spare room, and eventually he wound up in my shed.

It was even harder deleting my mother from my cell phone. I knew it was time when I absentmindedly called her as I walked out of a film, thinking she should see it. A stranger answered, and I was horrified. Not only had I forgotten she was dead, but the phone company had already reassigned her number. I took a deep breath and did what I knew I had to do. I scrolled down my contacts until I found *Mom*, hit the edit button, and answered *Yes* to the eeriest question I've ever been asked: *Delete Mom?*

Now here I was in a hotel called the Comfort Inn, feeling completely ill at ease. While the pressure in my head was starting to lift, and the nausea was passing, my laptop was just sitting there on the desk, reminding me of my impulse to purge my trip the night before. Though I still felt a sense of liberation for having had the guts to do it, I also felt the emptiness of the void I'd created. The pictures I'd taken weren't merely evidence of my journey; they were a means of sharing it with others. My trip wasn't anything like the fish that guy had caught. I wasn't capturing my experience for the hell of it, and without photos, people might think I was telling them just another "big fish" story.

Suddenly I *needed* evidence, and in one swift motion, I leapt off the bed and pounced on my laptop. Computers had backup systems, didn't they? There was always an undo function for morons like me, wasn't there?

Unable to sit still while my laptop woke up, I flew around the room like a trapped bird until a painting over the desk stopped me. It was a photo-realistic replica of a bowl of fruit, the likes of which probably hung in hotel rooms around the world. I stared at the painting, marveling at its detail, but only when I closed my eyes and thought of the bowl of fruit on my grandmother's kitchen table did my senses truly come to life. Only by looking away from the replica and into my past did I recall popping grapes into my mouth, turning them instantly into eyeballs. Fruit wasn't just fruit when I was a kid, and in my mind's eye I recalled how a banana became a pistol and an apple a target on my cousin's head. I opened my eyes and looked at the still life, and instantly the kinetic energy in my brain that turned fruit into playthings screeched to a standstill.

And so did my regret.

With the same resolve I'd found the night before, I shut down my computer, packed my bags, and closed the door on all thoughts of retrieving anything that wasn't already in my head. If a portrait of my father could replace the sound of him belting out a Russian folk song, or if a photo of my parents remarrying on their fiftieth anniversary could beat the thrill I got from walking them down the aisle, I would feel remorse. Instead, I felt like a living, breathing photo album, the keeper of my very own archaeological site that I could dig into whenever I chose. This journey was mine to experience, and even if I tried, I couldn't give it away.

As I swung onto my motorcycle, I smiled at the thought of the maid finding my five-buck tip tucked beneath my camera with a note that read: *I forgot this on purpose.* I wished I could see her face, and for a split second I thought of going back to give her the camera myself. But in the other half of that same second I realized there are few do-overs in life worth trying to make happen, so I fired up my Harley and headed out of town.

Soon I would be breathing in conifer and pine, and choking back road-kill. I would hear the wind through my visor and feel it pound against my chest. As landscapes flew by I would hang them in every chamber of my heart, and each person I met I would etch into the bone of my skull. From that moment on, I promised myself that I would experience everything and everyone to the hilt—as soon as I got out of this godforsaken town.

Twenty

A Woman of Extremes

———— ◆ ————

Sometimes **you have** to wonder why you wind up where you are, and I had a lot of time to think about that as I tried to get out of Gatlinburg. It wasn't easy. With only one road in and out of town, I baked in my leathers for at least an hour, pondering how I could be melting beneath this Tennessee sun when only four days ago I was freezing on the road between Buffalo and Rochester. My life had been like that too—hot and cold—and I suppose I'd have to admit that my personality has often followed suit.

"You're a woman of extremes," my old boyfriend Andrew told me once. "I have no idea what you're going to do next."

Andrew and I met at my cousin Ellis's wedding in Hennepin, Minnesota, on May 23, 1982. He'd flown in from Los Angeles, and I'd driven out from Missouri where I was in my second year of teaching at Stephens. A woman I'd been dating for all of a month had come with me, but her name escapes me now, because as soon as I laid eyes on Andrew's dark curls and cropped black beard I was desperate to be straight again. In fact, Andrew and I talked all night in his hotel room, talked and held on to each other . . .

because that was all I was able to do. As for the woman who had been my date, well, I think she flew back home, never to speak to me again. But I didn't care, Andrew was all I thought about when I got back to Missouri, and we made plans to see each other two months later in Hawaii.

"I can't wait!" Andrew had called, unable to contain his excitement. "We're going to have our second date in paradise!"

I was quiet. He probably heard me hyperventilating. I definitely heard him sigh.

"Look, you don't have to feel pressured," he said. "If you can't do it, we can just be friends."

I wanted more than anything to "do it." I was going to be twenty-seven. It was time to let go of whatever had happened at that frat house more than nine years ago. So I said I was excited too, and threw my reluctance, my sexual confusion, and my fear to the wind. I had been straight before I was gay . . . There was no reason I couldn't flip back.

"I'm really just a lesbian in a man's body," Andrew assured me. "I promise, no one is going to hurt you again."

We rendezvoused in Los Angeles, and then flew to Honolulu, where he'd arranged to have our hotel room filled with balloons. I knew what he was doing—trying to make the atmosphere more festive than romantic, trying to make our upcoming intimacy more of a celebration than a seduction. But we just ended up talking more, he coaxing me to communicate my feelings, me rambling on about which island we would visit next. In the end, we spent nearly every night in Hawaii either sitting on the edge of our bed crying, or holding each other in the dark, frustrated and upset. Whatever had happened in that frat house was wedged between us like a block of ice, and no man—not even the dearest of them like Andrew—was going to be able to melt it.

Years, and several girlfriends—both Andrew's and mine—went by. Then in 1990, I moved to Los Angeles, looked him up, and we became good friends. Finally, during the wee hours of the morning when the Northridge earthquake struck on January 17, 1994, Andrew and I were able to truly consummate our relationship . . . and though the earth actually did move in more ways than one, there had been too much time and friction between us. I was clearly ensconced in my chosen lifestyle, and he had given up on me and started dating someone else. To this day, one of my greatest regrets has been not trying harder to make my relationship with Andrew work.

Hot and cold, in and out of relationships, back and forth between sexual preferences, passionately kissing Andrew one minute, stiff as a two-by-four in his arms the next, I eventually embraced and was glad to have found my sexuality with women. I flew rainbow flags, marched in Gay Pride parades, but always I wondered why the rainbow couldn't encompass everyone, why being proud had anything to do with who you had in your bed. Certainly I wasn't ashamed of my sexuality, but the way I got there left me feeling as if I were in one world peering back at another.

When I was spat upon for holding Terri's hand in Santa Fe, I held on even tighter, but still cringed at being labeled a dyke. When I fell madly for Anna in Olympia, Washington, I wanted to announce to the world that I'd finally met the woman of my dreams, but she was way too politically correct, a very *out* lesbian who wore socks with her Birkenstocks and drove a pickup. I told her I wanted an open relationship until I was sure, and she swept me from her life like a cobweb. Why, I wondered, as I walked the timeline of my sexual maturation, did I always seem to be one step behind my liberal consciousness, always looking back at greener grasses and unable to see the beauty of the meadow I was walking in?

Now, as I found myself alone and sweltering in the heat of the Great Smoky Mountains, it was no surprise I was caught up in my past and unable to see the greatness around me. Of course I was balancing on a machine as extreme as a Harley, lamenting things I couldn't change, and dwelling on people whose memory of me had surely grown stale. I was definitely a woman of extremes, my life a mixture of fire and ice . . . the same as everyone's, I suppose, and yet I seemed to feel the mixture had left me with nothing.

Maybe it was just the goddamn heat pounding on my helmet, rising from the asphalt, and creeping through the soles of my boots. Maybe it was the fact that there was not a trace of breeze and I'd been idling in bumper-to-bumper traffic for at least an hour. Whatever the reason, my mind broke free and went off in all directions—it *had* to or I'd have left my bike and jumped naked into the Little Pigeon River. When I got to Nashville I was going to write a letter to the Tennessee Department of Transportation and demand to know why there weren't more roads out of Gatlinburg. Then I'd write to President Bush, asking him to enact a law making it illegal to honk in standstill traffic. Maybe he could issue an executive order to automobile makers to install horns that would deactivate when a car was stopped? I should write to helmet manufacturers too. Exhaust fumes shouldn't be able to seep through a person's visor. Maybe they could install tiny fans to blow the noxious vapors away and cool me down at the same time?

Just as I was wondering if I could get black lung without working in a coal mine, and praying that I could still hold up my Harley after sweating out half my body weight, the traffic thinned out. Soon I was flowing down the highway toward Nashville, bursting through fresh air, and energized by the ice-cold cocktail I saw in my future.

By six-thirty my prediction was dead-on, and I was sipping a triple platinum margarita at a guitar-shaped bar at the Hard Rock Cafe while I ate a Rock Your World quesadilla laced with Joe Perry's Mango-Peach Tango hot sauce. My throat on fire and sweating again because Aerosmith's lead guitarist's sauce was *not* for sissies, I quenched the fire with another triple platinum and got out of there while I could still walk.

As I weaved along the sidewalk back to my hotel, bluegrass wafted through the air, and I stopped now and then to listen to a riff or two. And that's when it hit me—a numbness so deep I felt I might fall down, paralyzed by the heaviness of this balmy Tennessee night. Then all at once, because yes, I am a woman of extremes, I went from feeling nothing to feeling way too much. I knew why I was alone on the road and in this life, and I knew it was no one's fault but my own. Putting distance between pain and myself, not dealing with upset, but running from it, was what I was all about.

After the incident at the frat house, I should have gotten a lot of therapy, but instead I got into a lot of short-lived relationships, trying as hard as I could to fall in love with a man and marry him. But eventually guys wouldn't put up with my ambivalence, and thankfully my graduate professor's kiss opened me up to a whole new world of sexuality. But even then my body and my heart just weren't getting the message, and I flitted from woman to woman like a bee chasing nectar.

In Santa Fe I met a perfectly wonderful woman, then crushed her heart like a walnut when I ran off to Denver for a PhD, and into the arms of Joanne. When she rejected me after six years of trying to make her see I was more than a perpetual student, I blew into the embrace of Andrea, and left my PhD in the wind. Andrea probably treated me better than anyone ever has, so of course I broke her heart by having an affair with one of our friends, whose heart I also broke. Confused, I ran off to Israel and lived on a kibbutz for a while, and when I came back to Los Angeles I tried to win at least one of them back, but neither would speak to me. They were too smart to have anything to do with a woman so careless with love.

Sure, I could blame my ex for running out on me when I finally believed—once again—I'd found *the one*, but I knew the truth. I knew why I was alone on the road, alone now in my Nashville hotel room on a night so humid the wallpaper was sweating. I knew why I hadn't found a proper mate . . . I had yet to grow up. I was still that child running after my mother for attention, still that high school pothead trying not to be different, still that newly minted, totally confused lesbian home on spring break, invisible on the couch under the wedding portraits of my sisters.

My ex, whose name I can't even say without upset, might not have been the most empathetic woman, but at least *she* was a grown-up. She was raising two adorable little girls, whose names I whisper in my soul, and her wonderful little family got such a grip on me I'll probably always ache for them. She could have picked a better time to skewer my heart, but if I choke back the ugliness, if I struggle for an adult thought, I have to admit that there's no point to a relationship if only one person is in it.

It was perhaps one of the first mature thoughts I'd had since my mom died, since my heart went into lockdown, and I eloped on my Harley. Was I finally growing up at the age of fifty? I ran to the mirror like a five-year-old to see.

But there, as I studied my face, as I examined the furrows in my brow and the wrinkles around my mouth, I also discovered a tiny bit of maturity, and as I did I realized I saw something else: my mother.

"Mom?" I whispered. "Good God, I miss you."

Watch out . . . I heard her say. *You're gonna smile.*

I stuck out my tongue like I did when I was two.

Careful, here it comes.

I frowned, suppressing a giggle, like I did when I was three.

Ah! There it is!

And sure enough, there I was beaming like a rodeo clown.

That's better. Now how about an ug?

I closed my eyes, and there was my mom, her arms outstretched.

Come here, little bug. Let me squeeze that sadness out of you.

And as I fell into her arms, I took myself to bed.

. . .

The next morning, I awoke with the same silly grin on my face. I was hangover free, feeling unusually happy, and strangely not alone. Dead or alive, my mom was always there with me, and so was my dad.

Now, in particular, I thought of him. After escaping from Russia during the Bolshevik Revolution, he lived in Europe for a few years and eventually landed in New York. As a young man, he wanted to see the country, so he joined the US Cavalry and was stationed at Fort Bliss in El Paso, Texas. There he went to synagogue and met my mother's father, a dairy farmer with four goats and three daughters. Several Shabbat dinners later, he married my mom, joined her father's business, and along with my uncle Bob, they turned four goats into Wholesome Dairy, a four-thousand-cow operation, and one of the largest dairies in Texas. If a six-year-old boy could make it from Eastern Europe to Ellis Island to West Texas and find happiness, surely I could get from the Atlantic to the Pacific and find contentment as well.

Now, lounging in a Nashville hotel, I longed to stake my claim to that elusive bliss I felt sure was in my future, and I grew excited thinking about the chase. Jumping out of bed, I went to my computer to see how far Memphis was. On Rolling Stone Dave's advice, I was going to Graceland, the second-most-visited private residence in the United States next to the White House. Elvis Presley had bought the 13.8-acre estate in 1957 for a hundred grand, and I'll bet he had no idea of its value. Most likely he felt insecure and misunderstood too, and just like everyone else, he probably had no idea who he was.

Twenty-one

Shelter from the Storm

———◆———

Riding *toward Graceland*, I felt like I was going to gawk at a car wreck. I didn't know why I was heading there, but I couldn't stop myself. I've never been an Elvis fan, but Graceland was an iconic American attraction, and I had a hunch I'd feel just like I did after visiting Disneyland—in total awe, and a little dizzy. As I sped along the interstate, I couldn't help but think of how tragically Elvis's life had ended, and with each mile I went toward Memphis, I fell back in time to that summer day when Presley fans around the globe stopped whatever they were doing and cranked up their TVs and radios.

It was August 16, 1977, and I was a confused twenty-three-year-old, wondering what to do with a journalism degree when I wanted to write fiction. By day I worked in an art gallery on the wharf in San Francisco, by night I waitressed at a Mexican food joint downtown. And when I wasn't peddling seascapes or serving enchiladas, I was smoking pot, playing my guitar, and drinking Scotch on my fire escape overlooking Alcatraz.

That particular afternoon it was slow at the gallery, so my co-workers and I had the radio blasting Bob Marley's "Stir It Up" when suddenly the

DJ broke in. "I've just been handed a bulletin, ladies and gentlemen," he said, his voice cracking. "Elvis Presley, the King of Rock and Roll, is dead at the age of forty-two."

Everyone—workers and customers—stopped in their tracks. Some broke into tears. I wasn't happy either. For at least a week, there'd be nothing but Elvis movies on TV and rockabilly on the radio.

A die-hard Dylan devotee when I wasn't crooning the Beatles, I didn't worship Elvis like everyone else. To me, the King had been dethroned well before he fell unconscious on his bathroom floor. So why was I driving to Graceland now?

To put it simply, Elvis was an oddity, and I had to admit I found him fascinating. I mean, the guy once showed up at the northwest gate of the White House with a six-page, handwritten note asking if he could meet with President Nixon to discuss becoming a "Federal Agent at Large." By using his celebrity, Elvis thought he could help straighten out America's problems. "I have done an in-depth study of drug abuse and Communist brainwashing techniques," wrote Presley. "I am right in the middle of the whole thing, where I can and will do the most good."

Scribbled on American Airlines stationery, the note made its way to Egil "Bud" Krogh, one of Nixon's top aides, who then arranged for the King to meet with the president a few hours later that same day—December 21, 1970.

Flanked by bodyguards, Elvis arrived for the infamous meeting wearing purple velvet pants with a violet cape. He carried a chrome-plated World War II Colt .45, which he planned to give to the president, and once the Secret Service confiscated the gun, the King was led into the Oval Office. According to Krogh, who took notes at the meeting, Nixon and Elvis talked about everything from Presley's daughter, Lisa Marie, to his cuff links, and then Nixon actually arranged for Elvis to receive an official badge from the US Bureau of Narcotics and Dangerous Drugs.

But what was most disturbing to me about the meeting was that Elvis reportedly attacked my beloved Beatles, suggesting that they were "anti-American" and should be banned from performing in the United States. Presley claimed that it was the Beatles' "unkempt appearance, suggestive music, and open drug use" that had laid the groundwork for the trouble America was having with its youth, and entertainers like Jane Fonda and the Smothers Brothers should be scrutinized as well for speaking out against Vietnam.

To be sure, long before Elvis himself became addicted to his own medicine cabinet, I went through a period of loathing the man for his zealous patriotism. So again, why was I so determined to visit Graceland? Why had I left Nashville without seeing the Grand Ole Opry or the Jack Daniel's Distillery to gawk at this man's wrecked life?

The answer, in one word, is history. More specifically, *my* history. While Gettysburg was amazing, I actually lived through the seventies when Graceland was in its prime. I remember the decade distinctly for its platform shoes, bell-bottom pants, lava lamps, and black-light posters. If nothing else, except for the mansion's opulence and garishness, I was excited to see the green shag carpet, the avocado appliances, and the wood-paneled den that would take me back to a time when my parents were alive.

And so, even though Elvis's estate had turned into a bizarre spectacle to be gaped at more than admired, I was hell-bent on visiting the sprawling eyesore, and I created a tight agenda to do it. My plan was to hit Elvis Presley Boulevard by ten, check into the Heartbreak Hotel, and jump on the shuttle to the mansion by eleven for the Platinum Tour. That would allow me to see Elvis's home, his airplanes, his auto museum, and a special viewing of his outlandish costumes. I gave myself three hours for the two-and-a-half-hour tour, certain I could explore all things Elvis in that time, but my plans changed.

Since the money I'd allotted for my trip was dwindling and a room at the Heartbreak Hotel was pricey, I decided to leave Memphis right after my tour and get a jump on my next destination—Little Rock, Arkansas. It was only two hours from the Tennessee border, and I figured if I pushed the speed limit, I could spend the next day exploring all things Bill at the Clinton Library. Since the Secret Service's code name for Clinton was Elvis during his bid for election in 1992, it would be two days of visiting Southern royalty—Elvis the king and Elvis the president—but again, my plans changed.

Three hours wasn't nearly enough time to take in the weirdness of Graceland. There was the Jungle Room, with an indoor waterfall and carpet that ran up to the ceiling. There was his thirty-seven-gun firearm collection, which included the pistol he used to shoot his TV while Robert Goulet sang, and the one he fired at his 1971 Pantera sports car when the engine wouldn't start. Of course his '55 pink Cadillac was cool, as was his room full of gold, platinum, and multi-platinum records. And, while his small fleet of airplanes—one of which was nicknamed Hound Dog One— was impressive, it was Elvis's Harley collection that finally connected me to the King.

Long before he became a pudgy caricature of himself, he was "Elvis the Pelvis," a sleek, handsome, very cool motorcycle enthusiast. Hordes of fans wouldn't leave him alone in broad daylight, so he would ride late at night through the streets of Memphis. I can imagine the freedom he felt on the 883cc Harley he bought in 1956, just days after recording "Heartbreak Hotel." Soon he graduated to a gigantic police cruiser called a Harley Dresser, and according to Ron Elliot, the proprietor of SuperCycle, where Elvis bought many of his motorcycles, that bike was probably the King's favorite.

As his fame grew, so did his stable of motorcycles, and in real life, it wasn't uncommon to see Elvis cruising Memphis with starlets like

Natalie Wood clinging to his rib cage. It was said that his dream was to be associated with cool bikers like Marlon Brando and James Dean, but in my opinion, he was neither a wild one nor a rebel.

Sure, Elvis looked cool on a motorcycle—hell, *everyone* looks cool on a bike—but after my last stop on the Graceland tour, any decent image I had of him was instantly erased. There, at Graceland's Meditation Garden, where the King was laid to rest, I was left with nothing more than a picture of a bloated, exploited man. Dry-eyed and standing among sobbing fans, I couldn't believe all the glitz around me. It was a monument to kitsch that made my eyes sore, and I wondered if Elvis would have wanted all this schmaltz around his death. It certainly wasn't a cool way to be remembered, not like James Dean, whose modest gravestone in Indiana simply marks the years of his birth and death; not like Marlon Brando, who had his ashes scattered over Death Valley and Tahiti. Let's face it, standing in this Meditation Garden in my leathers, a fifty-year-old woman alone on a cross-country adventure, even *I* felt cooler than Elvis, until I realized I'd wasted five hours of my life gaping at his extravagance.

With my day blown, I finally left Graceland, but not without dropping a chunk of cash at the gift shop. Sporting a pink Elvis watch and earrings shaped like guitars, I blew out of town, thinking about where I would want my ashes spread, and wondering if I would handle fame and fortune any better than the King.

"Free massages for everyone!" I yelled into my helmet. "Free tuition!"

I imagined myself hiring mediators for the Middle East, contracting builders to provide housing for the homeless, throwing money at science to find a cure for cancer.

"Free medicine!" I screeched. "Free therapy! A chicken in every pot!"

My mind was racing with humanitarian ideas, running wild with good deeds when suddenly a drop of rain splashed on my visor. I looked from the clouds overhead to Elvis on my wrist. His pelvis was pointing to five p.m. and I had the delusional thought I could still make it to Little Rock. And I might have, if it wasn't for the deluge about to fall.

Truth is, I remember a few ripples of thunder when I left Graceland, but I was sure I could escape getting wet. How could water land on a speeding bullet? Besides, I could always pull over and slip into my rain gear. But only nine miles away from Elvis's mansion, the skies ripped open and suddenly barrels of rain dumped on me. Since it had been in the nineties that day, the cold drops instantly turned to steam as they hit the burning asphalt, and just when my visibility was down to three feet, an overpass miraculously appeared, and I quickly took refuge beneath it.

I was already drenched anyway, so digging out my rain gear and stuffing my soggy leathers into Gore-Tex seemed pointless. I decided to wait it out, until the water began rising, and I realized I was in the middle of a flash flood.

As I watched the rain hiking up my boots and felt it seeping through my zippers, I decided to make a run for it. Wishing I had an ark instead of a motorcycle, I began to ride through the water streaming around me. In the distance, I saw a tiny green square of signage. It was exit 279A and it called to me. I was a boat lost at sea and it was my lighthouse. I was a castaway thrown overboard and it was my rescue party. It was a fucking exit sign and I could have eaten it—that's how delicious it looked.

Afraid I'd wipe out on an oil slick, I rode toward the sign at a sizzling fifteen miles per hour. I hoped there was a motel not far from the exit, but I'd have settled for sharing a cardboard box with a hobo if it got me off the slippery interstate. Thankfully, it didn't come to that, for not far off the ramp were a Travelodge and a Red Roof Inn. For a split second, I considered the Travelodge on my left because it advertised free Internet and bathtubs, but in order to cross over, I'd have to part the road like the Red Sea. Since I wasn't Moses and my bike wasn't a magic staff, I washed up under the Λ-frame awning of the Red Roof Inn like a piece of seaweed and splish-splashed into the office.

There, behind the front desk, was the woman Bob Dylan must have had in mind when he wrote "Shelter from the Storm," because I swear I was living in his lyrics: *With silver bracelets on her wrists and flowers in her hair /... [she] took my crown of thorns.*

Okay, so she didn't have flowers in her hair, but she did wear a medical ID bracelet warning people that she was allergic to penicillin. And no, she didn't do anything with a crown of thorns, but she did help me take off my helmet.

"Come here, you drenched thing." She clicked her tongue as though she were coaxing a kitten from a rain gutter. I splashed over and let her warm hands do what my frozen fingers could not—lift my visor.

"Oh, my God," she gasped. "Let me help you." She nimbly loosened my chinstrap, and a tug or two later, my wet head popped out into the lobby like a newborn chick.

She burst out laughing. "Oh, honey, you look just awful!"

I cracked a pathetic smile, then held up my sopping wet gloves, which she peeled off without my asking. She was my Florence Nightingale, my Mother Teresa, except she was neither a pious nurse nor a wrinkled nun. She was a sexy Red Roof Inn clerk, with laugh lines that revealed her age to be not far from mine. I loved the impish glint in her gray eyes, and if I didn't feel more like a sea creature than a human, I would have kissed her on the spot. Instead, I tried to utter a simple thank-you through my clenched teeth.

"Thu yeg," I said, spitting on her blouse. "Yerg gan gangel."

"I'm no such thing." She grinned, eyeing me up and down, and I wondered if she knew I'd tried to pay her a compliment. "Sit down. I'll get you some hot cocoa."

She pushed me gently into a chair, and I felt like I'd hallucinated her, for though she had disappeared, I could still feel her presence shimmering around me. Shaking, I almost felt a moment of happiness, but the puddle I sat in reminded me I was miserable.

"Are you still alive?" she called from the back. "I'm just warming up cookies."

I wasn't going anywhere. Instead, I stripped down to my saturated jeans and long-sleeved tee. When she returned, she set the cookies and hot chocolate on the table next to me. Then she saw my soggy leather chaps and waterlogged jacket crumpled on the floor.

"That looks like two cows ran into each other and died." She shook her head, bending down to scoop up the wet pile. "I'll hang these things up in the back to dry."

She was gone so fast she could have been on roller skates, and I sat there in awe of how wonderful she was. I wanted to apologize for the mess I was making, but first I had to unfreeze my jaw. I took a sip of hot chocolate, and though I burned the hell out of my tongue, I knew it was the best cocoa I'd ever had.

In truth, all my senses were discombobulated. She could have given me lighter fluid and I wouldn't have been able to taste it. All I cared about was the magic elixir that was now running through me, warming my insides and thawing my limbs. She went back behind the counter, and I watched her working at her computer, and when I was able to raise my arm, I lifted a cookie from the plate and took a bite.

"These are wonderful." I took another nibble. "And so are you."

She smiled. "Oh, you don't know the half of it."

My mind leaped to all kinds of ridiculous scenarios, but I knew I was delusional, so I let them go and hobbled outside to check on my bike dripping under the A-frame.

For a moment, I just stood there wondering how my stiff fingers were going to unstrap my pack, and as I tried to free the bungee cords, Mother Teresa came up from behind and put her hand on my shoulder.

My heart took a giant leap and I almost fell over.

"Sorry, I didn't mean to scare you. I just came out to help." She was actually yelling over the rain still pounding overhead, and yet somehow her voice sounded gentle. "Don't worry, I've got this."

I mumbled my thanks and stepped aside, convinced that love at first sight could happen across a crowded room or under an A-frame.

In seconds she had the pack undone and was slinging it over her shoulder. "You go on to your room and leave your bike here." She pressed a key into my hand. "And put your clothes outside the door. I'll get them washed and dried while you clean up."

I wanted to say forget the clothes and come take a shower with me. I wanted to say I hadn't been touched in almost a year. Instead I flashed her a mischievous smile and told her I'd like to take her for a ride when the weather cleared.

"On this thing?" She swatted my Harley playfully and grinned. "Well, maybe."

About three hours later, snug in bed and watching television, I heard a soft knock at my door. There was Mother Teresa with my socks, shirts, pants, and underwear neatly folded in her arms. She handed everything over, then tossed me a sly wink. "Would you mind if I give you a piece of advice?"

"What, wear scuba gear next time?"

"No, next time you give all your clothes to someone, empty your pockets."

She handed me my driver's license, credit cards, three hundred dollars, Lester's coin, and my father's gold ring.

I shook my head. "Wow, I'm lucky you're so honest."

She shrugged. "Most folks are—except around here. West Memphis has one of the worst crime rates in the country. Over three-and-a-half times the national average."

"Lucky you're not running for mayor. Didn't I just leave Memphis?"

"You just left *Tennessee,* but you're still in Memphis." She pointed to my *H.O.G. Touring Handbook* drying out on the dresser. "Check it out. When you took the bridge across the Mississippi River, you crossed the state line. Now you're in Arkansas—West Memphis, Arkansas, to be exact."

I raised an imaginary glass. "Well, here's to the crime capital of the world." Then by accident, I yawned.

She looked like I'd slapped her, and backed toward the door. "Oh, you must be exhausted and starving. I've got a pot of stew on the stove. You're welcome to join me."

I went to my backpack, dug out my mason jar of moonshine, and held it up. "And I've got some mighty fine turpentine. I'll join you if you join me."

So as it turned out I didn't get far away from Graceland that day, but I did get stewed with Mother Teresa at the Red Roof Inn. Her real name was something like Natasha Pugg, and when I told her what I called her, she snorted and knocked over her glass of hooch.

"I'm hardly a saint!" She gestured around the room where we sat on folding chairs at a metal table. "If I was, I wouldn't be working at this god-forsaken place."

I poured us more moonshine. "Well, you've been a saint to me. This rainstorm I got caught in—it was kind of fitting. My whole life got washed out about a year ago."

She grabbed our empty bowls, ladled out more stew, and sat across from me. "Go on. Tell Mother Teresa all about it."

I told her everything, not holding back, and it felt like a confession.

"So here I am—an orphan wandering around the country with no job and no girlfriend." I winked at her. "Unless you're free?"

"My folks are both gone too." She clinked my glass. "Here's to freedom . . . Without any parents we're free to do *almost* anything."

"Well, I guess that's my cue." I got up, thanked her for the stew, and went to bed.

Back in my room, I stared at the ceiling for a good hour, embarrassed as hell. Nothing, it occurred to me, rhymed with *orphan*, and like the word, I figured I'd never be paired with anyone again. I was working my way into a solid pout, thinking of the irony of how *alone* rhymed with *moan* and *groan*, when suddenly I heard someone knocking. Hoping to see Natasha, I threw on some clothes and opened the door to find a man standing in front of the room next to mine.

"Sorry, I forgot my key," he said. "I hope I didn't disturb you."

I almost said, *No, I'm already disturbed*, but my cleverness wasn't going over very well lately, so I just smiled and said, "No problem."

Then I went back to bed and fell into a delicious dream. In it the knock at the door had indeed been Natasha. I gently pulled her into the room, and together we sat on the bed. For a moment we just looked at each other, and then I asked if I could kiss her.

"Kiss me?" She swatted my leg playfully and grinned. "Well, maybe."

Twenty-two

No Exit

———————

The storm had passed in the night, and when I awoke to a clear day, I was feeling good, especially when the knock on the door in the morning actually was Natasha.

"Well, hello." I stepped aside and motioned for her to come in. "I was thinking of apologizing for—"

"Oh, no, I'm the one who needs to apologize." She brushed right past me and began taking my sheets off the bed. "I'm going to have to ask you to check out early. A convention of Elvis impersonators is coming."

"Huh?"

She stopped stripping the bed for a moment and looked at me. "I can give you a discount on your stay, but I can't pass up good money like this. I'll be vacuuming rhinestones for a week, but who cares!"

I started to laugh. "You're not kidding, are you?"

"Do I look like I'm kidding? I'm going to be up to my ears in idiots soon, and two of my housekeepers called in sick."

"Um, can I help?"

"Thanks, you're sweet, but I've already called in for backup. The best thing you can do for me is scoot before this place turns into Heartbreak Hotel." She grabbed my sheets and was out the door. "I'm serious about that discount!"

I watched her skipping off toward her big day, then I quickly gathered my things and slipped onto the long lonely highway.

About an hour down the road, I started passing people with jet-black hair and sideburns shaped like cowboy boots. I sighed with relief and chuckled at my insecurity, glad to see that Natasha hadn't made up the Elvis story to get rid of me. Still, I couldn't help but wonder what it would have been like if it *had* been her knocking in the middle of the night instead of the guy who'd forgotten his key. Since I had a two-hour ride into Little Rock, I had plenty of time to fantasize about it.

But instead my mind went back to high school and other rejections. Like the time I asked a boy to the Sadie Hawkins Day dance, and he said he was hoping my friend would ask him. "If she doesn't ask me, I'll go with you," he said. "But would you mind telling her I think she's cute?"

Or the time I was up late reading and my father poked his head into my room to tell me I'd better get to sleep because the Sweetheart Dance was coming up. "A little birdie told me the boys are kidnapping their candidates for queen tonight." He clapped his hands. "So lights out. Chop, chop!"

"It's not happening, Daddy. I am *not* Miss Popular, you know."

He grinned, refusing to hear me. "I know one thing. Your mother put some new pajamas in your dresser." He winked. "Why don't you wear them tonight just in case."

He clicked the door shut and I got out of bed to find white flannel pajamas with little red hearts on them neatly folded in my drawer. I rolled my eyes but had to smile. Parents could dream, couldn't they? Then I slipped out of my T-shirt, put on the pajamas, and lay awake all night, wishing for something I knew wasn't going to happen.

I was sixteen, in love with a green-eyed boy in my car pool. He lived a block away, and every time "Nights in White Satin" came on the radio, I would imagine myself slow-dancing with him. He would be among the boys doing the kidnapping and he didn't know I was alive.

I was different from my sisters. Each was whisked off in the middle of the night for a pajama breakfast when they became Sweetheart candidates. Each was the president of some club, captain of some team, and on dozens of pages in their yearbooks. I smoked pot in the desert behind the school and hung out by the 7-Eleven hoping some adult would buy me wine. I played guitar, wore tie-dyed shirts and ripped jeans, and fancied myself bohemian mostly because I liked the sound of the word. I was reading Nietzsche, Sartre, Dostoyevsky, and Hesse, spending as much time in my head and as little time in reality as I could.

Even now, on my Harley, when I had the chance to visualize the possibility of relationships in my future or even imagine a romantic rendezvous with Natasha under an A-frame, I raced straight back to Sartre so I could *think* rather than feel. Jean-Paul spoke to me, or at least his characters in *No Exit* did. "Hell is other people," said Garcin, one of the three damned souls locked in a room for eternity for committing crimes of the heart. But did they deserve to be tortured for making bad choices? Had *I* created my own hell just because my dating track record stank?

As I began to think about this, I rode past mutilated roadkill. Life, it occurred to me as I sped along risking my own, was fleeting and finite. It was easier and more secure to live a safe distance from others. Even animals, insects, and plants were safer in the wild, far from the lawnmower blades and poisons humans could inflict. It was certainly true for this animal. I was definitely more tormented in a relationship than out of one. I couldn't deny that, in the last two weeks, it had been easier to deal with strangers than anyone I knew or cared about. The more unfamiliar people were, the less harm they could do me.

This had to be what Sartre was getting at—hell *is* other people, because you can't stop thinking about them when they're not in your life, and when they are, they torture you. There is always a push and a pull going on, a desire to please and a resentment of having to, a hope for companionship and a need for space.

My head was beginning to ache. Hell, I decided, had *nothing* to do with other people; it had to do with trying to figure out your own life. Sartre should have called his play *No Entrance*. There is no door that leads to the meaning of existence, no window to enlightenment. If only we could enter life through the exit and live in reverse; then maybe we'd have a chance at understanding what the hell life is about.

My headache had spread to the rest of my body, and I longed for the off-ramp that would direct me to the Clinton museum so I could stop this hell of thinking.

But when the exit sign did appear, it also gave me the option to bypass it. Just an hour down the road was Hot Springs, Arkansas. It was where Bill Clinton went to high school, and it was known for having great bathhouses. As I drew within a mile of the Little Rock exit, I started to think existentially about why I was going to the Clinton museum in the first place. Was it because *I* wanted to go, or was it because I thought others expected me to go? When people asked me if all the presidential artifacts were interesting, what would happen if I told them I had bypassed the museum for a massage? Laughing, I blew past the exit without giving it another thought.

Twenty-three

Contemplating the Guardrail

———◆———

Time on a motorcycle is unlike time spent anywhere else. There are moments lost in the landscape, seconds devoted solely to balance, and long stretches spent spiraling inward. Between my last glimpse of the Little Rock exit and my turnoff to Hot Springs, the latter was true. No matter how hard I tried, I couldn't stop thinking about life, and even more so, the afterlife. If Sartre was right, there was no escaping either. As I watched the ground appear and disappear beneath my tires, I considered how control slips in and out of our grasp, but that's only on earth. Once we're buried beneath it or sprinkled somewhere upon it, we have no say in the matter.

My mom always claimed to know where she was going. Often she spoke of reuniting with my dad, as if they were in communication and he was ready for her arrival. Why else would she die so soon? He had to have called for her, and so she went.

When he had bypass surgery my sisters and I flew into El Paso to be with him, but really I think we flew in mostly for my mom. I can't speak for the others, but I was afraid she would do something drastic if the surgery went awry. She laid such a kiss on him just before the orderlies wheeled him away that everyone in the waiting room turned around as if they'd heard an orchestra crescendo. Then she leaned against a wall and slid down it, crumpling into tears. If only I could find a partner to love half that much, I'd be happy.

As I flew along the highway, I looked at how the ground dropped off beyond the guardrail. If I went full throttle and lifted my bike with every-thing in me, would my tires clear the metal bar? I could imagine the thrill and terror of sailing off into nothingness. If only I could surrender com-pletely, it would be an amazing way to go. But what if the impact didn't kill me? Would I have the courage to will my death before rescue arrived?

That's what I think my mom did when she found out she was termi-nally ill. She pushed herself over the guardrail between this world and the next and then sailed into my father's arms. The paramedics told Har riet they might be able to revive her, but she told them to let Mom go. It was a good thing her life wasn't in my hands. I might have had them drag her back. There were conversations I wanted to have with my mother, questions I wanted answered. I'm not sure what we might have discussed as she lay on her deathbed, but given the chance right here on this Harley to contact her, I had an idea of what I wanted to know.

"Were the answers all there, Mom?" I stared at the guardrail as if it were the only thing keeping us apart. "Was it worth rushing off?"

I have to admit, I would have done the same thing. Given the chance to see what's next rather than have people watch me die, I'd have blown this planet for sure—*if* I didn't have children. But my sisters and I simply weren't my mom's main concern. Our dad was her priority, and when he died, we were all amazed she didn't jump into the coffin with him. Theirs was a fifty-five-year love story, a quixotic pairing I used to watch from a distance, as though I were in a dark theater and they were a foreign film. Kids always seemed to spoil romance in the movies, but to my parents' credit, they never let us kill their passion. In fact, they remained role models of how to keep love alive, making me feel that much more a failure when my sisters followed suit and I wound up hugging the road.

Maybe that was why I'd been contemplating the guardrail lately. Since the here and now hadn't been offering much, the hereafter was starting to look like it might have some pretty awesome perks. Certainly the promise of reuniting with loved ones was a draw, but the idea that there might be answers to questions this earthbound life can't resolve is most intriguing. It's why I've always been lured to rooftops of tall buildings and edges of cliffs. To be sure, my mom and I were never alike, but I'm certain that on many nights after she buried my dad, she fell asleep thinking, as I often do now, that maybe not waking up would be okay.

"You'll see," she told me after my dad's funeral. "God has everything figured out, and now he's let your father in on it. When the time is right, I'll be in on it too."

"I wouldn't be in a hurry, Mom. God probably has his hands full with Daddy."

Sitting in my father's favorite chair, my mother grinned. "He *was* a character."

"Yup, he's probably already in charge of some big project up there."

"Oh, for heaven's sake, Barbara, you don't really believe that, do you?"

"Sure. Daddy's probably up there revamping the whole system."

"Up there?" My mother chuckled. "You can't be serious."

"Daddy had his faults, but if he's anywhere, he isn't down *there*."

"Of course he's not down there. He's down *here*. Can't you feel his presence?"

"On earth? Yeah, I guess I feel him around sometimes, but—"

"I saw him on the news yesterday." Naomi glanced up from the newspaper she was reading. "This guy tackled a bank robber, and I swear he looked like Daddy."

"Your father would never rob a bank." My mom winked at me. "Right, Barbara?"

"Yeah, Daddy might knock over a jewelry store or something, but—"

"Stop it!" Naomi's face reddened. "You know what I meant."

"Of course, honey." My mother rushed over to Naomi and gave her a hug. "I see your dad everywhere too. I half-expected him to be among the mourners at the funeral."

Naomi looked shocked, and I couldn't decide if it was because of what our mother had said or because she'd actually embraced one of us. Regardless, I was overwhelmed with jealousy, frantic to think of something to say so I too could be pulled into her arms. But before anything came to mind, my uncle Seymour walked in.

"Hello, ladies. What are we talking about?" He held up a pastrami sandwich. "By the way, whoever sent this deli tray is a saint."

I slid a look to my mother. "It probably came from Daddy."

We both burst out laughing, and Naomi stormed out of the room.

"Oh, honey, come back!" my mother called. "If we don't laugh, we'll cry."

Naomi sauntered back into the room, grabbed her newspaper, and sat primly on the couch. "I was just agreeing with you, Mom. I'll bet Daddy is with us right now."

I rolled my eyes. "If he's still on earth, he's probably playing pinochle."

"Maybe he'll make our game tonight?" Uncle Seymour grinned, and then headed toward the kitchen. "I'm getting another sandwich. Anybody want something?"

I shot Naomi a look. "No, but if you see my dad, tell him we're out here in the living room."

She threw her newspaper at me, and we both began to laugh, unaware that our mother had quietly slipped from the room. Later we found her weeping as she clung to the edge of her mattress, leaving the other half empty.

Now, as I rode along Interstate 40 with my father's death a memory and my mother's still a source of confusion, I turned my focus outward for peace I certainly wasn't finding inside. There I saw spruce, cypress, and pine along the highway, nothing like the brown desert of the border town where I grew up. As I ripped through the lush landscape, I realized that soon the green of Arkansas would blur into the beige of Oklahoma without my noticing it, and I began to wonder if maybe Naomi was right. Maybe the line between this life and the next was as imperceptible as nature bleeding from one state into the other.

Thinking about all this, I noticed a dull pain in my neck that ran through my shoulders and my back. My headache was getting worse too. Supporting a helmet buffeted about by the wind put a lot of strain on me. So did all this thinking, but I couldn't stop. I focused hard on the conveyer belt of asphalt beneath me and tried to stay in the present, but I drifted back to Natasha and wondered how she was coping with the Elvises. How could I even *think* she would sleep with me?

I started to sing "99 Bottles of Beer on the Wall," but at seventy-six bottles, I was bored out of my mind. Then my *haftarah* popped into my head. Astonished I could remember it, I began to chant in Hebrew at the top of my lungs until a creepy thought hit me. Except for my sisters and a few cousins, almost every relative who had attended my bat mitzvah was dead—*I* was thirty-seven years closer to dying myself. My heart fluttered and suddenly I felt feverish. My mother had died in an instant. Maybe I didn't have much time either. Where in the hell was the goddamned exit? I needed to stop and get some rest. I glanced down at my odometer and nearly fell off my bike. How could I have covered so much mental territory and logged only seven miles?

My heart fluttered again. My father had a six-way bypass. He had a stroke too. I could throw a blood clot at any moment and wind up with half my face frozen. Suddenly I tasted bile and thought I might be sick. I raised my visor a half-inch for some fresh air and in that split second a speck of something the size of a boulder flew into my eye.

"Fuck!" I threw back my visor. But with gloves on I was helpless. "Please, God." My heart slammed my rib cage. Tears flooded my eyes. *"Please*, don't let me die."

I clutched down from fourth, to third, to second. Then ripping into first gear, I dragged my boots on the tarmac to keep from going sideways. Nearly blind I finally felt gravel and miraculously came to a stop.

"Shit." I turned off my engine and tore off my gloves. "Holy fucking shit."

I managed to undo my chinstrap and pull off my helmet, and then I sat in my saddle shaking. The grit that had been scratching the life out of my eyes was running down my checks, and though I wasn't in pain anymore, I couldn't stop trembling. I felt so alone, so vulnerable out there in the middle of nowhere . . . and then I realized something. There was absolutely *no* traffic. Not a car, not a semi in sight.

I looked at my watch. It was just past noon. Had everyone pulled off the highway for lunch all at once? The nothingness around me was creepy. There wasn't even a breeze or a tree for the wind to blow. Where had all the evergreens gone? I looked around the desolate highway, and then in the distance I saw a single white billboard with black lettering. At first the words startled me, and then I began to laugh.

Don't make me come down there.

—God

Twenty-four

Playing Possum

———◆———

I *rode in silence* for the next twenty minutes into Hot Springs. I'd
been talking to myself way too much and was feeling kind of peculiar,
so I parked my bike in front of the first hotel/bathhouse that advertised
Bill Clinton had slept there, and walked in. It was definitely time to get
off the road and soak my head, if not my entire body.

As it turns out, Franklin Roosevelt, Harry Truman, George H. W.
Bush, *and* Bill Clinton had slept at the historic Arlington Resort Hotel &
Spa in downtown Hot Springs. But former presidents weren't the only
famous people who soaked, slept, or got rubbed down there. In fact, the
Arlington was host to the likes of Babe Ruth, Joe DiMaggio, Andrew Car-
negie, Tony Bennett, Barbra Streisand, and Yoko Ono, not to mention its
most infamous guest, Al Capone, who used to reserve the entire fourth
floor for his staff and bodyguards. I walked around the luxurious place in
awe, but decided that maybe I would treat myself to a few spa treatments
and stay somewhere I could afford.

The hotel I chose, on the other end of town, had a stained linoleum
floor, a sad breakfast area, and beds as lumpy as oatmeal. The decrepit old

man behind the desk looked like a walking stick in a Dickens novel—not even a character, just a gnarly cane someone might shake at a child. He was intently chewing on something, and if I hadn't seen it was a sandwich, I might have thought he had killed his meal with his bare hands. I cleared my throat and stood before him, wondering if he was deaf or had no peripheral vision, because he didn't react to my presence until I hit the reception bell, and even then he didn't look up.

"No air conditioner, connecting bathroom, double bed—take it or leave it, that's all I've got." He burped, then spat in a can behind him. "I can throw in an electric fan."

I ran my fingers through my gritty hair. "I'd pay a little extra for a private bath." I brushed a smashed dragonfly off my thigh. I was no prize either.

"Sorry." He smiled like it was painful, then handed me a pamphlet. "What I can offer is a discount for spa treatments at a bathhouse behind us. If you're looking for colonics, there's a few places in town I can refer you to, but they don't offer that there."

"Actually, I'll pass on the colonics." I handed him my Visa and scanned the pamphlet. "Hmm, what's—"

"I don't know, but everybody raves about it."

"How'd you know what I was going to ask?"

He rolled his eyes. "Fine, you tell *me* what ear candling is."

"Sounds exotic. Put me down for a massage, a mud bath, and that ear thing." I signed my receipt. "So why are your prices so low? I mean, ninety dollars for three spa treatments *and* a room? Is there running water?"

"Of course—hot and cold."

"Was someone murdered here?"

"Look, if you haven't noticed, this town is kind of glutted with bathhouses and hotels, so we offer an alternative to throwing your money away. It's your choice—you can spend more than three hundred to stay in a gangster's room or pay twenty-five for a tent, a pat down, and a happy ending. Personally, I'd stay here."

I looked around the lobby. "You do have other guests, right?"

"It's early yet. We cater to the leftover crowd."

I looked at my watch. It was half-past noon. "Wow, it's like I'm in a time warp."

"Tell me about it. I've been living in this hotel all my life."

"No kidding."

"Mother turned the third floor into her private suite, and I'm her personal servant." He curled his lip and picked up the phone. "I'm about to call the bathhouse to schedule your treatments. What kind of massage do you want: hot rock, Swedish, or Shiatsu?"

"Which do you like?"

"*No one* touches me." A visible quiver came over him. "I'm not into that."

"Okay, then." I stepped back. "I'll try hot rock. Just schedule all the other treatments whenever they have openings."

"Not to worry—they *always* have openings."

"Oh, really? Why? The place is clean, right?"

He chuckled. "Since when are mud baths clean?"

"You know, on second thought I think I'm going to splurge on some treatments at the Arlington." I handed him my Visa card again "Just charge me for the room and credit me back for everything else."

"Suit yourself, Mrs. Rockefeller." He reran my Visa and slid a key across the counter. "I assure you the bathhouse I deal with is perfectly fine. Mother and I soak there all the time."

"Well, that's nice." I grabbed the key, picked up my gear, and headed to the elevator. "I'm going up to my room to call the Arlington."

"Mind you, we don't actually soak in the same tub . . . That would be weird."

"Yes," I said. "That would be weird."

"Mother is a lovely woman. We're actually good friends."

I stopped and turned around. "Okay, now you're fucking with me. Who are you? Norman Bates?"

He raised an eyebrow. "What are you talking about?"

"Norman Bates—you know, Anthony Perkins—*Psycho*?"

"You got me." He grinned and raised his hands. "I was just messing with you. It's my favorite movie."

"Okay, Norman, as long as your mother is *alive* on the third floor, I'll stay." I jabbed the elevator button, but nothing happened.

"I wish my name *was* Norman. I got saddled with Melvin."

I pushed the button again and put my ear to the metal door. Nothing.

"It's not broken, just a little sluggish, kind of like me." He coughed and wheezed. "Bet you can't guess how many years I've been working here."

I kept my back to him. "I don't know, maybe a hundred?"

"Pretty much my whole life. My father died and left the place to Mother and me."

I turned around. "Are you operating this elevator by remote control?"

His body slumped. I was probably the only one he'd conversed with in a decade.

I mustered a smile. "Listen, it's not that I don't want to talk, but—"

He shrugged. "But you don't want to talk to a pathetic old man."

"You're not pathetic, just unusual." I hit the button. "You sure this isn't broken?"

He banged his fist on the desk. "The elevator is *fine!*"

I stared at him. "*You* need a massage, mister."

He looked like he might be sick. "I told you, I don't like to be touched. As the Bible says—"

I put up a hand. "Stop right there. I've already been preached to by a billboard."

Finally the elevator dinged and the doors creaked open. "Adios, Norman. I'm off to my room to Google ear candling. I hope they have that at the Arlington." I stepped to the back of the elevator mumbling to myself how the poor guy was probably a eunuch, castrated by his mother at birth.

"Excuse me?" Melvin stuck his hand between the elevator doors.

I froze. He couldn't possibly have heard me.

"I'm sorry," he said, his face reddening. "I've heard that word before, but now I *have* to know what it means."

I stared at him wondering what had stumped him—*eunuch* or *castrated*? I was about to apologize, when he blurted, "Tell me, what exactly is *Google*?"

Unfortunately the Arlington had no appointments available, but I was told of a spa nearby running specials. It was a similar package to Melvin's place and only slightly more expensive, so off I went and was soon in a vat of mud scented with clove and something that was either oregano or marijuana. I was happy as a dog rolling in dung, but couldn't stop thinking about sad-as-shit Melvin, afraid to be touched and crazy enough to tell a complete stranger about it.

"Yup, I'm the *lone* stranger." I leaned back and pretended I was in a pool of chocolate. "Roaming the highway with no one to give a rat's ass about me."

"I give a rat's ass about you, honey."

I whirled around to see a beefy blonde with a big fluffy towel, a garden hose, and an exaggerated tan. She looked like the love child of Ella Fitzgerald and Hulk Hogan.

"Hi, I'm Madeline, your massage therapist." She twirled the hose.

"Your mud bath is over, but if you've got more to say to yourself, I can leave you alone for a minute."

I looked at the hose. "You're not gonna spray me down, are you?"

"Not unless you want me to." She winked. "Me? I'd opt for a shower."

She twirled the hose again as though she was about to rope and hog-tie me with it.

"Come on, you big sissy. I just want to wash away your mud trail." She held out the towel and cocked her head toward the showers. "Snap to it, sexy. My eyes are shut."

I chuckled nervously and wrapped my muddy body in the towel. "You know carrying around that hose makes you look like a prison guard."

"Thanks, that's the look I was going for." She handed me a pair of flip-flops. "Better slip these on, sugar. There's enough fungus growing in here to make penicillin."

I did as I was told. "Could I have another towel?"

"Nope, only one per customer."

I stared down at my mud-splotched towel. "You're kidding."

"Of *course* I'm kidding. This is a classy joint. Why, I'll have you know I've had a Possum Queen or two on my massage table." She hung up another towel and a robe outside a shower stall. "Hop in before that mud gets crusty."

I stepped inside the shower and began lathering up. "So that sign I saw about electing so-and-so for Possum Queen wasn't a joke?"

"Hell, no! We're on our twelfth queen. There's a Possum Picnic to announce her, a Possum Coronation to crown her, and a Possum Parade she presides over."

"Wow, possums are a big deal around here, huh?"

"Yep, they're not just filthy varmints to us." She chuckled. "I've never had it, but some people actually make possum stew."

The shower was steamy but I shivered anyway. "Please tell me you're kidding."

She didn't answer. I poked my head around the shower curtain, but she was gone.

I stepped out, toweled off, and put on my robe. "Madeline?" I walked into the mud room, now watered down and slippery as hell. "Where are you?"

"I'm back here!" A voice echoed from down the hall. "Last room on your left."

I headed toward her voice, down the dimly lit passageway, until I found Madeline standing by a massage table holding a bucket of steaming rocks.

"Well, it's about time. I was beginning to think I should start working on myself."

I stared at the rocks and she followed my gaze. "Good God, they're not *alive!*" She tossed one to me. "Here, see for yourself."

I caught the hot rock and was surprised to find that it felt like a warm piece of soap. "Wow, this feels . . . *nice.*"

"Nice my ass. It feels like 'a hunk, a hunk of burning love'!" She juggled a few rocks and swiveled her hips. "Now strip and let's get this rubdown on the road!"

She left the room, clicking the door shut, then instantly cracked it open. "Facedown, sweet cheeks."

For the next hour, Madeline strategically placed smoldering rocks all over my body, but when she put a few on the backs of my legs, one of my calves began to cramp. I cried out in pain and started to jump off the table, but she held me down.

"Relax, I've got this." She pressed something on my screaming calf, and within seconds, the cramp vanished. "Amazing, huh?"

"Yeah, what the hell did you do?"

She flashed a silver spoon into my view under the face cradle. "It doesn't have to be silver, stainless steel works too."

"Seriously? A spoon cures cramps?"

"Yup, and if you're prone to getting charley horses in the middle of the night, just slip a bar of soap between the sheets before you go to bed."

"You're kidding." I laughed. "Any particular brand?"

"No, but I've been told Ivory doesn't work as well." She dug her thumbs into my neck. "You learn a lot in massage school."

I think she might have applied Mr. Spock's Vulcan nerve pinch because I either passed out or went to sleep. Either way, the next thing I heard was Madeline whispering in my ear, "Are you alive?"

All I could do was nod.

"You scared me. You stopped breathing for a minute there." She rubbed my back. "I'm afraid we've gotten behind schedule. I'll go get Gloria, your ear candler."

Instantly, I fell back asleep and didn't stir again until I felt something warm wafting in my ear. It was smoke.

"Lie still." Someone held my head. "You don't want to get burned, do you?"

"I'd rather not." I reached up and felt a long candle sticking out of my ear. "You must be Gloria. I didn't even hear you come in."

"Madeline sent you to another world. She does that to everyone." Gloria laughed. "Either that or your ear canal is clogged. Not to worry. I'm taking care of it."

I tried to keep still, but a crackling sound was freaking me out. "It sounds like Rice Krispies in here. Is everything okay?"

"It's just the candle burning. It's hollow, and the heat creates a vacuum." She tightened her hold on my head. "You're hearing the wax being sucked from your ear."

"Interesting, but don't I need a little wax in there?" I reached up to loosen Gloria's death grip. "You're sure this procedure won't hurt me, right?"

"It's perfectly safe." She was pinning me down with her full body weight. "And legal everywhere except Canada."

I was light-headed. "Maybe we should only do one ear just in case I go deaf."

"I know every ear candler in this town, and not one of them has reported a client losing any hearing." Gloria chuckled. "Besides, I've already done your other ear. You slept right through it."

"No way." I tried to get up but she held me down. "Did Madeline drug me?"

"Nope, she's just that good. We're all pretty amazing at what we do here. Wait till I show you the gunk I've sucked out of your ears."

Later, after seeing the unbelievable wad of coffee-colored wax Gloria vacuumed from me, I lost my appetite, but still I walked over to the Arlington's gorgeous Venetian dining room for a quick meal. It was only six-fifteen—the place was nearly empty—and I was glad because my hotel was kind of far away and I didn't want to be walking too long in the dark.

But even though I only had a salad and some wine, it was almost seven-thirty before I got the check, and I was growing uncomfortable as I walked away from the nicer part of town toward my grubby hotel. I hoped no one was lurking in all the alleys I seemed to be passing, or robbing all the liquor stores that suddenly appeared.

Where was that tough biker chick when I needed her? If only I had worn my scuffed-to-perfection leather jacket with the Screamin' Eagle spread across my shoulder blades. If only I had on my charcoal chaps with the ass cut out to show off my Levi's-clad butt. Then I'd be able to play it cool as I swaggered down the sidewalk like I couldn't give a shit about how freaking scary this neighborhood was.

I broke into a jog, wondering why in the hell I didn't ride my bike to the Arlington in the first place. It was only a twenty-minute walk from my hotel, but twenty minutes in daylight is never just twenty minutes when it's dark in a seedy neighborhood full of drunks and people who vote for Possum Queens.

Before my heart exploded, I slowed down to a rapid walk. Man, was I out of shape. I shouldn't be breathing this hard after a little run. My heart started flopping around. Had I missed my hotel?

I was working myself into a full-on panic and the thought of seeing Melvin's wrinkled face was starting to look pretty good, when suddenly a blissful relaxation washed over me. Yes, there in my newly cleared ear canal was my mother. She was singing nasally and wildly off-key; her voice was cracking and her words were almost completely incomprehensible, and yet they made perfect sense. In short, she was doing a fine Bob Dylan.

"Don't think twice," she sang. *"It's all right."*

And it was—my hotel was just steps away. I walked inside and, sure enough, there was Melvin, gross and crouched behind the front desk, looking oddly benign.

"Good evening, Mrs. Rockefeller," he said, flashing a friendly grin. "I trust the Arlington met with your satisfaction?"

I wanted to ask if his Prozac had just kicked in, but instead I laughed and said, "Good evening, Mr. Bates. Yes, it was lovely."

I pressed the elevator button and miraculously it arrived in seconds.

"I decided it was time to get the damn thing fixed," Melvin called after me as I stepped inside. "You never know when another heiress might show up."

I heard his laughter even as the doors creaked shut, then we disappeared from each other's sight. By morning I'd be on the road. He'd be out of my consciousness and I'd be out of his, a complete unknown . . . *like a rolling stone.*

Twenty-five

Roadkill or Buzzkill?

———◆———

A rooster crowed at the break of dawn, and I was gone not long afterward. For the first time in more than a year, I'd slept solidly through the night, and left the hotel as the sun rose behind me. Maybe it was because of the unique spa treatments, but it was probably because of the pill I took. I'd found it while rummaging through my backpack, looking for Shaggy Blond Dave's pocketknife, which I put under my pillow after freaking myself out on my walk back to the hotel.

At first I didn't see the tiny white tablet, I only heard it skitter across the floor when it fell from an envelope filled with assorted painkillers. I'd saved them from a root canal, a knee surgery, and a concussion—just in case—and I'd thrown them into my pack but forgotten about them. Back in Los Angeles I used to hold the pills in the palm of my hand and just stare at them, and now I ripped the envelope open, thinking I'd have one last look. Wasn't it time to throw them out?

But when a pill slid from the envelope, I didn't want some kid finding it, so I dropped to the floor and picked it out of a warren of dust bunnies. It was imprinted with AMB10, and I decided that perhaps it was a sign that ten milligrams of Ambien would do me good right now. The rest of the pills went back in my pack, and the next thing I knew, it was five a.m. and I was starving.

After a quick check of my *H.O.G. Touring Handbook,* I found that Mount Ida was the closest decent-size city and it was only forty-five minutes away. There, at a café that claimed to have "the best vittles in *Arkinsaw,*" I had biscuits, gravy, and grits while I figured out my timeline. If I rode directly home, I had only 1,640 miles to go—two days by car but three on a motorcycle. Of course, that meant my knees, back, and butt would have to handle eight-hour stretches in the saddle at seventy-five miles per hour. Doable if I was impervious to pain and met no hindrances, human or otherwise. But considering my penchant for detours and my ever-recurring reluctance to get home, I called Lynn to see if she could stay with my dogs for at least another week.

Having been dive-bombed by dragonflies, butterflies, and a kamikaze bird, choked to death by diesel fumes, gas fumes, and a tractor-trailer full of pigs, I was feeling invincible. Except for that speck that flew in my eye, a wad of gum that came out of nowhere and stuck to my visor, Melvin, and a possible rat sighting, I was having the time of my life.

"Don't you miss your dogs?" Lynn asked. "They ask about you all the time."

"Of course I do. It's people I've lost interest in."

My answer chilled me. On and off the road, I'd been keeping my distance from humans. I'd learned that getting too close to them could hurt you, and now on the highway, I was realizing they could kill you. Old people and new drivers were unpredictable, but it was the road bullies who really got to me. Often I fantasized about laying down my bike when some schmuck sat on my tailpipe or narrowly missed me whizzing by. What a power reversal it would be if I could pop a fake blood pill and skid off the road. Even a jerk would stop to see if he'd killed me. But I was not a stunt rider yet, so I usually accepted all the idiots on the road . . . except once somewhere outside of Nashville, when this guy blew past me in his convertible and touched a wicked nerve.

Driving a bloodred Stingray, he was tapping his steering wheel to heavy metal and letting his blond curls blow in the wind. I hated him on sight. The only thing missing was Marilyn Monroe riding shotgun, and I figured someone just like her was back at his condo watching a TV the size of a mattress and snorting cocaine. It was clear he had gotten plenty out of this life, and I'd be damned if I was going to let him have the road too, so I whizzed past him and planted myself on his front bumper.

He laid on his horn and I ignored him. He flashed his headlights and I tapped my brakes. I felt his impotence growing by the second, and power draining from him into me. I was having an *Easy Rider* moment, until I noticed I needed gas, so I waved over my shoulder like nothing had happened, and headed for the next exit.

But he followed me.

Panicked, I thought about zipping back onto the highway, but I knew his Corvette could blow my chaps off, and I had only a few miles left in my main tank before I had to stop to switch on my reserve. Besides, there would be people at the gas station, witnesses if he tried to kill me. My heart hammering, I pulled into a Phillips 66 and listened to him roar up behind me, get out of his car, and slam the door.

"Who the fuck do you think you are?" He thumped me on the back.

I didn't move.

"Take off your helmet, asshole. Take it off or I'll rip it off."

Through my peripheral vision, I saw a pinstriped pant leg and an Italian leather shoe. Then he waved a gun in front of my visor.

"Where's your nerve now, shithead?"

I sat there frozen, so he tapped my helmet with the barrel. "Look at me or I swear I'll blow your head off."

I looked at him and he burst out laughing.

"Man, are you lucky you're a chick!" Then shaking his head, he walked back to his Corvette and roared off.

I couldn't believe I was alive. Slowly, my hands shaking, I took off my helmet and shook out my sweaty hair, and that's when I saw a young couple at the pump across from me. They looked as scared as I felt, sitting frozen in their Chevy, staring at me as though *I* was the one to fear. I swung off my bike and tried not to faint while I pumped my gas, and all the while, the couple just kept staring. Then, suddenly energized by their terror, I grinned and whispered, *"Boo!"*

Their eyes widened and they sped off. I laughed because I did feel like a ghost on the road, slipping on and off exits, entering people's lives only to disappear the next day. I was like a specter speeding by on this Harley, this powerful machine that was all about being in one place one second and in another the next. Speed and power—what a beautiful combination, a constant reminder that life was miraculous and could swiftly be cut short.

Now as I buzzed through the Ouachita Mountains, cruising through all the shades of green Arkansas had to offer, I suddenly became aware of the increase in roadkill since I'd hit warmer climate. The number had grown from the north to the south, and now there seemed to be so many lifeless bodies I could feel their spirits rising from the asphalt. Rabbits and birds were easy to pass by—there were just so many of them—but the rare armadillo or porcupine, the random snake or skunk, often drew me to the side of the road to marvel at the many shapes and sizes of creatures that drew breath . . . and then didn't.

Why, I wondered, were some deaths so violent? I took my speed up a notch. Why did I feel like I was racing toward death and away from it at the same time? I glanced at my speedometer, my odometer, and then at my Elvis watch. My speed was greater than the number of miles

I'd logged—ninety compared to seventy-two—and nearly three hours had fled from my day. How had my mind covered more territory than my bike?

It's no wonder that the next town I came upon was called Y City, named that because it was at a fork in the road where travelers had to decide whether to bank left, right, or turn around. There was no going forward from this place, and as I sat idling at the only traffic light in town, I remembered the best advice my father ever gave me:

If you don't know where to go, take a step in any direction, he said. *You can always turn back and go another way. Just don't ever stand still.*

Y City, it seemed to me, was a place everyone comes to at some point, a place in the middle of nowhere that had to lead somewhere. I banked right onto Highway 71, north to Fort Smith, the last city in Arkansas before Oklahoma. It was a relaxing, two-lane blacktop with a series of hand-painted signs tacked to trees and telephone poles spaced out every five miles. Intrigued, I soon found myself eager to spot the next one.

IF YOU'RE BROKE I CAN FIX YOU—15 MILES

POWERFUL HEALING AHEAD—10 MILES

WANNA ROCK?—5 MILES

I was hooked, and when I saw the last sign: WORLD'S CUTEST SNAKE—500 FEET, I turned where the arrow pointed and parked my bike before a dilapidated junk stand.

"Hello?" I walked toward someone in a hammock. "I saw your signs."

If he heard me, he didn't seem to care. He was lounging under a straw hat embroidered with the same words that were spray-painted on the metal roof of his stand—THE QUARTZ KING—and now I realized why I'd been lured there. Throwing a rock with healing powers into my pack couldn't hurt. I cleared my throat to get his attention.

"Excuse me, but if it's true what they say about crystals, I'd like to buy one."

He didn't budge and I thought he might be dead. I stood over his hammock and looked down at him. "I'm not disturbing you, am I?"

He lifted his hat and a pile of dreadlocks fell out. "No, I've been expecting you. Heard those Screamin' Eagles a mile away."

I smiled proudly at my pipes and cocked my head at his stand. "So you're the Quartz King, huh?"

"Not today, I'm not." He scrambled out of his hammock and a wave of marijuana drifted off him. "Today I'm just Sawyer Finn. I've got plenty of junk, but no crystals."

I took in his wrinkled tie-dyed pants and worn-out huaraches. "Come on, I'll bet you have a crystal lying around here somewhere."

He shrugged. "Sorry, my supplier didn't show."

"Look, it doesn't have to be pretty. I'd even take one of your rejects."

He stroked his goatee. "How about a Pet Rock straight from the seventies?" He rummaged through his stand and handed me a smooth gray stone. "It used to have a training manual, but I lost it."

"How do I know this isn't a rock you found by the side of the road?"

"Does it look like an ordinary rock?"

I studied the rock. "Yeah, it does."

"Well, that proves it. The original Pet Rocks *were* ordinary rocks. That one there is one of the few left on earth, and I'm only asking five bucks for it."

I held up a plastic red, white, and blue donkey. "How much for him?"

"Seven bucks. And I'll throw in the rock for an even ten."

"Take a check?"

"Sure, just make it out to Bradley Forester Jr."

"I thought your name was Sawyer Finn."

"Is that what I called myself? Hah, that's a good one. I change it every day." He tapped his temple. "Good for the brain to tease it now and then, don't you think?"

I handed him a check. "Actually, I change my name from time to time too."

"Really? Who are you today?"

I shrugged. "Good question."

"Well, I wouldn't go stressing over it. We're all chameleons." He looked at the sun and then pulled a tiny wooden pipe out of his pocket. "Time to pretend I've got glaucoma." He lit the bowl, took a drag, and handed it to me.

"I'd better not." I pointed to my Harley. "I can hardly stay upright as it is."

"Suit yourself, but you're missing out on some damn good shit."

I sucked in the air around me for a contact high and held my rock and my donkey to my chest. My ex loved this kitschy stuff, and if we were still together, I'd slip them under her pillow to make her laugh. Now my donkey would end up on my fireplace mantel next to my rock and eventually they'd land in a drawer.

"Listen, how about we make a trade?" I set my purchases on the stand next to a Rubik's Cube and a dream catcher. "Just roll me a joint and we'll call it even."

He grinned and pulled a huge doobie from his pocket and handed it over. "You've made a fine choice. That there is primo shit."

I smelled the joint and tucked it into my breast pocket. "Thanks, I'll save this for a celebration. One's bound to come along soon."

He took another drag off his pipe. "Had a dry spell lately?"

I inhaled his exhale. "A setback or three."

"We all have 'em." He snuffed out his pipe and tucked it in his pocket. "Say, how about checking out my snake before you go? It's awful cute."

"Um, we're talking about a reptile, right?"

He laughed. "Follow me."

We walked around the back of his stand to a cage that held a little striped snake wrapped around a toy mouse.

I peered at the truly gorgeous reptile. "Um, it's not poisonous, is it?"

"Not if I got the right kind." He produced an earthworm from a sack and dropped it into the cage. "Dinner time, Eve. Come and get it."

I watched Eve, who really was kind of cute, swallow her worm whole. "What do you mean by the right kind?"

"Well, snakes aren't that different from humans—they can look real nice, but be mean as hell. Eve here is a milk snake, harmless as a cow, but she *looks* like a coral snake, one of the most venomous reptiles on earth. Get bitten by one of those little suckers and you're dead before you know it." He laughed. "They paralyze your larynx—literally take your breath away."

I took a step back. "I've been bitten by a few nice-looking humans."

"Me too. Why do you think I'm living off the grid?"

"So how do you know Eve *isn't* a coral snake?"

"Ah, now that's where humans and snakes part ways. All you have to do is look at the color pattern on a snake. If it's red then black, it won't attack. If it's red then yellow, it's a deadly fellow. Doesn't matter what color a human is—they can all turn on you."

"Well, I'm glad to see you're not a racist." I put my helmet on and headed toward my bike. "Thanks for the herpetology lesson and the weed."

"Smoke with care and try to stay happy. Nobody likes a buzzkill."

I swung into the saddle. "Who you calling a buzzkill?"

He laughed. "Sorry, I thought you were gonna unload on me back there when you mentioned those setbacks. That's why I took you over to see Eve. Parents are always stopping by with their cranky kids. I got her to keep the little brats amused."

"So now you're calling me a brat? Thanks a lot."

He raised an eyebrow. "Okay, then what are you?"

"Huh?"

"Let me put it this way. I'm a pothead who's happy just kicking back and selling junk. And you're a . . . ?"

"I'm a . . ."

He burst out laughing. "Well, don't bust a brain cell over it." He climbed back into his hammock. "Just figure out what makes you happy and keep on doing it."

I sat there on my Harley watching him stare up at the sky, swinging in his hammock, happy as hell. Then I flipped down my visor, flipped on my ignition, and rode off to think about how to finish my sentence.

Twenty-six

Reality Check

———◆———

After struggling for a few miles over the question of who or what I am, I decided that no one is the same person from start to finish. In half a mile, I could come upon an accident and instantly be a hero by pulling someone from a wreck. Later, I could witness a murder and cower behind a tree. The more important thing to consider was that the junk man wanted no part of my grief and had used a snake to keep it away from him. Wasn't I using the road in the same way? Wasn't this whole trip a big decoy to distract me from my life back home?

I thought about pulling over, lighting up the joint, and blowing off the whole day. Maybe I would never go back. The junkman was right—I just needed to figure out what made me happy and keep doing it.

I whizzed past a poster taped to a tree that advertised squirrels for sale. *That* made me happy. I threw back my visor and let the wind clear my head.

"There are squirrels to buy out here!" I yelled. "I want a whole family of them!"

For the next few miles, I giggled at the thought of owning my own pack of rodents, and I might have turned around if I could have found a way to carry them. No wonder I was on my third day of roaming through Arkansas. Sooner or later I was going to have to focus on getting back, if only for my dogs. The last time I spoke to Lynn, she held the phone out to them, and I swear they said they missed me.

"Go home," I muttered, watching the sun begin its afternoon descent. "Go home," I said, a little more forcefully, remembering how neighborhood mothers and fathers used to shoo me toward my house at suppertime. "It's late, sweetheart. Go home. Your parents will be worried."

As a child, I didn't know how to tell them that my absence at the dinner table could easily go unnoticed. I was lost in the cross fire of my sisters' dialogue about boys and prom dresses, puzzled by my parents' talk about finances and board meetings, and always eager to run next door to another family that at least noticed I was there.

Was that why I bought this motorcycle . . . to get some attention? And was that why I chose a Harley . . . to make more noise? No doubt, *I* was the one people heard coming now, and *I* was the one who earned a wide berth on the road. It was *me* who kids waved at from backseats, who husbands looked at with envy, and who wives pretended not to notice. Even out of the saddle, *I* was the one who sparked curiosity when I entered a room. Certainly no one shooed me away or told me to go home. For the first time in a great while, I was getting some recognition, and I loved it.

Leaving Highway 71 and passing by the gallows of Isaac C. Parker, the "Hanging Judge" of Fort Smith, I was now cruising on Interstate 40 and buzzing through eastern Oklahoma. So what if my life had capsized— I was on a fucking Harley about two hours away from linking up to Route 66. I could be whoever I wanted to be, and so I morphed into Dylan and Kerouac, feeling cool as hell.

"Well, I see you got your brand new leopard-skin pill-box hat!" I sang out like a lunatic. *"Well, you must tell me, baby, how your head feels under somethin' like that!"*

As I burned up Interstate 40, which in my mind was Dylan's Highway 61, my 2004 teal Sportster turned into Bob's 1964 red-and-silver Triumph. He'd wreck that bike somewhere in Woodstock, but for now his Tiger 100 was reassembled into vintage perfection, and even though it spat out less than half the horsepower of my ferocious Harley, Bob's bike was cool because it was his, and I was cool by proxy.

As I rode west, I wailed out a few more tracks from Dylan's album *Blonde on Blonde,* and then lapsed into a delicious silence as his Triumph vanished and my Harley reappeared beneath me. For the next few miles, I blissfully thought about nothing, and my head felt like it was decompressing with the freedom of a quiet mind. After a while, I pulled over and bungee-corded my helmet to my backrest so I could give my brain even more room to wing out, but the words of Bart Mange instantly flew in my face.

"I don't give a flying farm animal what the law says! *Always* wear your skid lid!"

Someone had asked if helmet laws varied around the world, and Bart exploded like a land mine. "If I hear you're bareheaded in *Zimbabwe,* I will find you and kill you!"

Bart claimed to have spies everywhere, but I felt so free with loose locks that I rode helmetless all the way into Oklahoma City. There I planned to see the memorial dedicated to victims of the 1995 Federal Building bombing. But first, I wanted to keep a promise I'd made to AAA Lester, so I veered off at exit 153 and headed to the National Cowboy & Western Heritage Museum.

"If you miss that place, you might as well quit calling yourself an

American," he told me. "I don't believe in all that past-lives stuff, but I swear I was a Cherokee warrior once. Promise me you'll check it out."

"It's only a museum, right? I mean, what's in there, scalps?"

Lester handed me a brochure. "*Reality* is in there—American history we'd like to forget. If you don't shed a tear when you see the statue in the entryway, then you're probably made of plaster yourself."

I promised him on the spot, but by then I'd already made a few promises I never intended to keep—like call my niece every day once I got off the road, and check in with Lynn now and then to tell her I was alive. In fact, I rarely used my phone for anything but navigation, but Lester had made such a compelling case about that statue, I parked my bike in the museum's free lot and headed in, prepared to be underwhelmed.

Instead I understood why the old guy had gotten so emotional, and I also realized the real reason I needed to stop at this museum. It was time to be reminded of grief greater than my own. Oklahoma City was where almost an entire nation of people had been herded like animals. It marked the end of the infamous death march known as the Trail of Tears, during which a fifth of the Cherokee nation was wiped out.

Like most American children, I grew up streaking my face with "Injun" war paint. I banged on toy drums and danced around trying to make it rain. But my play had been influenced by television, not by anything I'd read in a history book. While I'm sure my teachers must have mentioned Andrew Jackson's Indian Removal Act, I can only remember how Indians were always depicted as savages.

But now as I looked up at James Earle Fraser's eighteen-foot sculpture, called *End of the Trail*, I saw the real victims of the war between the United States and the Indian Nation. Fraser's depiction wasn't of a proud Native American warrior, but of a man and his people in total defeat. Everything about the piece was cast downward—the man's eyes and the spear he held, even his horse's head was bowed in submission. It was a portrayal of a broken people, and I felt suffering so great it put my own sorrow into perspective. Lester had nailed what I felt with one word—*reality.*

Riveted by the sculpture, I finally managed to pull myself away and wander through a few of the museum's exhibits. But the cowboy pop culture was dwarfed by the scope of that single statue in the entryway. I did enjoy watching clips of old Westerns starring John Wayne and Ronald Reagan, and I got a kick out of seeing Annie Oakley's first water pistol, but after buying my own musket in Gettysburg, I was hardly impressed.

It was the Oklahoma City National Memorial I visited the next morning where I was really taken by surprise. There, with about twenty other visitors, I was led into a replica of a hearing room. The doors closed and the actual recording of a Water Resources Board meeting began with the stating of the date, April 19, 1995, and the time, nine a.m. About two minutes into the recording of the meeting's routine agenda, an enormous bomb blast went off, followed by breaking glass and screams, and instantly the lights went out. As I stood there in the dark stunned into silence with my fellow visitors, I realized that many of the people we had been listening to—first sounding bored and now screaming for their lives—were likely dead. Finally the lights came on and somehow the room was suddenly filled with photographs of those who had perished on that day at the hands of Timothy McVeigh and his accomplice, Terry Nichols.

The doors opened and we all walked into the rest of the museum, complete with television footage of first responders, interviews with survivors, and glass cases filled with everyday articles like briefcases, eyeglasses, and shoes found in the rubble. I was shaken by it all, just as I had been watching the coverage of Columbine and 9/11. Like the Oklahoma City bombing, those events captured people in the midst of ordinary days and in seconds ended their lives or changed them forever.

I walked around the field of 168 glass, bronze, and stone chairs that represented the people who had died, and stood by the reflecting pool, keeping my distance from a woman clutching a picture of a child and shaking with grief. As I stared into that thin sheet of clear water, I could almost see the child within me tugging on the adult trying to pull away. My evolution back to my life—back to *caring* about living it—was beginning.

In fact, it had all started the night before at the Holiday Inn when I called Lester to tell him that I understood why he had wanted me to see Fraser's statue. His first response was total disbelief that I'd called.

"You know I give my card to a lot of young travelers, and they all say they're going to call, but you're the first one who actually did it."

"I'm not young, Lester, but thanks."

He laughed. "You're young to me. Anyway, I just knew you'd appreciate suffering like that . . . being a Jew and all."

I didn't have a response to that so I ignored it. "The rest of the museum was pretty cool though, don't you think?"

"It's always been one of my favorite places. I tell everyone to go there. By the way, did you see the re-creation of that turn-of-the-century cattle town?"

"No, I'll probably go back tomorrow," I lied. "I could explore that place all day."

"Make sure you see the Kit Carson gallery. Did you know he couldn't read or write, but he spoke Navajo, Apache, Comanche, Cheyenne, Arapaho, Blackfoot, Ute, Piute, Shoshone, *and* Crow? The man wasn't just a friend to the Indians, he married one."

"I can't believe you remember all that."

"I have a photographic memory. I can tell you what you wore the day we met."

I laughed. "I don't remember what I wore yesterday."

We talked awhile longer, and then I said I had to go scrounge up some dinner.

"I sure hope you're not eating pizza every night," he said. "I don't mean to be acting like your father, but you seem like a young lady who could use some parenting."

I told him I'd only had pizza one time and then hung up and ordered my seventh pie. I'm not sure what made me lie so much while I was on the road, but after I washed down my pizza with shots of Scotch and a bottle of club soda, I came to the conclusion that lying was my way of keeping people at a safe distance. Maybe I'd done that all my life, even with my own mother, and now that she was gone, it was time to give her a break and admit my part in the shortcomings of our relationship. In fact, if I didn't take too many more detours, I could make it home on the exact anniversary of her death, and then I could celebrate—not *mourn*—her. Maybe then, wherever she was, she'd feel a little closer to me, and I to her.

"Fuck sadness!" I said, tossing back a shot. "To the death of mourning!"

As I flopped on my bed, slightly buzzed and oddly happy, I decided to check my cell phone messages for the first time on the trip. None of my friends were too concerned about my not responding because they had no clue I was riding a Harley across America. The few who did find out had left messages encouraging me.

"*Insanity becomes you,*" said Carl. "*Wish my wife was as cool as you.*"

"*Lynn told me what you're up to,*" said Nancy. "*Get back safe so I can kill you.*"

"*You don't call, you don't write?*" said Annie. "*I hate you.*"

My sisters had all left messages too—mostly just comments about how I was worrying the hell out of them—and my niece had left word that my sisters were driving her crazy. I knew I should call everyone back, but I was feeling too peaceful to listen to anyone's angst, so I decided not to return any messages until I got home, and only to answer calls from Lynn in case my dogs needed anything. Of course, I had to pick up if one of the

Daves called. They'd threatened to organize a search party if I didn't stay in contact.

"You drop below our radar, and my buddy in the FBI will throw a net over the entire country," said Shaggy Blond. "Don't you underestimate me. I've got connections."

"Fuck the Feds," said Rolling Stone. "I'll come find you myself."

Twenty-seven

The Mother Road

———————

I **woke up knowing** the night before had been important, but I couldn't recall why. Then I saw the hotel stationery with my scribbled handwriting on it: *There is no reverse on a motorcycle.*

Slowly something was dawning on me, shaking me awake. I felt it pushing me out of bed, and though I was still sore as usual, I was also giddy with epiphany. I'd finally decided to grab reality by the horns and wrestle my life into submission. No more dwelling on what I couldn't change, no more avoidance of what was ahead. I was going to hit my reset button and reactivate my life . . . after aspirin and food.

I was on the road by nine and by noon the state of Oklahoma was well behind me. Soon I found myself deep into the Texas Panhandle, which was really a frying pan. The scorching sun bouncing off the asphalt and filtering through my hot engine made me wonder why my tires weren't melting. The Scotch, the sand, the wind, and the heat—all of it made me feel like I was riding inside a hair dryer. I had hooked up to the historic Route 66 where it bisected Interstate 40 almost three hundred miles ago, and while at first I was definitely "getting my kicks" from the famous highway, now it was kicking me.

I pulled over to consult my *H.O.G. Touring Handbook* for the closest town, and decided that given the choice between McLean, Texas, and purgatory, I probably wouldn't know the difference. Hell, in fact, might have been more interesting, but McLean was at least on the map, so I scooted off at exit 146 and went straight to the Red River Steakhouse.

Since I planned to have dinner in Amarillo, less than two hours away, I decided an appetizer would be enough, so I ordered Texas Toothpicks because I liked the name. The waitress delivered a nifty collection of beer-battered jalapeños and onions. It was a zesty little snack that might have blown my head off if it weren't for the dipping sauce called Red Mud, good enough to drink straight from the bottle and conveniently packed for mailing home. I sent a few bottles to myself, and one to each of my sisters, and then I walked over to see the enormous balls of barbed wire my waitress said I shouldn't miss.

Sure enough, in front of the Devil's Rope Museum were two gigantic wads of prickly metal cable with a sign, TRIBUTE TO BARBED WIRE, below them. Since I'd yet to honor any kind of wire, I went inside to pay my respects. There, staring at *fence wire* used to corral animals and *war wire* used to imprison people, I was captivated. So when the man next to me drawled, "You sure can get hooked on this stuff," I had to agree.

"Who'd a thunk it?" I grinned. "Suddenly I feel like crawling on my belly."

He tugged on one side of his horseshoe mustache and then the other. "Do you know what happened to the cow that jumped over the barbed-wire fence?" His eyes twinkled. "Udder disaster."

"Ugh . . . I'm going to start singing 'Don't Fence Me In' if we don't quit this."

We both laughed, exchanging puns until we ran out, and then he pointed to a copy of the *Barbed Wire Identification Encyclopedia*. "Buddy of mine just bought a ranch in Abilene. You think that book would make a nice ranch-warming gift?"

I saw the thirty-two-dollar price tag. "Hmm, back in El Paso, you can buy a steer skull for less. This town has to have one."

"That your home, El Paso?"

I was jarred for a moment. I'd lived in Los Angeles for more than a dozen years and only got to El Paso on holidays. I wasn't even planning to stop there this trip.

"Yup," I said. "Born and raised."

He looked me over. "You sure you're not one of them San Francisco types?"

I knew what he meant. "Nope, I'm Texan head to toe, except now I live in L.A."

"So the truth comes out." He stared at my breasts. "How 'bout I buy you a beer?"

"Thanks, but the truth is I am one of those *types* you were talking about."

"Really?" He ran his fingers over his mustache. "Well, you're a fine-looking one."

"Why, thank you, and I'd take you up on that beer if I didn't have to hit the road."

"Going to see your folks in El Paso, are you?"

It was odd to hear myself say the truth out loud. "No, both my parents are gone."

He expressed his condolences and we soon went our separate ways—he probably to find a woman straighter than I; and me, off to embrace the bend in the road.

The West Coast was practically magnetic now, drawing me home no matter how many interesting sights threatened to distract me. Still, I couldn't help but be lured off track now and then by oddities like the hundred-ninety-foot cross clearly visible twenty miles off Route 66 in a tiny Texas town called Groom. Since I needed to give my knees a break, I figured I couldn't pass up the chance to see 1,250 tons of religion.

"That is the biggest damn cross I've ever seen." A skinny young man hugged a skinnier girl as they gazed up at the nineteen-story structure. "Just *makes* you want to sin, doesn't it?"

"Jesus, Jonathan!" She wriggled from his grasp. "You're going to get us killed."

The boy crossed himself. "Sorry, God. Just kidding. Please don't strike us dead."

"I wasn't talking about *God*." The girl looked around at several people on their knees. "There are some serious believers here." She turned to me. "I am *so* sorry, ma'am. My boyfriend thinks he's funny, but he's not."

At first I was embarrassed to have been caught eavesdropping, then upset that she'd called me ma'am. Then I realized she thought I was there for religious reasons and had to laugh. "Oh, you don't have to worry about me. I don't believe in anything."

Someone behind all three of us let out a deep sigh. "I'm sorry to hear that."

We all turned around to find a combination of Moses, Santa Claus, and a little old Jewish man wrapped up in one. He had his eyes cast upward at the mammoth cross, and when he got our attention he looked at us and frowned. "I know it's none of my business, but I couldn't help overhearing you and it makes me kind of sad."

"Doesn't that beanie you're wearing mean you're Jewish?" asked the boy. "I mean, what are *you* doing here?"

Santa Moses winked at me. "Who can pass up a cross on Route 66? The question is, why are *you* here?"

"You talking to me?" I asked.

"Don't be silly. I know why you're here. I'm talking to these two young people."

The boy started to speak, but I jumped in. "Hang on. I want to know why this guy thinks he knows so much about me."

"*This* guy is Rabbi Jerry." He lifted his yarmulke and settled it back on his head. "Anyway, I'm certainly not Solomon the Wise, but even I know a thing or two. You're here because you *do* believe in something. You just don't know what."

I hugged my helmet to my chest. "I stopped here out of curiosity, that's all."

"*Ahh*, so I'm right."

"And, that's our cue to get outta here." The boy took his girlfriend's hand and started to walk away, but she pulled him back.

"Wait a minute. This man asked why we're here, and I want to tell him."

"Oh, jeez." The boy rolled his eyes. "Here we go."

"Let her talk," I said, and then I turned to the old man. "Unless Nostradamus here already knows what she's going to say."

He shrugged. "I said I knew a thing or two, not three or four."

At the mention of Nostradamus a few people gathered around and the girl looked ready to bolt. Then she gathered herself and looked angrily at her boyfriend. "Tell them why we're here, Jonathan."

He rolled his eyes. "You're the one who wanted to stop. Crosses creep me out."

She frowned at him. "*Tell* them, Jonathan."

I looked at the boy, his hands shoved in his jeans. He couldn't be more than nineteen. "I don't think Jonathan wants to talk."

"Damn right." The boy gave his girlfriend a kiss, then walked away. "When you're through telling strangers our life story, I'll be in the car."

The girl's eyes welled with tears. "Nothing's been the same since I got pregnant. I'm already a few weeks along, and I'm excited to be a mom, but . . ."

I looked over toward Jonathan in the car. "But he's not so excited to be a dad?"

"Oh, no. We both want the baby, and we're going to get married. It's just that our parents, they—"

The rabbi put up his hand. "Don't tell me. They're against it. I'll bet they don't even know you're pregnant, right?"

Her mouth dropped open. "How did you know?"

"You were knocked up by a boy who stomps off like a child." He shook his head. "If your parents do know, they shouldn't be parents."

I rolled my eyes. "Oh, now that's the right thing to say." I cocked my head toward the girl's future groom. He was drumming on the steering wheel, either listening to music or more pissed off than I thought he was. "So tell me, why's your boyfriend so upset?"

"Oh, he wanted to drive straight to Las Vegas, but I wanted to make this into a pre-honeymoon trip—you know, see some of the country before the baby arrives. Neither of us has ever been out of Nebraska—the *only* state in the whole country where you have to be nineteen to get married." She shrugged. "Anyway, we were heading to the Alamo and this cross just appeared out of nowhere. It was like a sign, and I thought maybe we could get some kind of blessing."

"I see . . . Couldn't get your parents' blessing, so you ran away, right?" The old man pulled out his cell phone. "I ought to call the police."

The girl's face went ashen, and motherly instincts I never knew I had rose within me. I threw my arms around her and told Rabbi Jerry to back off. "You are *not* helping."

After that I had no clue what to say, so I held the girl at arm's length and looked her in the eyes. "Does *anyone* know where you are?"

She shrugged. "We told a couple of friends."

"But your parents don't know a thing." Rabbi Jerry held out his phone. "Now's your chance to call them."

"I'm turning eighteen tomorrow. You don't need a blood test in Las Vegas *or* parental approval if you're eighteen." The girl's cheeks flushed with defiance. "Jonathan was right. You can't trust anybody."

She turned away and briskly walked off, leaving the old man and me staring after her, helpless as a couple of Jews in the shadow of a giant cross.

All the way to Amarillo I thought of that poor girl, so young to get married, a child having a child. I thought of Jonathan too, wondering what he really thought about marriage and being a dad. As for the rabbi and me, well, we discussed calling the police, decided there was no point to it, and then got to know each other. It turned out he was from the Midwest, and had been kicked out of his congregation for cheating on his wife.

"I was a bad boy." He grinned sheepishly. "But you're no saint either, are you?"

I smiled at my new pal. "You got that right."

"So what are you doing on *that* thing?" He cocked his head toward my bike. "You part of a girl gang?"

Left with the perfect opportunity to launch into whatever story I liked, I couldn't believe it when I laid out the truth. "I'm not part of anything."

"Sure you are. Why, you're part of Americana just by riding the Mother Road."

"The *what*?" My knees went weak. "Did you say the *Mother* Road?"

"Yeah, that's what they call Route 66."

"Now that you mention it, I think I knew that on some level." I almost started to tell him about my mother and about how ever since I'd hooked up to this highway I'd felt a need to cling to it. "That sure is a coincidence."

"I know what you mean—that girl we just met." He shook his head. "She has no business becoming a mother at her age."

"I don't want to talk about her. I'll get upset again." I held out my hand for him to shake. "Listen, Jerry, it was nice to meet you, but I gotta fly."

He raised his eyebrows. "Another coincidence?"

"What do you mean?"

"You've read *The Grapes of Wrath*, right? Well, it was John Steinbeck who dubbed Route 66 the Mother Road. Do you know what else he called it?"

"What? The road to barbed wire?"

He grinned. "I see you stopped in McLean. Anyway, he also called Route 66 the Road of Flight. Fits those runaway kids, not to mention you." He pointed toward his Volvo. "I've got the book in my car. I just finished it. You can have it if you like."

I thought about strangers luring kids to their cars with puppies. "Thanks, I'm just gonna take off." I offered my hand again.

Jerry gave me a hug instead, and then pulled off his yarmulke. "I don't know why I still wear this. I lost my religious way a long time ago." He handed it to me. "Here, need a nice coaster?"

I laughed, took the skullcap, and shoved it into my jeans next to my father's ring. Then I left the fallen rabbi standing under the cross, climbed onto my Harley, and hugged the road all the way into Amarillo.

Twenty-eight

Gluttony, Violence, and Art

———

The final sunset in *Indiana Jones and the Last Crusade* was filmed there, and Georgia O'Keeffe taught art in public schools there, but other than that, Amarillo is known for one thing—the free seventy-two-ounce steak at the Big Texan Steak Ranch. As I rode into town, I wasn't hungry, but after passing dozens of billboards advertising the place, I wasn't just a woman on a motorcycle, I was a carnivore salivating for charbroiled beef.

Dating back to 1960, the idea of offering a four-thousand-calorie slab of sirloin *free* to anyone who could eat the whole thing came to the Big Texan owner, Bob Lee, when a local cowboy walked into his restaurant and claimed he was hungry enough to "eat the whole darned cow." That's when Lee decided to feed the man steak after steak until seventy-two ounces later, the cowboy finally quit. Today you have to eat the super-sized steak in an hour or less. You also have to polish off a baked potato, beans, a dinner roll, a salad, and a shrimp cocktail. Failure means not only an upset stomach, but also a check for seventy-two dollars.

When I strolled into the Big Texan, I wasn't even going to try the steak challenge, but I did hope to catch some idiot going for it. I flagged down a waitress racing by with a bucket of beer and asked her if anyone was vying for the free meal.

"Stick around." She threw a menu at me. "Gluttony is guaranteed."

She dumped her beer at a table full of drunks, then in the middle of her U-turn back to me she stopped and yelled across the room, "Somebody better handle that puke situation. We're just *asking* for a lawsuit!"

Now standing at my table, her pen poised over her order pad, she stretched a tired smile across her face. "Just another night in the pigpen. So, what'll it be, honeybee?"

"I'm just going to have a petite filet and some cabernet. No sides."

"No *sides*?" She popped her gum. "What's the matter with you?"

"Nothing. I'd just like to fit into my jeans tomorrow."

"Suit yourself, skinny minny. How'd you like your steak—still mooing, like shoe leather, or somewhere in between?"

"In between but closer to mooing."

"Still bleeding then." She wiped up some goo on my table. "Sorry for the slobber. How about a free taste of fried rattlesnake to make up for the mess?"

"Damn, I had that yesterday."

She didn't crack a smile. "Yes or no?"

"Sure, why not?"

She shrugged. "Reptiles are a delicacy, but some don't like swallowing scales."

She took off and a plateful of snake arrived in seconds. After some serious chews I got a bite to slither down my throat. It was like eating a flavored extension cord.

I flagged down a busboy. "Listen, this snake is—"

"Gross, I know." He whisked the rattler away. "We should serve it in a trash can."

As he took off snickering, the room erupted in cheers. A bald guy in uniform and a scrawny kid had climbed onto the challenge platform and donned bibs.

"You can do it, Isaac!" someone shouted at the boy. "Pace yourself, son!"

"Chuck-*ee*!" a bunch of army guys chanted. "Chuck-*ee*!"

Forty-five minutes later, I'd finished my meal and Chucky was upchucking in a bread basket. Since vomiting disqualifies a contestant, it was up to Isaac, who was still going strong. The crowd was on its feet, and so was I.

"Go, Isaac, go!" we all screamed. "Eat, Isaac, eat!"

But with twenty-six ounces of steak to go and fifty-six seconds on the clock, Isaac was history. Still, he stuffed his face, and as he turned green, so did I with half my filet on my plate.

My waitress flew by and threw down my check. "My gerbil eats more than you."

I watched Isaac staggering by covered in food. "How can you stand it here?"

"I turned vegetarian years ago." She shrugged. "Besides, drunks tip big."

She'd called me skinny and given me free snake, so I tipped her big too. Then I bought a scorpion sealed in Lucite in the gift shop and waited for the free shuttle to take me back to my motel. It was a white limo with a longhorn tied to the grille, and as soon as I climbed into the cracked leather backseat, I felt sick all over again.

"It smells a little funky in here," I said. "Something die?"

"Sorry, the fellow I just dropped off stepped in horseshit." He looked over his shoulder. "A stick of spearmint gum might take the edge off. Want some?"

"It's okay. My motel is just up the road. It's the one with the Texas-shaped pool."

He laughed. "Half the pools in Amarillo are shaped like that." He pulled into the gravel lot of the Sleepy Palomino, and I scrambled out.

"Thanks for the lift." I handed him five bucks and wrinkled my nose. "You know, I grew up around horses and it sure doesn't smell like—"

He threw his hands in the air. "Okay, ya got me. I've got a dead body in the trunk." He tossed me a devilish grin and stepped on the gas.

Pretty sure he was telling the truth, I ambled toward my motel room while a yawning neon horse flickered on and off overhead. Exhausted from riding and cheering on gluttony, I crashed into a deep sleep. But just a few hours later, I bolted upright in bed. Something—like a body—had slammed against the wall.

"What the fuck?" Then came another thud, followed by a scream. I dialed 911.

"I'm at the Sleepy Palomino, room 118," I whispered. "Someone is getting beaten up in the room next to mine."

"I'm sorry, ma'am, you'll have to speak up."

"I *can't* talk any louder," I rasped. "I don't want them to hear me next door."

The operator must have understood me, because within ten minutes I saw flashing lights through my drapes. I put on some clothes and waited, expecting to hear the police busting into the room next to mine, but instead they banged on *my* door, announcing themselves loud enough for wife beaters across town to hear.

I cracked the door as far as the latch would allow and saw two cops whose ages combined didn't equal mine. "I said it was *next* door!"

"We listened on either side of you," one officer said. "There weren't any signs of trouble. Would you mind if we came in for a moment?"

"Why? I'm not the one getting beaten up—at least not yet."

The policemen exchanged glances. "What do you mean by that?" The taller one frowned at me. "Are you protecting someone in there?"

254

"Yes!" I cried. *"Me!"*

"Could you let us in?" his partner asked. "We just want to see you're okay."

"Fine, give the guy next door time to hide the body." I removed the latch and waved the men inside. "By the way, I'll be the one in the Dumpster tomorrow."

They stepped inside and made their way around an explosion of leather as they inspected my bathroom and closet. "Do you ride?" one of them asked.

"No, I'm a dominatrix. Of course I ride!" I pointed to my helmet. "What do you think that's for—*bowling*?"

"So that Harley outside—it's yours?" the other asked. "She's a beauty."

I couldn't believe we were talking about my bike. Still, it was gorgeous. Who could blame them? "Yeah, it's mine." I tried to stifle my pride. "You really should check the room to the left of me. I swear something awful is going on."

I finally convinced them to have a look, and while they were next door, I stood with my ear to the wall trying to eavesdrop, but all I could hear was a lot of mumbling. A few minutes later, the officers stepped outside and were apologizing.

"No problem," the batterer said. "You were just doing your job."

"Really, I'm fine." The victim laughed. "Those bathtubs are *very* slippery."

As I heard the door close, I hoped the officers wouldn't incriminate me by coming back to report their findings, and luckily they just drove off. I figured it was only a matter of time before the guy next door came after me, so I packed up to make a fast getaway.

Lying on my bed in full motorcycle gear, I waited for sunrise, and the next thing I knew it was ten-thirty and the maid was vacuuming next door. I popped my head inside.

"*¡Ah, dios mio! Me espantó!*" She clutched her heart. "*¿Se olvidó algo?*"

"*Perdón, pero creo que dejé mis llaves.*"

She smiled and then spoke in perfect English. "They're in your pocket."

I looked down and saw my keys poking out of my jeans, so I told her everything and then asked if I could look around.

"Go ahead, but I haven't seen anything unusual." She dumped the trash can into a large plastic bag, then pulled out a crumpled page from a phone book. "What about this?"

"Wow." I scanned the page. "It's a list of women's shelters in the area."

I raced to the office, and when I told the guy behind the desk what had happened, he just yawned. "I got here at five this morning. What was it this time? Drugs or alcohol?"

I showed him the page from the phone book. "The maid found this."

He shrugged. "All that page proves is that the world is screwed up."

I wanted to kill him. "Would you look up who stayed in that room? I'm calling the police again, and I'd like to give them a name."

"Come on, lady. Would you want me to give out your personal information?"

"I would if it saved my life."

"Look, I can't give out any names, but I'll call the police myself, okay?" The clerk offered a half-baked smile. "I promise."

But as I headed out of Amarillo, I wished I could have done more. Why hadn't I written down the license plate numbers of the cars next to my bike? If the couple were headed west, I might spot them at a gas station or a restaurant. Then I could pull the woman aside to ask if she needed help. It didn't matter that I hadn't seen either of them. I would know who they were. He'd be the one looking relaxed and in control, and she'd be the nervous wreck beside him.

I know how it feels to be hit. The pain is staggering, probably because you don't expect it, mostly because you can't believe it. When it happened to me, I just stood there. After the first blow you'd think I'd have covered my face; certainly after the second and third, you'd think I'd have cowered. But I just stood there, numb with shock. I *knew* this man. I *loved* this man . . . and he loved me. It was as though his mind had snapped and my brain had powered down. We both stood there for a moment dumbfounded, and then I took off.

Later, when he saw the bruising and welts on my face, he was unable to speak. Finally, he burst into tears, and though a large man, he looked very small as he begged for my forgiveness.

At the time when he hit me, I had wanted to fight back, to pummel him with my fists or at least spit in his face. But the power I felt the next day telling him that if he ever hit me again, he would never see me again was much more satisfying. Even more empowering, however, was when he did raise his fist to strike me again, only to cower back before releasing a blow, stopped by the strength of my glare.

Maybe that was why I was having so much trouble letting go of what had happened at the motel. I knew how hard it was to find my own power, and I wanted to help this woman find hers. In my heart, though, I knew what was really bothering me was that smug clerk's indifference.

While I, too, have been cynical throughout much of my life, my losses and this ride were bringing me out of that heartless place. Even now as I rode out of Amarillo, I made no jokes about the nothingness around me, and I could see, and *feel* the beauty of the naked desert. There was potential in this dusty Texan landscape, room for growth out here in the middle of nowhere . . . and ten vintage Cadillacs buried nose-down in the dirt?

At first it looked like a hallucination, a mirage solely for travelers thirsting for something interesting to spring from the desiccated earth. But there was no denying it—out in the middle of a barren cow pasture was an unusual art installation—ten upended 1949 to 1963 Cadillacs. It was a tribute to the tail fin, the epitome of creative expression, and to my mind, some road whimsy I had to check out.

Funded by millionaire Stanley Marsh 3, who didn't use the Roman numeral III because he thought it was pretentious, *Cadillac Ranch* was created in 1974 by a group of artists who called themselves Ant Farm. For me their installation was the perfect mood-changer, the artistic antidote to that hotel clerk's blasé attitude. Even from the highway, it looked amazing, but like other curious travelers wandering around the pasture, I had to see the Caddies up close.

I pulled onto the shoulder and walked past a sign that read NO GRAF-FITI, toward at least a dozen people defacing fenders and tail fins with spray paint. One vandal, a teenage girl, was christening the windshield of a 1963 Sedan de Ville with a dripping red heart.

"Do you have any paint?" She shook an aerosol can as if her life depended on it. "I ran out after I wrote my boyfriend's name and I *need* to write mine."

I was afraid she'd start crying, until a guy in a tie-dyed vest with a salt-and-pepper ponytail threw a can to her, then offered one to me.

"Care to break the law?" he asked. "Vandalism is kind of encouraged out here."

I took the can. "Cool. If you don't count speeding, I haven't broken the law since I slipped a donut over a soldier's rifle in front of the Pentagon."

"You're lucky he didn't shoot you."

I shrugged. "Well, he was a statue."

"Okay, then. Pick a car and have at it."

I shook the can and then sprayed my artistic contribution to the underside of a 1949 Club Sedan.

"*BS?*" Mr. Ponytail looked at my boring artwork. "Not too original, are you?"

"Those are my initials—I'm Barbara Schoichet." I handed him back his can. "My middle name is Mae, so that kind of makes it worse."

"I drew a peace sign and a dove." He shrugged and waved his ponytail at me. "Most people made it out of the sixties. Guess I got stuck."

I studied some of the graffiti around me. There was the usual profanity and several body parts, but mostly people just swirled designs, scrawled important dates, and proclaimed they ♥ed someone.

"All you need is love," I sang. *"Love is all you need."*

He shrugged. *"All we are saying is give peace a chance."*

I thought of the night before. "The world can be a pretty messed-up place, but at least there are still some people drawing doves and singing the Beatles."

He swept his arm toward the nose-down Cadillacs—all once state-of-the-art automotive designs, and now junkers turned into creative expression. "It's hard to think about anything bad in the presence of this." He laughed. "Genius kicks Evil's ass again!"

I thought about Hitler and Lex Luthor. "Yeah, usually the Dark Side loses."

"I know what you're thinking. There's a lot of very smart, terribly fucked up people out there." He nonchalantly sprayed *RIP* on a fender. "So Barbara—or should I call you Phaedrus—what brings you to this humble cow pasture?"

"Phaedrus?"

He pointed to my motorcycle. "Well, you're traveling on that gorgeous hunk of machinery and at least *I* feel like we're having a karmic moment."

I smiled. "I assume you're referring to *Zen and the Art of Motorcycle Maintenance*. I'm always amazed at how many people have read that book."

He rapped on a nearby tail fin. *"The truth knocks on the door, and you say, 'Go away, I'm looking for the truth.' And so it goes away."* He grinned. "Chapter One."

"I'm impressed."

"Don't be. I'm one of those space cadets who read it three times."

"Twice for me." I picked up a rock and studied it as though it held the answers to all things. "It's weird. I'm on a trip so much like the one Robert Pirsig took—except for the going-crazy part—but this is the first time his book has entered my consciousness."

"Wow, you must be unconscious then." He laughed. "Well, just leave it to an old hippie to bring it to your attention." Suddenly his good humor vanished. "I wish I was out here for the same reason you are. I'm just a baby boomer from New York who flew out yesterday to buy some cheap land."

"And why *do* you suppose I'm here?"

He shrugged. "Maybe the truth came knocking?"

Mr. Ponytail looked like the kind of guy who might start quoting whole paragraphs from all kinds of books, so I told him I had a highway to catch and headed off through the cow pasture to my bike.

"Hey, Barbara!" he called after me. "Stay conscious, all right?"

I waved over my shoulder without looking back, and then I realized something. I'd told him my name but never got his. It was peculiar how so many people on this trip seemed to care about me when I volunteered so little. Except for giving a few basics to the Daves, I rarely talked about my life, and yet here I was readily coughing up my arrest record to this stranger without even thinking. I was definitely coming back to my old self—maybe to a new and improved one—and I wondered if it was time to revisit where I came from—El Paso. Up until now I'd seen no reason to go back to the lazy border town, especially since I was afraid I'd feel nothing but my parents' absence. Still, my sister was there, so I dug out my *H.O.G. Touring Handbook* to see how far off course I'd have to go.

But as soon as I saw that El Paso would add four hours of ride time to my trip, and realized that Harriet would probably make me stay a few days, I decided against it. Even though I still had nothing waiting for me in Los Angeles, I was ready to be there, and in my heart I knew El Paso wasn't the detour I needed to make. It was Santa Fe.

Twenty-nine

The Last Detour

Back in the 1980s, when I was still denying my sexuality, I lived in Santa Fe, going out with a handful of guys, but usually sleeping with women. One was a sexy waitress named Polly, whose boyfriend threatened to kill me. One was a friend named Maria, whose girlfriend almost strangled me. Most were very nice people, except a poet named Blanca, whose crack dealer nearly shot me. He looked like Fagin from *Oliver Twist* and I wouldn't have let him into the house if he hadn't walked right in.

"Blanca said you'd let me keep this at your place." He set a briefcase on my kitchen table. "It's only for a few days."

"What's in it?" I asked, not knowing Blanca's drug history at the time.

The guy didn't even have to look sinister, he simply was. "Just a little candy." He smiled crookedly and popped open the case. "You can have some for your trouble."

I never really thought about how eyes can actually pop out of your head until mine did. I was looking at a huge pile of little white packets . . . with a gun resting on top.

"Get out," I said. "Get out or I'll call the police."

He grabbed the gun and snapped the briefcase closed. "You're Blanca's friend, so I'm just going to leave quietly." He backed toward the door with the gun at his side. "I guess she was wrong about you."

I swallowed hard. "I guess she was."

I never saw Blanca again, and I hope I never will, but I had to revisit Santa Fe. Even though a detour there would add hours to my trip, Santa Fe held the promise of running into Mai, a Navajo woman with whom I never connected, but always wanted to. We'd met at Color Me Purple, a gay bar I tried not to frequent, but nevertheless wound up dropping by most weekends. She was sitting at the bar and I noticed her immediately. It was summer and she was the only one there wearing mukluks.

I sat next to her and ordered a glass of wine, and before I had a chance to introduce myself she said, "My mother hates you."

"How's that?" I raised an eyebrow. "I've never met your mother."

"My mother hates any woman I like—it could never be *my* fault I might be gay."

She had dark brown hair tied back in a ponytail. Her John Lennon glasses were adorable and her suede mukluks were hot in every sense of the word. "So you're not gay . . . you just *might* be?"

"Yup." She nodded to the bartender and ordered a Johnnie Walker Black with a Rolling Rock chaser. "I just *might* have to give in to it."

I wanted to ask why she was wearing such heavy boots in July, but instead commented on her drinks as soon as they arrived.

"You'd have to carry me out of here if I drank that." I raised my merlot to her whiskey and beer. "Put your keys on the bar now or I might have to frisk you later."

"No worries. This is all I'm having." She tossed back her shot, then took a sip of beer. "I need liquid courage if I'm going to ask you to dance."

I wondered if the shiver she sent through me was visible. "What if I asked you?"

"I might need another shot. I haven't quite accepted this new *thing* I'm into."

"This *thing* you're talking about, does it involve a detour you hadn't planned?"

"Uh-huh." She grinned. "Maybe someday I'll let you be my detour guide."

Just then, Marvin Gaye's "Sexual Healing" began to play, so I cocked my head toward the dance floor. "It's risky to start with a slow one, but I'm willing if you are."

As it turned out, Mai was an awful dancer, and by the time the song was over, she'd crushed two of my toes. I limped back to my stool, thinking she was behind me, but she'd walked out of the bar, leaving me alone and disappointed as hell.

A few minutes later she tapped me on the shoulder. "If I promise not to maim you, can we try that again?" She showed me her sneakers. "See, no more weapons."

I laughed. "What happened? Your feet start to melt?"

"No, I shouldn't have worn those boots. My family makes them. We own a leather shop in town."

"So you were advertising." I grinned. "Maybe I'll buy a pair next time it snows."

We had another round of drinks, and when Tina Turner's "What's Love Got to Do with It" began playing, Mai led me onto the dance floor.

"Careful now." I put my arms around her waist. "I've only got eight toes left."

"Shut up." She placed her hand over my heart. "I could still hurt you."

I held this feisty brunette at arm's length to get a good look, then pulled her in close, and we danced like that for the next two songs. At the end of the evening we exchanged phone numbers, but we never called each other, and she never introduced me to her mother. Shortly after we met, I started getting threatening calls from a guy down the street, so I moved out of my apartment in the middle of the night to my friend Terri's house, and started learning self-defense from a wise sensei. It wasn't long before Terri became my lover and I talked her into moving with me to Denver where I'd been accepted into a PhD program. She didn't want to leave Santa Fe and she shouldn't have—only a few months after we moved, I met Joanne, who I was sure was the love of my life, and Terri was history.

I got what I deserved though. Six years later, good and hooked and ready to settle down, I asked Joanne if she would consider adopting a baby. But she wasn't anywhere near where I was in the relationship, and quickly became unsettled. That's when she spat out my heart like a cherry pit, and I ran off to Los Angeles with no doctorate, and found nothing but trouble awaiting me.

And Mai, well, even though her phone number probably got washed with my jeans, and my miserable love life twisted around until it finally disintegrated, I never forgot her. She became my Cinderella fantasy—the relationship I always imagined would have been perfect if it had ever actually happened. But finding perfection in one person, as many therapists have tried to tell me, is impossible. It's like trying to locate wet pieces of paper in a washing machine and then reassembling them. It's like discovering a single suede mukluk on your doorstep.

It had been more than twenty years since I left Santa Fe, around the time when Coca-Cola changed its successful formula and introduced New Coke, a product that bombed about three months later and was taken off the market. Also that spring, President Ronald Reagan went to Germany to lay a wreath at a cemetery in Bitburg where forty-nine Waffen-SS soldiers were buried. Many thought his actions were insensitive, and some thought the president, who later succumbed to Alzheimer's, had lost his

mind, especially when he fueled the controversy by saying he believed the
SS soldiers "were victims, just as surely as the victims in the concentration
camps."

The trip, a huge fiasco, gave rise to protests, and the Ramones, an
American punk rock group, had an instant hit on their hands—"Bonzo
Goes to Bitburg." The song gave voice to Reagan dissenters around the
world, and when it was rereleased a year later with a new title, "My Brain
Is Hanging Upside Down," I truly related to it. As it turned out, my depar-
ture from Santa Fe, and my time in Denver, were disasters as well. In fact,
I still get a bad taste in my mouth when I think of how my life might have
ended right-side up if I hadn't made such poor choices. Then again, maybe
Mai just dodged a bullet.

But now, leaving caution in my wake and hoping I was less toxic, I
was speeding right toward her, intent on recapturing a flirtation that had
happened more than two decades ago. The past year had upended my life
in a big way, and I felt it was time to stop being a *luftmensch*, time to pull
my head out of the clouds and turn a far-fetched dream into an enchant-
ing reality . . . or finally let it go.

Spinning one romantic scenario after another about a woman I'd
known less than three hours, I flew down the highway, determined to
keep sensibility at bay. But just after I blasted through Tucumcari, level-
headed thoughts wormed their way into my head and I began reaching for
my handbrake. What if Mai had moved out of town? What if she didn't
even remember me? Six presidential terms had gone by, the Twin Towers
had fallen, a *lot* had happened. It was likely Mai hadn't given me a second
thought.

Still, I kept riding west, and when I hit Moriarty, a little more than an
hour outside of Santa Fe, I decided to find a Wi-Fi spot and locate her on
the Internet. Although I don't think she had ever given me her last name,

I remembered her telling me about her family's business. It was called Trickster Leather, and sometime around my third merlot, she had told me how her first name and the store were linked.

"I was always a little prankster when I was growing up," she said, tipping back her beer. "I drove my parents crazy—hiding from them until they were frantic, wearing my dresses backward, just basically living up to my name." She grinned. "Mai means 'coyote' in Navajo. It's a playful animal in Native American mythology, but also a rascal."

"Looks like we have something in common. Barbara means 'mischievous' in Spanish. I throw my parents a surprise or two myself."

"Anyway, coyotes have always held a prominent place in Navajo lore . . . but not always in a positive way." She laughed. "My parents named their shop after me. It's called Trickster Leather, and business has always been kind of up and down."

"I like you, Mai." I raised my glass. "Can I call you Coyote?"

"Not if you want me to answer you." She grinned, but it was more like a warning not to mess with her. "It's like calling me a mangy dog."

Now in Moriarty home to the annual Pinto Bean Fiesta—I Googled "Trickster Leather" only to find a bunch of sites that had nothing to do with a leather shop. Had I remembered the name wrong? I Googled gay bars in Santa Fe, and Color Me Purple was not among them. Deciding that if it was meant to be, I would find Mai, I jumped on my Harley and sped along Interstate 40 toward the girl of my dreams, paying as little attention as I could to the uncertainty that clung to my back.

Dreams have always been important to me—those I have in the night as well as those that enhance my day. They help me work out difficulties as I sleep, and lift me over impossible ruts as I work my way through life. One dream I had not long after my dad died often comes to mind when I'm troubled or indecisive, and sure enough, it popped into my head as I rode toward Santa Fe. It was a vivid dream, and it played out in my brain so often that sometimes I wondered if it actually happened even though I know it couldn't have—my family just wasn't that playful.

It takes place at the kitchen table in our Texas ranch house. I'm ten years old, and my sisters and parents look vibrant and full of color, while I look pale and transparent.

"Barbara looks worried," my mother says. "Let's play a game to make her problems go away." She produces six pieces of paper and six pens, and then turns to my dad. "Okay, Ben. You go first."

"I don't like games," he says. "I'm not playing."

"That's not setting a good example." My mother frowns. "Come on, Ben. Play."

"Fine, that's my biggest problem. I don't know how to play." He writes down *I'm too serious*, folds his piece of paper in half, and shoves it into the middle of the table.

"Good, I'll go next." My mother looks at my sisters and me. "My problem has to do with you girls. I'm afraid I never should have had kids."

We all start to protest, but she puts up her hand. "I'm serious. I've never hugged you enough, and I swear you would have had peanut butter and jelly sandwiches for every meal if I could've gotten away with it."

No one says a word, and my mother writes down *I've never tried hard enough*, then tosses her paper next to my dad's.

"Well, I think El Paso is my problem," Harriet says. "I'll never be anything but a small-town girl." She writes down *I'm too naïve*, and shoves her paper into the pile.

Naomi suddenly looks very uncomfortable. "I know everyone is going to laugh, but my biggest problem is self-confidence."

"Oh, please." Sandra rolls her eyes. "Everyone stops what they're doing when you walk into a room just to see how gorgeous you are."

"But no one thinks I have a brain!" Naomi cries. "I'm smart and I'm funny, and no one knows it." She scribbles down *I'm insecure*, then folds her paper into an exact square and places it in the exact center of the pile.

Sandra's eyes fill with tears. "My problem is that I say things I don't mean." She writes down *I'm misunderstood*, and quietly slides her paper in with the rest.

My mother looks around the table and smiles. "Well, I think we've made a lot of progress here. How about you, Barbara? What's your problem?"

I look at my family all looking at me. "I think I'll pass. Just pretend I'm not here."

"But you *are* here, honey." My dad lights up his cigar. "If I played, you can."

"I don't want to!" I crumple my paper into a ball, throw it into the pile, and sit there like a five-year-old.

"You're ruining the game," Harriet says. "We've all played, why can't you?"

"Yeah," says Naomi. "You think it was easy for me to admit I'm insecure?"

Everyone starts badgering me, until I can't take it anymore. "Look, I don't have a clue what my problem is."

My father bangs his fist on the table. "Case closed. *That's* your problem."

"Excellent!" my mother cries. "Now, let's finish the game. Everyone grab a problem. Ready . . . *go!*"

All at once everyone grabs a piece of paper, leaving my crumpled wad behind.

My mother shoots me a look of disappointment. "Fine, don't play."

As everyone reveals that they've chosen their own piece of paper, my father puts his arm around me. "Who wants someone else's problem, right? Of course we picked our own." He grabs my wad of paper and hands it to me. "You actually nailed it, kiddo."

And that is how the dream ends—my dad never explaining what he meant, and me wondering how in the hell I nailed it.

Throughout the years, I've had therapists offer lots of interpretations, but the best was that my father was congratulating my waking self, saying that by having the dream I had identified *all* of my problems in one fell swoop—I was too serious, I didn't try hard enough, I was naïve, I was insecure, and because I often said things I didn't mean, I was misunderstood.

And so I acknowledged that I was a basket case full of problems and moved on, taking my overthinking, negligent, immature, apprehensive, misjudged self toward an unsuspecting woman who possibly was no longer there. I felt like a nut, and although I wanted to get to Santa Fe and finally scratch this itch, I decided to prolong it just a tiny bit more by taking the scenic route—Highway 344, otherwise known as the Turquoise Trail. It was a longer, more reflective stretch of road, and it would give me the extra time I needed to accept that if I actually did find Mai, she might laugh in my face . . . or even more frightening, turn my fantasy into reality.

Thirty

Exposure Is the Enemy

————

I could blame it on the heat, but I hold Dr. Death and a guy wearing overalls responsible for my delay in getting to Santa Fe. They chatted me up and bought me beer at the Mine Shaft Tavern, and I wound up spending the night in a B and B over a coffee shop named Java Junction.

It was early June, and though there probably was a cool breeze still lingering in New York, in New Mexico it was much too hot to be riding in cowhide. I was beginning to melt right into my leathers, so I pulled over halfway up the Turquoise Trail to gaze at the Sandia Mountains while I stripped down to a T-shirt and jeans. Bart Mange would have killed me for two reasons: exposure and exposure.

"Letting a body part see daylight is like *asking* to have your skin ripped off." He slapped his butt. "Exposure is the enemy. If your ass hits asphalt, *you're* the ass!"

My motorcycle class was full of idiots, and one right next to me raised his hand. "But what if it's nighttime?"

"Get the hell out of here." Bart pointed to the door. "I'm begging you, ride naked. And don't wear your helmet either!"

Now, standing alone under a blazing sun, my skin exposed and my helmet bungee-corded to my pack, I knew I was subjecting myself to peril. But I loved defying Bart, and as I looked up and down the desolate highway, I smiled at the idea of defying him again.

"Now, fellas, you oughtta ride with a buddy as often as you can, but *you*, Grandma"—he pointed to me—"you should *never* be on the road by yourself. No matter how tired you are, unless your bike is broken down and you can't push it to the next exit, do *not* stop on the highway alone."

He fixed his gaze on me and kept it there.

"What?" I looked around the room for support. "I heard you."

"Did you? I *know* women like you. You think you're invincible, right? Well, I'll give you this, you're probably smart enough to avoid an ugly bastard like me in town, but what if you stopped on the highway and some schmuck *worse* than me showed up? What if you were all by yourself and some Tom, Dick, or Ted Bundy came along? How do you think you're going to roll up your windows and lock your doors on a motorcycle?"

Often Bart's words made sense, but now alone on this magnificent two-lane blacktop, I didn't care. The only human for miles, I was empowered not scared, and if some monster were to spring from the desert, well, I could think of no better place to die.

Named Sandia—"watermelon" in Spanish—the ruddy mountain range rose all around me with a meaty red terrain and lush green conifers. From a distance, the gorgeous peaks looked so much like their namesake, I actually grew hungry and thirsty, and so I decided to stop thirty miles south of Santa Fe in a ramshackle town called Madrid for an iced tea and a snack.

As I rode down the main street—and probably the *only* street—in Madrid, I was glad to see that the Mine Shaft was still standing. I'd been there years ago to hear the Rhubarbs, a funky bar band that featured wild-haired Sky Fabin on the washtub bass fiddle. Now, except for a few hippie art galleries, there was little left to Madrid except this rugged saloon and an old fire engine. In fact, rumor had it that the entire town was up for sale once for two hundred fifty thousand dollars . . . there were no takers.

Pronounced *Mad*-rid and known for attracting offbeat types, the town was nothing but a memory of itself, and for a long time, the Mine Shaft was all that brought anybody there. Built in 1899, it quenched the thirst of a large community of coal miners, but when the bar burned down on Christmas Day 1944, Madrid itself began to die as well. Though the Mine Shaft was rebuilt in 1947, the collapse of the coal industry pretty much finished off Madrid, and today its population tops out at maybe four hundred. Now riding into town on a hot June afternoon, I thought half the population was outside on the saloon's raised wooden deck . . . chairs tipped back, feet propped up, and mugs of beer in hand.

I stopped across the street, and I admit I sat there idling for a moment just to show off. When I finally threw down my kickstand, swung out of the saddle, and strode toward the bar, I was sure I was being watched with envy, until everyone started to laugh.

"What?" I looked at them, confused. Then, seeing several people point behind me, I whirled around just in time to see my bike going horizontal as my kickstand sank into the hot sand I'd mistaken for solid ground.

"Need a little help?" A man with untamed Einstein hair grinned down at me.

"Wait up, Doc." A guy in overalls vaulted from his chair. "That bike is way too big for an old fart like you to lift alone."

As it turned out, my bike was pretty much suctioned to the ground, and it took all three of us, encouraged by cheers from the crowd, to right it. When the job was done, I looked up and bowed. "I'm glad to have provided some entertainment." I felt my face reddening as several people chuckled. "And now, I'll be on my way to Santa Fe."

"Oh, come on now, you stopped here for a reason." Einstein pushed my bike to a square of asphalt and parked it. "Let me buy you a beer."

"I'll buy you another." Overalls glared at the crowd. "These people are idiots."

I said I'd have one round, but three beers later, I found myself staring at a tattoo on Einstein's neck that said *Dr. Death*. "What are you, a serial killer?"

He reached up and caressed the ink running from below his left ear to his shoulder blade. "It's an homage to my hero—Jack Kevorkian."

"Some *hero*." Overalls belched loudly. "That dude puts people down like dogs."

Einstein raised his hand. "I'm done talking about this. All I can say is that man put a lot of people out of their misery."

Overalls drained his beer. "Well, I'm sorry to rain on your cloud, but if you ask me, Kevorkian was just a publicity hound."

I could see Einstein was getting emotional, so I jumped in. "I think it was the media that latched on to him, not the other way around."

Einstein winked his thanks to me. "Actually, you're both right. Kevorkian exposed himself to the media to get his message out."

"And the media ate it up." I shrugged. "The public wants what it wants."

"Let's change subjects." Einstein stood up and looked at me. "So, Madame Harley, tell me if I'm right. Are you a lesbian?"

Overalls let out a wolf whistle. "That's a *fine* change of subject. Well, are you?"

"I think so." I laughed nervously and cocked my head toward my Harley. "What gave me away, my bike or the string of women following me?"

Einstein, who everyone called Doctor D, chuckled. "I didn't mean to offend you, it's just that most girls that know about this bar are of that *persuasion*."

"No offense taken." I took a long draw from my beer but it went down the wrong pipe. Tears welled in my eyes as I tried not to choke to death.

"You okay?" Doctor D laid a calloused hand on my back.

"I think so."

He laughed. "That's the same answer I got when I asked if you were a lesbian."

"Really?"

"The Doc's right." Overalls grinned. "You thinking of trading teams?"

I gave him a look. "Not anytime soon."

I had meant for my look to be playful, but I think I forgot to smile.

"Now don't get me wrong," Doctor D jumped in. "I only brought the subject up because I know a few girls in Santa Fe . . . when you're ready."

"What do you mean, when I'm ready? I'm ready as long as it's not one of *them*." I nodded toward two women kissing over a plate of tacos. "They're not my type."

"The Marys?" Doctor D didn't even look over. "Everyone wishes they'd just get a room. No, I was thinking of a couple of friends of mine."

"Any of them named Mai?" I asked, spelling it out. "I don't know her last name, but she might work at a place called Trickster Leather. I met her a long time ago and—"

"How long ago was that?" Overalls asked. "If you're on some kind of lesbian treasure hunt, I'm gonna need more details."

My face flushed. "A little over twenty years."

"Now let's see . . ." Doctor D ran his fingers through his wild white hair. "You don't have a last name and this girl *might* work at this leather shop?"

"Right. I would call her, but I kind of washed her phone number."

Both men burst out laughing.

"Man, was I right." Doctor D tipped back his chair and grinned. "You are *not* ready for a relationship."

"Who the hell are you? Dr. Freud? You don't know me, so what makes you think I'm not ready to get involved with someone?"

"Well, for starters, you don't look like you're on solid ground. I could see that *before* you parked in quicksand."

I had to laugh. "Guess I'm not fooling anybody, am I?"

He waved his arm around. "Look, none of us are stable. But come on—what kind of person peacocks like you did when you pulled up? An unstable person who's trying to *look* stable, that's who."

I stood up. "What do I owe you for the beer?"

"Nothing, and I'm sorry if I hurt your feelings, I just like talking to pretty girls."

I smiled. "Thanks, I needed that. But I'm kind of talked out."

As I went into the sun, the beer and the heat made it clear I shouldn't be on a bike. I looked at Doctor D and Overalls sitting on the deck and ambled back over to them.

"Pretty *and* smart." He tapped his temple. "Kick back and let's fix your love life."

"What was I thinking? I can barely hold up my bike as it is."

"Don't give yourself grief over enjoying yourself." He patted the seat next to him. "Now, sit down, accept where you are, and be happy you didn't kill yourself."

I woke up to the smell of coffee in a double bed over Java Junction. Doctor D, Overalls, and even the Marys had proved to be good companions—talking politics, philosophy, and just generally bullshitting around. I told them all about the few hours I had spent with Mai, and how I still held out hope there was more than a mere flirtation between us. Everyone concluded I was delusional, wished me luck, and told me they liked my chutzpah. No one had heard of Trickster Leather or Mai, and I was beginning to wonder if the entire evening at Color Me Purple was just a figment of my imagination.

I showered across the hall, got dressed, and went downstairs for a breakfast burrito, then headed over to the Mine Shaft to say goodbye. I was sure everyone would still be there, but the only one I saw was Overalls, bellied up to the bar drinking a beer and eating enchiladas.

"Good morning, sunshine." He tipped an imaginary hat. "A little hair of the dog for you?"

"God, no. I just came to say goodbye. Where is everyone?"

"Well, Old Doc is probably in Santa Fe by now. He likes to get into the office early. And the Marys got a room. I'm the only loser still here."

"Doc still works? I just thought he was retired."

Overalls laughed. "I thought you'd have him figured out by now. Old Doc D is a psychiatrist. He loves telling people how to live their lives."

Thirty-one

The Horse Fetish

———

Ifound a number of leather shops in Santa Fe, but none of them was named Trickster Leather. Still, I strolled into a few and asked if anyone knew a woman named Mai. No one had heard of her, and I began to wonder if she had made up the whole story about her family's shop. Maybe her name wasn't even Mai. More than anything, I couldn't stop thinking about Doctor D and how he had decided so quickly I wasn't ready for a relationship.

It was at this moment in my trip, and perhaps in my life, that I was faced with a hard truth that I could no longer deny. I was *not* in a romantic comedy. I was *not* a character in a novel with a feel-good ending. I was a hopeless romantic with the emphasis on hopeless. I was *not* going to walk into one last shop and meet a woman who was Mai's mother, and she was *not* going to say, "Well, it's nice to finally meet you. Here's my daughter's address. She's been pining away for you for years."

It was the death of a dream, but I wasn't sad. My time with Mai *had* been wonderful, and now I would have to accept that my evening with her was nothing more than a fish I had caught long ago. It was time to release her into my memory, where perfect slices of life fit snugly and never have to change. And Mai, well, she was surely out there in the world or in the universe. Certainly, like me, she wasn't in a film or a novel, and in that case, we *might* just run into each other . . . someday.

I strolled around the town plaza shaking my head at my ridiculous self, especially since—if I'm honest—I still half-expected to run into Mai. What happened instead, though, was just as magical.

I'd decided to buy myself an appropriate gift for letting go of my obsession: a fetish, a small stone carved into the shape of an animal. There were dozens of them in shops all over the plaza, but I was drawn to a few displayed on a colorful striped blanket among strands of silver necklaces, lots of turquoise earrings, and several clay pots. The heavyset brown woman who was selling these items sat under the portal in front of the Palace of the Governors. She looked wise, kind, and very stern, and I remember thinking that buying something from her seemed not only important but also a privilege.

Of course I was drawn to a tiny white coyote, and when I pointed to it and asked how much it was, the old woman just shook her head.

"What? It's not for sale?"

She had to be a hundred years old, and when she grinned at me, I saw more spaces than teeth. "Coyotes can be great teachers, but you need a healer." She pointed to a small onyx horse. "This is the fetish for you."

I looked at the little horse. It had a jagged streak of turquoise and I liked it, but I was bent on my first choice. "No, I want the coyote. How much?"

"Take the horse for thirty," she said. "You are not ready for a coyote."

It was as though she'd punched me in the stomach. I didn't have to ask what she meant because the old woman had seen right through my present directly into my past.

"You're sure about the horse?" I picked up the coyote. "I really like this one."

She frowned, gave me a severe look, and her eyes said, *Take the damn horse* . . . And so I did.

"Thanks, now I have luck and healing on my side." I patted my pocket where I'd shoved the tiny horse next to my father's gold ring. "Maybe someday I'll come back and get that coyote."

As I rode out of Santa Fe, I took with me not only the fetish but also some of the best advice I've ever gotten.

"Stop wanting things you can't have," the old woman said, putting my money into a tin can by her side. "If something is to be yours, then it will be."

Thirty-two

Acting Like a Grown-up

———

With only thirteen hours of ride time to the Pacific Ocean, I was glad to realize I would make it home on the anniversary of my mother's death. Split into three days, the trip put me in Holbrook, Arizona, the first night, Needles, California, the second night, and in my own bed the third. If I could avoid road whimsy, fatigue, and surprises, I could ride up to my house with time to chat with Lynn, feign exhaustion, and politely kick her out to be alone with my dogs and the memory of my mom.

But by three o'clock, road whimsy hit. I was well into New Mexico and about to bypass Gallup, when a sign caught my eye that reminded me of the day I left Los Angeles. It was then that a chatty cabdriver had noticed my motorcycle gear and told me about a ride he'd never had the guts to take—the Devil's Highway loop on Route 666. Now here I was, speeding past the turnoff for that very ride, and I wondered if I should circle back to take a short cruise on this supposedly haunted highway. Deciding that it was now or never, I made a U-turn back to town, where I stopped at a gas station for some water. If Route 666 lived up to its name, it was bound to be hot as hell, and I wanted to be prepared.

"What's wrong, young lady?" An elderly gentleman wearing a red bow tie winked at me as he rang up my water. "Ninety degrees and no humidity too much for you?"

I laughed. "Actually, I thought I might give Route 666 a whirl."

"Well, then I guess you've already had a heatstroke." He shook his head. "Why would you want to do something foolish like that?"

"Oh, come on. You don't buy into that satanic hype, do you?"

"*I* don't, but lots of crazy people do. They're the ones you have to worry about." He handed me change for my twenty. "It doesn't happen often any-more, but a while back, some lunatics were sacrificing animals out there."

"Well, that's just sick. But the highway itself is safe, isn't it? I mean, it's properly maintained, right?"

"I don't know and I don't care to find out." He rolled his eyes. "*I'm* a grown-up."

"And what makes you think I'm not?" I pointed to the loose skin on my neck and made an exaggerated smile to show the crow's-feet around my eyes. "I earned every one of these wrinkles."

He grinned. "Have you ever seen a newborn?"

"Point taken." I picked up my water and headed out.

"Be careful, kiddo," he called after me. "I don't want to be hearing about you on the news."

"Don't worry, you won't," I said over my shoulder. But when I got to the door I turned around. "Hey, can I ask you something?"

He shrugged. "Sure, but if you're looking for ghost repellent, I'm fresh out."

"Very funny." I took a swig of water. "Actually, I was wondering if you could tell me when you realized you had become a grown-up?"

"That's a good question." He rubbed his chin. "I'll have to think about that."

"Just tell me the first thing that comes to your mind."

He smiled. "Well, for one thing, I wasn't so impatient anymore."

I rolled my eyes. "I'm serious. Think about it for a second."

"Only for a second?" His eyes twinkled. "Actually, I know exactly when I became an adult. It was when my first grandchild was born. I should have been a grown-up when I had my own children, but it takes some of us kids a little longer, right?"

I walked out of the store carrying a weighty thought that slowed my step. An old regret had resurfaced, and I wanted to ride off and leave it behind. Children—at least not my own—were never going to be a part of my reality. I swung heavily onto my bike and sat there idling. Then I broke into a knowing smile. I'd been my own child for a long time. Maybe it was time to try this adult stuff.

I kicked my bike into gear and headed out of New Mexico. Taking a spin on a highway known to be particularly dangerous was more of a childish dare than a challenge, so I left the Devil's Loop in my wake . . . grinning like a smart-ass teenager when my speedometer hit a hundred as I flew toward Holbrook.

Now in Arizona, the last state I would hit before California, I began to think about what I was going to do when I got home—besides look for a job. The euphoria I got from accelerating, the power I got from blowing past cars, instantly dropped away. Without the road propelling me forward, without a clear destination, all I could picture myself doing on the day I woke up in Los Angeles was lying in bed with no place to go.

By the time I veered off at the Holbrook exit, my mood swings had me exhausted and depressed, so I headed down the main drag looking for a hotel. Instead I saw a neon sign that made me laugh. It asked: HAVE YOU SLEPT IN A WIGWAM LATELY? Since I had not, I pulled into the Wigwam Village, and my blue mood gave way to silliness.

"I'll take your finest wigwam, please," I said to the clerk. "Your eighteenth wigwam would be nice if you have it, but—"

"We only have fifteen." The woman didn't bother to suppress a snarl. "They're all rented except number sixteen. Sixty bucks plus tax—take it or leave it."

"Number sixteen? But you just told me you only have fifteen."

She rolled her eyes. "We skip number thirteen."

Someone walked in behind me.

"Sixteen it is," I said. "By the way, I see you're right next to some train tracks. Trains don't run at night around here, do they?"

"Have you slept in a wigwam lately?" she asked drily. "If you want to, you'll be sleeping by some train tracks."

Located on West Hopi Drive off Route 66, the village's fifteen wigwams—which looked more like teepees—each stood thirty-two-feet tall with round bases that were fourteen feet in diameter. Vintage cars from the fifties and sixties were parked on the grounds to give tourists that nostalgic feeling, but it was hard to lose sight that I was in the twenty-first century when I knew that my wigwam was made of concrete instead of sticks and mud. Truth be told, I was a little disappointed with the interior, which looked something like a Motel 6 room, and I thought they could have at least thrown an animal hide on the floor.

Still, I loved my weird little wigwam with its slanted walls, single tiny window, and prison-style toilet. There was a claustrophobic coziness to it, and to remember the experience, I bought an *I Slept in a Wigwam* T-shirt from the snarly clerk so I wouldn't ever forget that I had indeed slept in a wigwam . . . and never had to do it again.

After settling in, I went about exploring Holbrook, reading historical plaques and marveling at all that had happened in this odd little town. Once said to be "too tough for women and churches," Holbrook was the site of the Pleasant Valley War, one of America's most costly feuds. Beginning in 1887, the dispute erupted over grazing rights between the sheep-herding Tewksburys and the cattle-ranching Grahams. After nearly a decade of violent bickering, the families wiped each other out, and some say that's how Bucket of Blood Street got its name.

Hoping to get a scoop of Rocky Road on a waffle cone at the Horsehead Crossing Deli at 112 Bucket of Blood, I learned otherwise from a talkative fellow in line.

"Guess what this street used to be called." He pulled on his suspenders and looked around the deli, but no one said a word. "Plain old Central Avenue! Can you beat that?"

A little girl giggled and her mother dragged her outside, but the old man just rambled on. "It all started when a poker game went sideways down the block. A gunfight broke out, and so many people got shot, the saloon was covered with buckets of blood!"

No one said a word. It had cooled down to a survivable eighty-eight from a high of ninety-five, and I'm pretty sure everyone just wanted to get their ice cream and find some shade to eat it in.

"And that, my friends, is what put Holbrook on the map. In fact, Bucket of Blood is ranked *sixth* on the top ten list of wackiest street names in America." He wagged his finger at a teenage boy eating a hoagie. "Do you want to know what number one is?"

The boy stopped midbite and shrugged.

"It's Psycho Path, located in Traverse City, Michigan." The old coot popped his suspenders against his potbelly and grinned proudly. "I can name all ten if you'd like."

"Go for it," the boy grunted. "You're a real wealth of information."

"*Useless* information." A red-faced woman burst through the door and grabbed the old guy by the arm. "Sorry, folks. This old hound of mine gets loose now and then."

Sad for both the lunatic and his wife, I headed for the door with my ice cream.

"Watch out for meteorites!" he shouted. "They aim for tourists!"

I turned around. "Come again?"

Mrs. Hound twisted the old man's arm. "Would you quit terrorizing folks?"

But later, after beers and a burger at a bar called Empty Pockets, I was telling some folks about the grizzly old nut and was told that a meteorite *had* fallen on Holbrook in 1912. Apparently it had broken up into more than fifteen thousand fragments, and Jill and Margaret Shnook, twin sisters sitting next to me, had come to town to find a few.

"Gonna snag some frags." Jill poked her sister. "Right, Mags?"

Margaret nodded, looking embarrassed. "Yeah, we're meteorite hunters."

"Been at it for years." Jill beamed. "Did you know even slivers are worth a lot?"

"I did not know that." I suppressed a grin for Margaret's sake. She was obviously shy and I suspected would rather have done anything other than discuss her peculiar pastime.

Jill slugged her beer. "Found as much as fifty bucks' worth in a single day."

"Wow." I tried to sound excited. "So how much money have you two hauled in since you became meteorite hunters?"

Margaret looked at her hiking boots. "Maybe four hundred fifty dollars."

"But we have fun just looking." Jill poked her sister again. "Don't we, Mags?"

They were both kind of homely, probably in their mid-thirties, and I figured they hunted meteorites because the search for men was out of their wheelhouse. "Well, I'll keep my eye to the sky." I grinned. "Or maybe I should say to the ground."

Jill frowned. "It's not as easy as you think. Takes time, energy, and equipment." She drew a photo of a metal detector from her wallet. "That's our new baby. She's top-of-the-line with an 18.75-kilohertz frequency coil. Cost damn near a thousand bucks."

Since I hadn't even considered owning a cheap metal detector, I told the twins I was tired, wished them good luck, and made a beeline for my wigwam.

I crashed like a meteor and slept like a rock until four a.m. when I awoke with a fierce hot flash. As I lay there melting into the sheets, I suddenly became aware of being watched. Peering through the square glass window built into my wigwam's wooden door was a pair of eyes. At first I thought it was one of the meteorite twins, since I was pretty sure Mags had a crush on me. But slowly I connected the eyes with a small freckled nose and straw-colored hair, all of which were glowing. It was probably just the fluorescent lights in the parking lot, but the figure looked ghostly, and judging by the small hands at the base of the window, I figured my Peeping Tom was about four feet tall.

Now in a complete eye-lock with what I decided was a child, I was determined to win this staring contest, but the kid was good, and soon I felt myself breaking. Besides, it was time to stop. A child should be in bed at this hour, and a woman my age needed her sleep. Clearly someone had to be the adult here, and since I was taller, I pulled the sheet around me, crawled out of bed, and retrieved some clothes from my backpack. Then I flung open the door to find a little boy who squealed, giggled, and scurried away

I managed to grab him by his pajama bottoms as he rounded the last wigwam.

"I'm sorry! I'm sorry!" he squawked, trying to wriggle away from me.

But I was in full adult mode now and held tight to his chicken-bone wrist.

"What are you doing out here?" I squatted down and took hold of him by the waist. "Do you know that peeping into windows is against the law?"

He looked up at me with light brown eyes and lashes so long they could have been whisk brooms. "I was just playing."

"Playing? At four in the morning?" I tried to frown but couldn't help smiling at his shirtless little belly puffing in and out above his pajama bottoms. "How old are you?"

"Nine and a half. My birthday is in two weeks."

"Wow, you're gonna be in double digits. My name is Barbara. What's yours?"

"James." He blinked hard. "Sometimes my daddy calls me Jimmy."

"Can I call you Jimmy?"

"No."

I laughed. "Well, okay then, James. You can call me Barbara Roller Coaster Tomato Pie."

"That's a silly name."

"I only use it for silly people who go peeping into wigwam windows."

He looked at his filthy bare feet. "You're not gonna tell my daddy, are you?"

I didn't know what to do. Here was this unattended unkempt kid running around a motel parking lot at four in the morning. "I don't know," I said. "Where *is* your daddy?"

"With Cathy." He pointed to wigwam 3. "I'm supposed to be asleep in the car."

"In the car, huh?" I wanted to kill Daddy and Cathy. "Which car is that?"

He pointed to an old station wagon. "Daddy locks me in with his clicker. He cracks the windows a little, but tonight he left one open all the way." He looked like he was about to cry. "You're not gonna tell on me, are you?"

"Not if you promise not to go spying on people anymore."

He nodded. "I promise."

"Then your secret is safe with me." I took his hand and we walked over to the station wagon. His daddy was probably someone I shouldn't confront, the kind of guy who would accuse me of kidnapping if I let his boy sleep in my room.

"Listen, James, I wish I could invite you to stay with me, but I think your daddy might get mad." I poked my head through the station wagon's window. There was a nice little setup in the backseat . . . for a dog. "You'll be okay in here, right?"

"I like it in the car. Daddy and Cathy make too much noise."

I squatted down to meet his eyes. "I'm going to lift you through the window, and if you go right to sleep, no one will know about this." I stuck out my hand. "Deal?"

"Deal." He shook my hand like he was pumping water. "It was nice to meet you."

I laughed. James had nice manners for a Peeping Tom. "It was nice to meet you too, James." I lifted his thin frame through the window. "Happy birthday in two weeks."

I crept off to my wigwam, feeling like I should call Child Services, and after a restless sleep, I awoke in the morning with the conviction to have a word with James's father and Cathy. I put on my motorcycle gear to look tougher than I felt. Then I strode over to their wigwam, and that was when I realized the station wagon was gone.

Later that morning, when I was already on the road, I offered up a silent prayer for James, and then the boy vanished into the sinkhole of my consciousness . . . like global warming, terrorism, and other things I could do nothing about.

Thirty-three

Take It Easy

—◆—

The only thing interesting about Needles, California, was riding through Arizona to get there. I loved the road signs, and watching for the next one saved me from losing consciousness in the heat. There was a turnoff for Two Guns, once a tourist spot with a thriving zoo but now a ghost town with empty cages. Then came Twin Arrows, a run-down trading post marked by two telephone poles with pointed ends and feathers stuck on the top. I could see the makeshift arrows from the highway, and I swear my bike headed there all by itself. Devil Dog Road, known for a naked woman found dead there in 2003, was after that. To this day she has never been identified and is referred to as Devil Dog Doe. My favorite sign was HOLY MOSES WASH, which warned people of flash floods. I couldn't even imagine a drizzle in the area—when I passed through, it was a hundred and two degrees.

But well before I encountered an abandoned lion cage or was lured off the road by humongous arrows, I was just a hungry biker amazed by how fast the memory of James had given way to thoughts of breakfast.

Since I was helpless to do anything about the former, I rode into the first decent town west of Holbrook to take care of the latter. That was Winslow, Arizona, made famous by the Eagles with their 1972 hit "Take It Easy." Today, people flock there just to stand on a corner and sing the song. I called my friend Norma and got past only the first verse before she stopped me to say she was in a meeting.

"Good God, Barbara, we've all been worried about you!" She sounded jazzed on coffee. "And now when you finally call, I can't talk. Will you pick up when I call back?"

"I will. I promise."

"Swear it, or I'll walk out of this meeting right now. I don't care if I get fired."

"I swear on the life of Devil Dog Doc."

"Who the hell is *that*? Never mind. I'll call you in thirty."

Later, while I was eating breakfast downtown at the Falcon, Norma called. I didn't pick up till the last ring just to yank her chain, and when I did I started singing again.

"Enough," she snarled. "Tell me why on earth you're in Winslow, Arizona."

I laughed. "Taking it easy."

"I'm not kidding, Barbara. Do you know half of Los Angeles is looking for you?"

"That's impossible. I don't know an eighth of Los Angeles."

"Are you *high*? Everyone here is freaked out about you."

I thought of the joint I'd gotten from Sawyer/Bradley Finn/Forester and decided what I was going to do as soon as I landed in Needles. "I'm not high. I'm having an omelet."

"Well, everyone's been calling me to ask if I know where you are. Even—"

"Do *not* say her name."

"Fine, even *she* called me. She went by your house when you stopped answering your phone, and someone was there taking care of your dogs."

"That would be Lynn. You don't know her."

"Well, Lynn wouldn't say where you were and was very rude to—"

"Don't—"

Norma sighed. "Jesus, Barbara, when are you going to grow up?"

"For your information, I don't think being a grown-up means I have to be sensible all the time. Right now, hearing her name upsets me. Can we just leave it at that?"

"Well, if it makes you feel any better, I think she's single again. Anyway, you're right—let's not talk about her. Let's talk about why in hell you're in Winslow, Arizona."

I giggled. "Because it's *such a fine sight to see*?"

"I will climb through this phone and strangle you if I don't get a straight answer."

I swallowed hard. "I don't know, Norma. Maybe I just needed to get away."

"People who need to get away go to Hawaii."

I was getting rude looks for talking on my cell, so I paid my bill and stood outside in soul-sucking heat, trying to calm down my friend. Secretly, I was glad she was upset.

"Look, I understand you've been worried, and I appreciate it, but remember how frustrated you were six months ago when I wasn't coming out of my depression?"

"Yeah, so?"

"Well, I know everyone meant well, but I got frustrated with them for trying to fix me. I guess I just needed to be broken for a while, so I took off."

"But you're okay now, right?"

"Yeah, I'm okay."

"Really? I swear, we were going to have an intervention before you disappeared."

I laughed. "Don't worry, I had an intervention all by myself."

"Good, tell me about it when you get home. You *are* coming home, aren't you?"

"I'm on my way."

"Great, I'll be excited to see you. Do you need a ride from the airport?"

"Don't worry, I'm on a motorcycle."

She burst out laughing. "Man, did I ever dodge a bullet by not sleeping with you."

"Norma, you're straight."

"That doesn't mean I never wanted to."

I laughed. "Okay, now I'm *definitely* coming home."

After hanging up with Norma, I was in a great mood, and I couldn't wait to get home to everyone who cared about me. I hopped on my motorcycle and took a spin through downtown Winslow, whistling "Take It Easy," feeling like this trip had indeed *loosened my load.* Then, sure enough, I saw a woman *in a flatbed Ford.* She wasn't exactly *slowin' down to take a look at me,* but she *was* looking at me.

To be honest, she was looking at everyone who passed by this part of town, specifically the corner of Second Street and Campbell, where muralist John Pugh had painted a two-story image of her on a brick wall that looked down upon a six-foot bronze statue titled "Easy" sculpted by Ron Adamson. It was all part of a shrine called Standin' on the Corner Park, which opened in 1999 to commemorate Winslow's one claim to fame.

Now, idling on my bike across the street, I debated whether I wanted to be a geek and have my photo taken with "Easy" like everybody else. He looked like Jackson Browne, who wrote the song with Eagles founding member Glenn Frey. Though Browne supposedly did break down in Winslow on his way to give a concert in Flagstaff, I saw the cast-iron guitar player with his thumbs hooked in his jeans as simply the embodiment of cool. I parked my bike and was walking over for a better look, when someone behind me said, "Wow, he looks a lot like you."

I turned around and must have looked upset because the teenage girl standing there backed up and raised her hands. "Hey, take it easy. I meant that as a compliment."

I frowned. "Saying that I look like a guy is a compliment?"

"I wasn't saying you look *masculine*." She grinned, clearly flirting with me. "I mean, aren't you aware of how cool you look?"

I looked at my distorted image in her mirror sunglasses. "I have my moments."

She couldn't have been more than sixteen, cute as hell, and clearly out of her mind for flirting with me. I was just about to say something wise to let her off easy when she said, "My mom loves the Eagles. It was her idea to come here."

I felt like Grandma Moses. "So where is your mom?"

"Oh, she's back in the hotel moping over my dad. They were high school sweethearts and supposedly danced to this song at her prom." She rolled her eyes. "I keep telling her to get over him. I mean, even *I* think my dad is a jerk."

"Maybe you should cut your mom some slack. It's hard to get over somebody."

"They've broken up five times." She popped her gum. "You have kids?"

My heart dropped. "No, never seemed to find the time."

"Smart." She glanced over at my motorcycle. "Keeps you free."

I was thinking about having her take my photo with the hitchhiker, but I didn't want to blow the cool image she had of me. Then all of sudden she read my mind.

"Hey, do you have a cell phone? I'll take your picture with that statue."

"Yeah, thanks." I handed her my phone. "Do you know how it works?"

She rolled her eyes. "Go stand over there. I'll take a few different shots."

Walking toward the hitchhiker, I ran my fingers through my helmet hair, got into a nonchalant pose, and then looked over to the girl . . . but she was gone.

"Hey!" I whirled around looking for her. "Some kid just stole my cell phone!"

A pack of tourists surrounded me asking questions all at once. I described the girl the best I could, but she looked like any teenager in faded jeans. Then I pointed like an idiot to the mural of the girl in the flatbed Ford. "Actually, she looked like *her!*"

Someone laughed. "Every girl looks like her when they're in this town. You might as well kiss your phone goodbye."

The crowd dispersed, everyone going back to their own business and basically not giving a shit about mine. I thought about going to the police and then decided to find a mobile phone store instead. Within an hour, I had my old phone canceled, my new phone programmed, and my old number ported into it. Praising technology and cursing my dependency on it, I headed out of town feeling anything but easy and sure of nothing except that I wanted to be home. The worst thing was that I felt extremely uncool, stupid really, as I sped down the road with my tailpipe between my legs.

After a dozen miles or so I was finally able to shake off that wicked little thief, and even laugh at myself, but the continuous loop of "Take It Easy" that had been blaring through loudspeakers everywhere in Winslow was stuck in my head. I tried thinking about all the truly good-hearted people I'd met before running into that brat—the Daves in Buffalo, Amrita and Achnir in Gettysburg, Mother Teresa in Memphis. And I thought of the odd but harmless ones too—gun-toting Sandy in Virginia, the stoned-out junkman in Arkansas, and Rabbi Jerry under the cross. All of them canceled out the rotten teen, but nothing was getting rid of that song, and on top of that, I was feeling pretty lethargic. Had the evil girl sprayed me with something that turned me into a gullible ass *and* made me drowsy? I was probably wiped out from being up late with poor little Peeping James. Either way, I had to pull over for some coffee or learn how to ride with my eyes closed.

Luckily I discovered the Late for the Train café in Flagstaff just a half-hour down the road. There I had a cup of coffee, fortified by two shots of espresso, called a Locomotive. It was like drinking cocaine, and if it wasn't for the triple splash of cream, I think my heart would have run all the way to California by itself.

I only had to pull over two more times during the next three hours to Needles—first to use the restroom at the Roadkill Café in Seligman, where they served "off-the-fender" dishes like Smear of Deer and Flat Cat—and next at a biker bar in Kingman, not far from the California border.

Judging by all the Road Kings, Dyna Wide Glides, and Fat Boys parked out front, the Route 66 Roadhouse was clearly a Harley hangout. Not a single Suzuki, Ducati, Honda, or Kawasaki was in the lot, and though my Sportster hardly fit in with all the monster cruisers, I found a nifty little spot by a sexy V-Rod, and strolled into the saloon like I belonged there. Since I still had more caffeine in me than a case of Red Bulls, I figured one beer wouldn't hurt, so I sidled up to the bar and said one word: "Heineken."

"Hey, Felix!" The bartender put a bottle of beer in front of me and then threw a dishrag at a bald guy at the door. "We got us a real talker here!"

Wide and cuddly, Felix lifted himself onto the stool next to me. "Some-body die?"

I turned my Heineken upside down against my lips. "Probably some-where."

"She's a keeper." Felix slapped my back hard enough not to ignore, but easy enough so I didn't fall off my stool. "Where you from and what brings you to nowhere?"

I figured saying I was from LA would bring me grief, so I laid out a slick line that was true and safe. "I'm from El Paso, and I'm just passing through." Then seeing Felix about to gear up for a conversation, I excused myself to go to the restroom. I didn't have to ask which way to go, I just headed toward a neon sign that read: IT'S BACK HERE.

"Hey!" Felix called after me. "While you're there, check out our Wall of Shame!"

What he was talking about was a hallway covered with photographs of famous bikers. Peter Fonda, Jay Leno, James Dean, and Elvis were no surprise, but I didn't expect to see Roy Rogers and Jimmy Carter. I was also a little taken aback and mostly weirded out to see a framed ponytail. I made a mental note to ask Felix what he knew about the hair, but first I followed arrows directing me to CHICKS or NOT CHICKS. I chose the appropriate door and went in to find two young women in skintight leather. One had cakes of mascara on her eyelashes; the other had streams of it running down her cheeks. Both had stringy blue-black hair, pasty skin, and white powder rimming their nostrils. "Sorry." I turned to walk out, but the one who was crying grabbed my arm.

"Wait, tell me if a man who looks like a giant asshole is out there?"

"Felix? Yeah, I just left him."

"Do I look like someone who'd cry over *him*? I'm talking about Jack."

I removed my arm from her grasp. "You'll have to be more specific. There are a lot of guys out there who look like assholes named Jack."

"I'm talking about *Big* Jack. He'd be the jerk with more tattoos than skin."

"Hmm, I did see some guys playing cards. I'll see if he's out there."

"No!" The girl jumped in front of the door. Then she took me by the shoulders, looked deep into my eyes, and said, "Would you?"

Her pupils were so dilated I figured she was high enough to hurt me, so I popped outside and made a quick study of the guys at the card table. All of them had tattoos, all of them looked like assholes, but only one had ink over every inch of his skin.

I headed back inside. "He's there. What did he do to you?"

"He dumped me!" She stomped her fuck-me pump so hard the heel nearly buckled.

"When? Just now?"

Her friend stumbled out of a stall looking like she'd just eaten a powdered donut. "It's been over a fucking year, but she still goes bat-shit when she sees him."

I looked away from these girls, both probably in their twenties, and stared at myself in the mirror. "How old do you think I am?" I asked, not looking back at them.

For a second I think they thought I was asking myself, and I suppose I was.

"Forget it, I know." I grinned at my reflection. "Too old for this shit."

I left the girls staring at me and walked back to the bar to find the half-bottle of Heineken I'd left replaced with a fresh one. I thanked the bartender, but said I had to go.

"Don't thank me." He cocked his head toward Felix. "Thank the boss."

I laid a ten on the bar. "I believe I will." I started to head out, then turned around. "Hey, I've got a question for you. Whose ponytail is framed back there?"

The bartender laughed. "Used to be Felix's. He and a bunch of guys cut off their hair in solidarity for a fellow dying of cancer. You know something—I think the old bastard's still alive. Probably will outlive us all!"

Thirty-four

What Would Lucy Do?

———

Not long after I checked into my motel in Needles, I found the joint I'd gotten from the junkman, so I poured a hot bath and got high. I was lucky I didn't drown because an hour or so later I woke up in a tub of cold water. Starving, I put on some sweats and walked to the diner across the street. Everything looked greasy, but I took a chance on the chicken-fried steak. It was fabulous, and the mashed potatoes might as well have been manna.

I was just plowing through my apple pie when I noticed a guy two tables over reading a newspaper. Maybe it was just paranoia mixed with my munchies, but I was convinced he was watching me and decided I shouldn't let him see me walk to my motel alone. I thought of my sensei in Santa Fe, who would tell me to play it cool and let the guy leave first. But thirty minutes later, he was still there and I had worked myself into a genuine state of fear.

My sensei would remain level-headed; he wouldn't pretend to be choking or set his menu on fire, both of which I considered. But I was not my sensei, who probably never felt vulnerable, and he was not me. He was a six-degree black belt who had conquered his mental, physical, and spiritual selves to live a life of harmony. He was not a restless, insecure woman who had once split in two to feel whole again.

So I stopped thinking about what my sensei would do and began imagining what someone like me would do. And that's when Lucille Ball came to mind. Although she might actually set her menu on fire or even *yell* fire, most likely she would just cry. So channeling my inner Lucy, I picked up my napkin and began to sniffle.

The waiter raced over. "Are you okay? Can I get you something? Maybe a glass of water?"

"No, I'm fine." I wondered if I could trust him to walk me to my motel.

"Well, how about another slice of pie—on the house."

And then suddenly I had my story. "Oh, that would be nice. My husband and I had a terrible fight. The pie will be a nice peace offering."

The waiter smiled. "Then I'll wrap that to go."

I slipped a knife into my sweatshirt and carried it out with my pie.

Later in bed, laughing over my story and worrying that the serial killer behind the paper hadn't bought it, Annie Edson Taylor came to mind. On her sixty-third birthday—October 24, 1901—she became the first person to go over Niagara Falls in a barrel and survive. She'd done this crazy feat to secure her financial future, but she died in poverty nearly two decades later. Then there was Bobby Leach, the first man to do the same stunt, on July 25, 1911. He also lived to tell about it, but died fifteen years later after slipping on an orange peel, breaking his leg, and getting gangrene. John Glenn had also succumbed to Murphy's Law, though his adventure was aboard the spacecraft *Friendship 7*, not inside a barrel. The first American to orbit Earth, Glenn circled the globe three times on February 20, 1962, and came home unscathed. Later, however, he slipped in the bathroom, hit his head on the bathtub, and damaged his inner ear. Irony could be a bitch, and I was aware that with the end of my journey so near, there might still be a few pitfalls and probably some psychopaths between Los Angeles and me.

As I lay there thinking about all the hazards I'd avoided on this trip, I wondered if my luck would hold out until I got home or if I had used it all up. I'd already had my share of narrow escapes in my life—car crashes, bicycle wrecks, and out-of-control skiing accidents. I'd been crushed by a crowd at a rock concert in Colorado, clipped by a taxicab stepping off a curb in London, bucked off several horses throughout the Southwest, and almost drowned by rogue waves and riptides in both the Atlantic and Pacific. Though I'd never been mugged, shot, or stabbed, there was plenty of road between my home and this motel, and fate's fickle finger could point at me at anytime.

I'm not sure when I finally dozed off, but the sun had yet to peek through the curtains when my cell phone began ringing. I reached for it but knocked it to the floor. When it stopped ringing, I pulled the sheet over my head and went back to sleep. Then once again . . . there was my mom.

"Wake up, little bug."

Through the sheets, I could see her silhouette standing over me.

"Time to get cracking," she said. *"It's been a year."*

I smiled . . . It was so nice to see her, but then the damn phone rang again.

I found it under the bed and was about to shut it off when I realized that when my cell phone hit the floor, it must have landed on the snooze button. It was the alarm that was ringing now. I'd set it to wake me at five a.m. on June 13—the hour and the day I'd learned of my mother's death.

But now, as I lay there exhausted from having obsessed the night before over all the ways I had almost died, I wondered why I wanted to resurrect that horrible day. I was angry with myself for having set the alarm and felt ghoulish for doing it.

"Idiot," I mumbled into the darkness. I rolled over and tried to doze off, but after fifteen minutes, I figured I might as well get up and have an early start.

But while my mind was road ready, my body was not, and I knew I needed more sleep to make it home alive. And so I started thinking about all the times I had awakened in the middle of the night as a small child. Whether it was from a bad dream or the excitement of what I was going to do the next day, I would creep into my parents' bedroom and watch them sleeping until one of them woke up. It was always my mother.

"What is it?" she'd grumble.

If I told her it was a nightmare, she would tell me the story she always did about her father and the broomstick he kept under his bed.

"This is *not* a broomstick, it's a rifle," she would say in a gruff, grandfatherly voice. "Show me the culprit keeping you awake and I'll shoot 'em."

If I told her I was too excited to sleep, she would tell me she was going to paint a picture of me dreaming. "Go back to bed, little bug. I've got to get my paints."

I'd race down the hall to my room, and after a few minutes, she'd show up with a basket of hot towels she'd heated in the dryer. One by one, she'd lay them on top of me.

"This is the first coat of paint," she would whisper. "And this is the second."

By the fourth or fifth towel, I'd start drifting off; and now, in my darkened motel room, I could hear her whispering, "And this is the *sixth* coat."

Without the shock of a horrible phone call, with a year's worth of time between me and that terrible day, my mother was able to be there for me once again, warm towels in her arms, to paint me back to sleep.

A few hours later, I woke to my phone alerting me that I'd gotten a text. Sandra was asking if I would be available for a conference call at eleven with her, Naomi, and Harriet. I typed back, *OK*, then I lay there for a few minutes. It was already after eight, and though I was still groggy, I was definitely rested and excited to go home.

As I went about repacking the explosion of stuff that seemed to detonate the moment I entered a hotel room, I tried to imagine what my sisters wanted to talk about. I could see how they might be angry with me for not answering my cell throughout most of my trip, and I wouldn't be surprised if they had tracked down some of my friends or badgered my poor niece for information. I didn't worry too much about it, because I knew things would go back to normal soon enough. Eventually, my sisters, my friends, and I would be talking regularly again, and then they would hang up and go back to their normal routines. I too would go back to whatever my normal was going to be, but with my life stripped of all schedules, I had no idea what normal was anymore.

When I walked through my front door later that afternoon, there would be no Hollywood ending—no job offers on my answering machine, no letter from the building inspector saying I could keep my guesthouse, no flowers from my ex, and certainly no miraculous communication from Mai. As I thought of this, I felt myself rapidly slipping into a depression, so I raced to the bathroom mirror.

"Do *not* go down that rabbit hole again." I jabbed my finger at my reflection, then smiled. "It's time to get cracking, damn it. It's been a fucking year."

I was in Barstow, California, trying to turn a cup of Starbucks coffee into a Locomotive with a double shot of espresso when Sandra called with Naomi and Harriet on the line. I knew I was in trouble when Harriet began with, "Okay, now listen to us."

But I was wrong.

"The bottom line is we love you," Naomi said. "That's the most important thing."

"Yes, we love you," Harriet said. "And we want you to know that—"

"Oh, would you *please* quit the bullshit," Sandra broke in. "The reason we called is that we *never* want to go through anything like what you put us through again."

"This is not the way we said we were going to handle things, Sandra." Harriet kept her voice level. "What we're saying here is that we—"

"No, Sandra is right," I said. "I should have kept in contact."

"You called us *once*," Harriet said.

"To tell us you'd seen Mom and Dad on a battlefield," Naomi said. "For God's sake, Barbara, you never answered *any* of our calls. I don't think I've had a decent night's sleep since we heard from you."

"I'm sorry I worried you. Really, I am. I just needed some time away from everybody . . . and it worked."

"It *worked*?" Sandra let out a sigh. "So all of sudden you're fine?"

"Well, I'm relieved," Naomi said. "At least you did what you had to do and—"

"And everyone else can go to hell?"

"Sandra, please." Harriet was stern now. "I think it's clear that Barbara is sorry she worried us. What we need to establish here is that she promises never to do it again."

"I'm sorry, Harriet, but I can't do that."

"Okay, I'm hanging up now," Sandra said. "Barbara is no longer my sister."

"What I was trying to say is that I can't promise I won't make you worry again. I really like motorcycling, and I might take another trip. Hell, I might go skydiving. But I promise I'll never disappear again, okay?"

"Swear it." Naomi sounded like she was about to cry. "I really don't think I could handle another day of what we went through. I must have called you fifty times, and your phone went straight to voice mail. Do you have any idea what that was like?"

"Fine. Unless I'm kidnapped, lost at sea, or my plane goes down, you will always know where I am. I swear it."

Sandra laughed. "You are so sick . . . and you are now my sister again."

We talked a little more about the upcoming unveiling of our mother's headstone, about how we couldn't believe a year had gone by, about how our parents were probably happy as hell they were alone together without any of us to drive them crazy. Then I said I had to go because I still had at least another two hours before I got to Los Angeles.

"Well, that lasted about fifteen minutes," Harriet said. "Now I'm worried again."

And then I hung up . . . and disappeared onto the highway.

Thirty-five

Twenty More Minutes

———◆———

I **can't explain it,** but when I got to my street, I kept riding west toward the ocean. I wanted twenty more minutes of this trip, and it had to be without my Harley, with no leathers, no boots, and no helmet. I rode straight to the Santa Monica Pier, parked my bike, and changed into my shorts, T-shirt, and sneakers, then I walked along the boardwalk, had an ice cream, and won a stuffed bear by breaking balloons with a dart. It was a gorgeous summer day, and I soon discovered that Uncle Buck was right. Twenty more minutes is never just twenty more minutes, and before I realized it, I'd been walking along the midway for more than an hour.

But I wasn't ready to go home, so I walked down to the beach. It was packed with lovers and families, and while I felt like I was the only one there who was alone, I wasn't.

Rolling Stone Dave jumped into my head: *Just because you've got sand between your toes doesn't mean you're free of surprises. There's broken glass and pointy seashells everywhere. Watch where you step, goddamn it.*

I picked up a stick and threw it into the surf. It disappeared, resurfaced, and then washed back to my feet.

Dry out that sucker and you can whittle yourself a nice whistle, Shaggy Blond Dave suggested. *You still have my pocketknife, don't you?*

I picked up the stick and was nearly plowed over by a kid catching a Frisbee.

"Sorry, lady!" He tossed it back to his friend and ran off. "I didn't see you!"

Sorry, I didn't mean to scare you. Natasha Pugg popped into my head. *I just came out to help.*

I wiped away a tear as I felt her arms encircle me. *Here's to freedom . . . Without any parents we're free to do almost anything.*

Vulnerable without my helmet, I felt more visible than I'd ever felt before. Exposed without my leathers, I felt the wind rushing through my hair and the sand biting my arms and legs. Then all at once hot tears flooded my eyes and streamed down my face, bursting the dam erected by my losses. And I cried. Oh, how I cried.

But I *was* happy . . . *really* happy as I sat on the sand hugging myself

At first people walked by, giving me my space, but as I continued to sob and tremble, as I kept on weeping and actually let out an honest-to-God wail, a few people stopped to see if I was okay. A young couple slowed down, but kept walking when I waved them away. An elderly man bent toward me and whispered, "Come on, now. It can't be that bad." And I began to cry anew over his kindness.

Finally, when a child dropped his ball in my lap, I stopped.

"Thanks." I smiled at him. "I needed that."

I gave the boy his ball and he looked relieved. Then I watched him run off to his parents, waiting a few steps away.

"I gotta go home!" he called back to me, waving. "See ya!"

"I gotta go home too!" I yelled back.

And so I did.

Thirty-six

A Union of Opposites

——◆——

When I walked into my house on the anniversary of my mother's death, my dogs flew out of their fur to greet me. Lynn had my mail and notes that people had left, most expressing concern, some threatening to cut off all ties if I didn't respond immediately. After chatting awhile, I thanked Lynn for everything and politely shoved her out the door. I had a lot to do that night—celebrate my mom, think about what I was going to do with my life, and grow the hell up.

To be sure, I was not the woman who had left them more than three weeks ago. That woman had almost stopped eating completely. She would never be savoring the lamb chops I now devoured by candlelight, alone and happy. That woman felt nothing, certainly not the mixture of opposites I felt now—content but not satisfied, eager but not impatient, tired, stressed, and frightened, yet energized, carefree, and calm.

I raised my glass in tribute to my mom, my dad, my sisters, and my friends. I toasted Bob Dylan, squirrels, and possums, wigwams, Cadillacs, and Daves. It felt so good to be drinking to remember and not to forget.

I finished my last bite of lamb, blew out the candles, and escorted my dogs outside. "And to you, my loyal friends." I held up two bones. "May you not choke on these offerings of my love, and may you savor them for more than two minutes."

Since I knew tomorrow was coming whether I was ready or not, I went to bed, but a barrage of opposite feelings wouldn't let me sleep. I was happy to be home but sad not to be on the road. I was looking forward to reconnecting with my friends and family, but apprehensive about all the questions they'd soon be asking and advice they'd want to give. And my mom, well, there was still a strange confusion about her absence, and a longing I realized might never go away.

Exhausted but awake, I lay there staring at the ceiling, afraid I'd still be doing that by sunrise. When I closed my eyes, the road stretched before me and then suddenly I was surrounded by velvet and Madame Zabrina's words came to mind: *A great deal has happened to you . . . A great deal lies ahead.* But why had she put her hand over that one particular card? Was there something about the Chariot I should know?

I dove out of bed and found the deck of tarot cards I'd bought and located the card. On it was a stern-faced charioteer dressed in armor. He was trying to control two wild horses—one black, one white—pulling in opposite directions. The charioteer was as wild-eyed as the stallions he was trying to rein in. Did Madame Zabrina see a wreck in my future? Did she cover the card to protect me?

I got into bed, but couldn't stop imagining what the old gypsy had seen, and then I broke into a fierce grin, thinking I should call her to tell her I'd gotten my horses under control and had made it back okay. Instead I picked up the phone and called Muriel.

"I'm back and ready for therapy," I said to her voice mail. "When can I see you?"

. . .

The following week, as I rode to my appointment, it was too hot to wear my leathers, but I did wear jeans, boots, and my helmet just in case I ran into Bart. The minute I walked into her office, Muriel gave me a huge hug—something she'd never done before—and she held on so tight, I thought she might never let go.

"You scared the bejesus out of me." She finally stepped back and held me at arm's length. "I swear I could kill you if I wasn't so happy to see you."

"I scared the bejesus out of me too." I flopped onto her couch and just sat there grinning. "But here I am, alive—arthritic knees, helmet hair, and, well, kind of happy."

"That smile of yours is nice to see," she said, settling into her leather chair like a hand in a glove. "I'm guessing your trip was successful?"

I launched into the highlights—the ghosts of my parents at Gettysburg, in particular—and I even talked a little about wanting to jump the guardrail to be with my mom. I told her how I'd started out feeling split in two, and how the motorcycle chick and I had returned as one. "Yeah, I'm feeling full of life now," I said, ending with my huge cry on the Pacific shore. "I'm glad to be home and ready to figure things out."

"Full of life, huh? Well, that's great to hear. The last time we met, you didn't believe in life at all." Muriel leaned in and smiled warmly. "You've certainly come a long way, haven't you?"

"Yup—3,988 miles to be exact." I grinned like a maniac. "But who's counting?"

We talked a little more about continuing therapy, and I agreed it was a good idea. Incorporating the concept of being an adult orphan into my identity was challenging, especially the part I had control over—being an adult. While the trip had helped me come to terms with being in a world without my parents, riding a motorcycle had infused me with a giddy freedom, and once I'd arrived in one piece after such an undertaking, I began to struggle with a sense of invulnerability similar to the one I'd had as a child.

"So next week?" asked Muriel.

"Absolutely," I said, giving her the Harley wave, low and slow, just shy of the thigh. "See you then."

I left her office, swung onto my sweet Sportster, and listened to Bob Dylan all the way home. Feeling sexy as Catwoman, tough as Darth Vader, as I rode down my block I fantasized about seeing my ex's car sitting outside my house. There she'd be when I pulled into my driveway, wolf whistling at my Harley and at me.

Wow, she'd say, walking over to where I sat in my saddle. *Things change, don't they?*

I'd slowly take off my helmet, but still I'd hover over my chrome pipes, hot enough to melt off her skin if she got too close. Then I'd swing off my bike and stride toward my front door, letting my swaggering butt say *fuck you* for me.

You're right, things change, I'd say just before I closed the door in her face. *The girl you left is gone.*

Of course when I rode down my block my ex's car was not sitting outside my house, so I turned up Dylan's sound track to *Pat Garrett and Billy the Kid* and rode right past my driveway. I turned the corner and cruised toward the liquor store to pick up some Glenlivet because since I'd already been home a week my bottle was already half full.

I was up to about thirty-five, maybe forty miles per hour, and screaming, *"Knock, knock, knockin' on heaven's door,"* which turned out to be kind of ironic since a woman was getting out of her parked car and opening her door . . . right into my path.

There are no ifs in motorcycling! Bart screamed in my head, just as I thought *if* there's no one on my left, I can swerve out of her way . . . *if* I don't check my side mirror, I'll get by her just in time . . . *if* I slam on my brakes, I might not hit her.

Surprise! Rolling Stone Dave reared back in his easy chair and laughed.

My bike began to wobble sideways and nothing seemed to be in my control. Suddenly I was Annie Edson Taylor and Bobby Leach going over Niagara Falls. I was John Glenn slipping in his bathroom. I was Uncle Buck's friend wrestling a steer backward from the ground up.

As I slid with the bike on top of me, I thought I smelled barbecue cooking. The friction of the asphalt against my jeans was hot and I could feel the heat flaming up my right side.

It seemed like an hour but it was probably only about ten minutes before a firefighter was squatting next to me and shaking his head. Up until then, the man whose car I was under had been trying to console me.

"You're gonna live," he said, then began to ramble. "I saw a show once where someone didn't know a motorcyclist was underneath him and he dragged the poor sucker more than a mile. You're lucky I was sitting at the light."

"Damn lucky," I said, looking up at his beer belly. "Thanks for telling me that. Now I think I might throw up."

He took a step back from where I was wedged beneath my bike and his car. "Now you stay calm, okay? I've called 911. Someone will be here any minute."

"I'm not going anywhere," I said. "You're okay, aren't you? I slammed into you pretty hard."

"Me? I hardly felt a thing." He laughed. "You and your bike took the brunt of it."

Just then I heard a siren in the distance. "Thank God," I mumbled, fighting back tears. "You wouldn't have a pillow to put under my head, would you?"

"I'm not sure I should move you." He looked over his shoulder. "Help is on the way. Just hang in there."

Sirens were coming from everywhere now, and in seconds we were surrounded by two cop cars, a fire engine, and an ambulance.

"Well, what've we got here?" A firefighter squatted down to check me out and tsk at my poor Sportster. "That was a nice Harley you had there. I'm afraid it might be cooked." He called the paramedic over. "My buddy here is going to check your vitals before I move you. Can you just sit tight?"

"Sitting isn't exactly an option." I tried to smile. "Um, I don't think anything's broken but I feel like my left leg is on fire."

"Probably a little road rash." He stood above me shaking his head, then bent down to take off my helmet. "You're lucky you were wearing this. Might have saved your life."

The paramedic took my blood pressure and pronounced me in good enough shape to move. Then, together, he and the firefighter lifted the bike off me.

"Can you stand?" the paramedic asked. "If not we can put you right on a gurney."

I was shaking so bad I wasn't sure. "If you help me, I think I can get up."

He offered me his hand, then carefully hoisted me to my feet just in time to see a cop walking toward us. "She okay?" he yelled. "Can I arrest her now?"

"Arrest me?"

"I'm just kidding." He walked up grinning. "I'm not even going to give you a ticket if you apologize to the lady you almost hit." He pointed down the road behind him to the woman who had been getting out of her car. "Poor thing is pretty shook up."

"Wow, I'm sorry." I stood there shaking, blood oozing out of my Levi's, Bart screaming in my head, *Where in the hell are your goddamn leathers?* I looked back toward the woman I could have killed. "She's all right though, isn't she?"

"She's more worried about you." The cop looked me up and down. "You sure are a lucky idiot. I just measured your skid marks. Do you know you slid a good forty feet?"

My knees almost buckled, and the firefighter lunged for me. "Steady there. I think you ought to get into that ambulance."

"No, I'm okay. I don't have health insurance." I looked at the cop. "Do you think you could give me a lift home?"

"No health insurance? How about life insurance?" The fireman grinned. "I wouldn't trust you on a bicycle."

"Which reminds me," the cop said. "You do have motorcycle insurance, don't you?" He pointed to my mangled bike. "And a license to drive this thing?"

I nodded.

"Well, good. Like I said, I'm not writing you up, but you have to take care of the car you hit." He squatted down to have a look. "There's damage to the trunk and the underside, but your bike is probably a goner."

The firefighter and paramedic left once I'd signed a waiver, the cop had written his report, and I'd exchanged insurance information with the guy I'd hit. Then I apologized to the woman I'd nearly mowed down, who pretty much couldn't stop crying.

"Consider yourself lucky," the cop said as we drove to my house in his squad car. "When it's a motorcycle versus a car, the motorcycle always loses." He looked over and must have seen me grimacing in pain. "Aloe vera is the best thing for that road rash . . . You might consider taking a bath in some cold milk too."

I'd hardly said a word the whole ride, but the cop didn't stop talking until we pulled into my driveway.

"Your bike will get towed to the nearest Harley dealership," he said, walking me to my front door and carrying my helmet. "Now can I ask you to do me one favor?"

"What? Consider skydiving?"

He smiled. "Just promise me you won't buy another bike."

You Can't Teach an Old Dog

Two **weeks after** I destroyed my Sportster I was at the Harley dealership not far from my house talking to Burle about my trip and eyeing a gorgeous pearl-white Fat Boy.

"There's something different about you." He looked me up and down. "You're not the same woman who showed up here a few months ago, are you?"

"Yeah, I'm a badass biker now—not just a wannabe."

"So let me guess. You're here for a new bike." He shook his head. "Unbelievable . . . We've hooked another one."

I'd washed the blood off my Levi's—now fashionably ripped from the wreck—and they were still my favorite pair, so there I was standing in them, my hands thrust in their pockets looking as badass as I could. "Yup, I'm hooked. I don't just want another bike, I *need* one."

"I see. So I guess that means you figured out something every biker knows, huh?"

"What do you mean?"

"Four wheels move the body. Two wheels move the soul." He winked at me. "Welcome to your new addiction. I saw a teal Sportster 1200 Custom with maroon pinstriping hauled in a couple weeks ago. Looked just like the picture you showed me—except for the asphalt tattoo and the hunk of crunched chrome. I see you survived?"

I grinned. "Yeah, the burns on my leg have healed nicely, thank you."

"My burns have healed too." He showed me the scars on his forearms and wrists. "So now you think you're ready for a bigger motorcycle. You think it's going to be more solid, more stable, easier to handle. Well, you're right and you're wrong." He cocked his head toward the Fat Boy. "Go on—sit on her—you'll see."

I did as I was told, and as soon as I managed to hoist the bike upright and was straddled over it, I understood what Burle was talking about. "Wow, do you think I can handle something this big?"

"You just rode across the whole damn country—you can handle anything, girl!" He threw an arm over my shoulder and gently guided me off the motorcycle and toward a line of Sportsters. "Now these bikes are more nimble and quick. That old Fat Boy is gonna feel like a Clydesdale—the most comfortable fucking Clydesdale you'll ever ride, but *definitely* more lumbering and sluggish." He winked. "Until you give her free rein."

Of course I bought the Fat Boy, and in a month or two, whatever confidence I'd lost from wrecking my Sportster came roaring back. Soon I was out for a spin every day, tooling down the freeway and giving the Harley wave—low and slow, just shy of the thigh—like the badass biker chick I was.

But confidence, while a prerequisite to riding a motorcycle, can also be a detriment. Just ask Evel Knievel, whose confidence landed him a place in the *Guinness World Records* book for the "most bones broken in a lifetime"—35 bones and 433 bone fractures, to be exact. Confidence can get you pretty banged up on a motorcycle, but in my case, it gave me a quick and painful lesson.

I was wearing shorts, a T-shirt, and tennis shoes for a quick ride to the store. I was going only a few blocks, and didn't crash, thank God, because I wasn't wearing my helmet either, but I did sear off a patch of skin when I was idling at a stoplight showboating my Fat Boy to some teenagers in the car next to me. I swear, the second my calf touched the drag pipe I went from grinning like an idiot to screaming like a spider monkey, and I thought I was going to pass out on the spot. If it wasn't for Bart Mange whispering in my head, *Breathe, sweetheart. You're okay,* I don't think I'd have made it home. From that day on I always wore my protective gear. As any *smart* biker will tell you, "It's better to sweat than bleed."

About nine months after my return to Los Angeles, I found a job as a marketing writer for a huge law firm in Century City, and the only thing good about the job was that I rode my Fat Boy to and from it almost every day. In less than a year, I felt my principles were being compromised and my spirit caged, so I quit and went off on another adventure. I moved to England and got my PhD from Lancaster University, thereby finishing something I had failed to complete thirty years before. My sisters, who have always been my emotional support, were with me all the way via texts, e-mails, and Skype, driving me crazy with advice I hardly ever listened to. After I passed my orals in January 2014, each of them in one way or another told me that our parents were smiling down on daughter number four, the newly minted Dr. Schoichet.

Today, I live in Soho on the border of Greenwich Village, own a sky-blue Volkswagen Beetle convertible that I keep at a friend's house in Long Island, and drive maybe twice a year. At the moment, I don't own a motorcycle, but I'm probably going to sell my car and buy one of the Harleys I keep drooling over on eBay. I'm also considering getting a sidecar for my dogs. I think it would be a blast to take them on a cross-country trip, and they'd look adorable in goggles. But no matter what I buy, I'll definitely send the details to the Daves for their approval first.

As for my ex, she tried to contact me repeatedly for about three years, but I wouldn't pick up the phone or answer an e-mail. Then one day I called her, and we became distant friends. Sometimes I fantasize about slitting her tires or keying her car, but it's a seven-hour flight and at least four hundred dollars to get to her. Besides, I'm a grown-up now.

After I left England, I moved to Santa Fe for a while, and I wish I could tell you that I ran into Mai and we lived happily ever after. But I left my storytelling days on the road. I still like a good adventure, though, and that's why I moved to New York. I'm also experiencing the beginning of the last act of a romantic comedy   Notice I said *beginning*. I live in the real world these days . . . not between the pages of a book . . . not inside a television . . . not on a movie screen. But I am living in something of a romantic comedy—turns out I've been in one all along—I just have no idea how it ends.

ACKNOWLEDGMENTS

At times our own light goes out and is rekindled by a spark from
another person. Each of us has cause to think with deep gratitude of
those who have lighted the flame within us.

— Albert Schweitzer

To be sure, the reason I wrote *Don't Think Twice* is because my "light"
had pretty much gone out, and I wanted to remember my journey back to
life. I was on the road alone for those twenty-one days, just as I was during
the five years it took to write this book, but I certainly had support along
the way. With me every mile and every page were my wonderful sisters—
Harriet Roth, Naomi Caspe, and Sandra Shahvar—who kept me balanced
on the road (even when they had no clue where I was) and who continue to
keep me afloat every day. Without them and our parents, Bernard and
Florence Schoichet, I never would have found the tenacity to complete the
ride or find the will to tell my story.

I am filled with tremendous gratitude to those who guided me through

Acknowledgments

the writing itself. My graduate professors at Sarah Lawrence, Grace Paley and Cecil Dawkins, and my PhD professors at Lancaster University in England, Graham Mort and Lee Horsley. They deserve my sincere thanks, as do my faithful readers, Jeanette Holling, Joyce Wilson, Lynn Ferro, Anna Schlecht, Reginald McKnight, and Rick Ramage, who boosted my spirits whenever I feared my book would never be published.

For putting me on the road I'd like to thank Harley-Davidson for making such an amazing machine, and especially Jill Close, who leads Harley-Davidson's Outreach to Women Program. Mike Schwartz, of Mike's Famous Harley, helped me years after the ride, and of course I'll never forget the two Daves in Buffalo: Rolling Stone (Dave Hames) and Shaggy Blond (Dave Swart), who will forever remain in my Harley-loving heart.

For putting me on the road to publication I want to thank Bruce Mahler, Susan Ciccone, and Darlene Chan, who led me to my agent extraordinaire, Linda Chester. Without her and Jen Charat I am certain *Don't Think Twice* would never have seen the light of day. And finally my heartfelt appreciation goes out to Sara Minnich, my editor at Putnam, who took the leap of faith and told me to simply tell the truth. Her wisdom and guidance has made this publishing process a complete joy.

———